The Coburgs

Theo Aronson

First published in 1968 by Bobbs-Merrill Company

Copyright © The Estate of Theo Aronson 1968

This edition published in 2021 by Lume Books
30 Great Guildford Street,
Borough, SE1 0HS

The right of Theo Aronson to be identified as the author of this work has been asserted by them in accordance with the Copyright, Design and Patents Act, 1988.

All rights reserved. No part of this publication may be reproduced, stored in a retrieval system, or transmitted in photocopying, recording or otherwise, without the prior permission of the copyright owner.

for Peggy and Jean

Table of Contents

Author's Note	7
Prologue: The Prince, *1790–1831*	9
Leopold I: King Against Europe, *1831-1865*	26
Chapter One	27
Chapter Two	49
Chapter Three	70
Leopold II: King Against The World, *1865–1909*	90
Chapter Four	91
Chapter Five	111
Chapter Six	130
Chapter Seven	163
Albert I: King Against Conqueror, *1909-1934*	190
Chapter Eight	191
Chapter Nine	210
Chapter Ten	240
Leopold III: King Against Countrymen, *1934-1950*	261
Chapter Eleven	262
Chapter Twelve	277
Chapter Thirteen	309
Epilogue: The Reluctant King	327
Bibliography	339

Author's Note

The title of this book indicates its scope. It is the story of the Coburgs of Belgium pictured, as it were, in their more defiant attitudes. It is not a definitive, day-by-day account of the reigns of the various Belgian sovereigns; still less is it a history of their country. The focus, throughout, is on the dynasty, with domestic politics being relegated, wherever possible, to the background, thus allowing the monarchs to be seen in their more embattled moments: Leopold I safeguarding his newly established kingdom in the face of a hostile Europe, Leopold II founding and defending his notorious Congo Empire, Albert I challenging the German invader, Leopold III fighting to retain his crown. It is, first and foremost, a family history; a study, not only of the monarchs themselves, but of the various members of this colorful and ill-starred dynasty. It is a book about people.

I am grateful for all the help I have received from the Musée de la Dynastie, the Bibliothèque Royale and the Commissariat Général au Tourisme, Brussels; the Bibliothèque Nationale, Paris; the Library of Congress, Washington; the British Museum, London; the State Library, Pretoria; and the Mbabane Library Association, Swaziland. I must thank also Mrs. C. Webster, Mrs. J. Gaydon, Miss A. T. Hadley, Baron du Bois de Chantraine, Mr. L. de C. Bucher, Mr. E. Verhille and those many people who have gone out of their way to help me during my visits to Belgium. Two recently published books to which I am particularly indebted are *My Dearest Uncle* by Joanna Richardson and *The King Incorporated* by Neal Ascherson. My greatest debt, as always, is to Mr. Brian Roberts, whose encouragement, enthusiasm and advice have been invaluable.

T. A.
Bruges, Belgium
1967

Prologue
The Prince
1790–1831

1

Prince Leopold of Saxe-Coburg owed almost everything to his looks. As the eighth child, and third son, of a petty German princeling whose domain covered less than eighteen square miles, he had started life with very little else. But by the time he reached manhood, during the years when Napoleon's armies were tramping across the face of Europe, there were few young men as handsome as he. With his broad chest aglitter with orders, his chin firm above his high, gold-embroidered collar and his hair swept forward with the studied abandon of the period, Prince Leopold had the looks to draw every eye. Whenever someone was needed to play the god Jupiter in a *tableau vivant*, the choice was always Prince Leopold whose beauty, says one contemporary, was "remarkable." The Emperor Napoleon was to remember him as the handsomest young man he ever saw at the Tuileries.

The Prince was by no means insensitive to this very valuable asset. Although handsome, he was no fool. With an eye ever open to the main chance, Leopold never hesitated to put his charms to good use. When, in 1807, at the age of seventeen, he accompanied his eldest brother Ernest, now Duke of Coburg, to Paris to petition the all-conquering Napoleon, he managed to insinuate himself into the good graces of those two most susceptible of women—the Empress Josephine and her daughter Hortense. There was even a rumor that Hortense, although seven years his senior, managed to seduce him. But however close his association with Napoleon's step-daughter might have been, Leopold was careful not to associate too closely with Napoleon himself. Even on coaxing from the Emperor a promise to enlarge the Duchy of Coburg, the adroit Leopold refrained from giving him his full allegiance. And after Napoleon's retreat from Moscow, he ceased even to consider it. Finally, nailing his colors to the mast, he joined the Russian Army. When, on the last day of March, 1814, the victorious Allies came clattering into conquered Paris, the handsome twenty-three-year-old Prince Leopold, now a lieutenant-general, was to be seen leading a brigade of the Empress Marie Feodorovna's cuirassiers.

It was just over two months later that Prince Leopold, visiting London in the entourage of the Czar, met Princess Charlotte, only child of the Prince Regent of England and thus Heiress Apparent to the British throne. Here was an opportunity indeed and one that the Prince was not likely to let slip through his fingers. To become the consort of the future Queen of England would satisfy even his overweening ambitions. The very fact that he was a humbly born prince, free of any dynastic entanglements, improved his chances and won him some powerful backing. Within a few days of their meeting Princess Charlotte broke her engagement to the Prince of Orange. Leopold promptly proposed himself to the Regent as her suitor. In a letter to his brother, however, he admitted that his chances were very poor "because of the father's opposition." But he was resolved, he wrote, "to go on to the end."

It was not for the sake of Prince Leopold's hazel eyes, however, that Princess Charlotte had broken her engagement to the Prince of Orange. An attractive and high-spirited princess, Charlotte of Wales (who had never much cared for her fiancé) had fallen in love with a Prussian prince. The affair came to nothing, but at least the broken engagement cleared the field for Leopold. Anxious to free herself of her father's restricting authority and as a cure, perhaps, for her broken heart, Princess Charlotte now turned to the eager Leopold. She could, she realized, do a great deal worse. Leopold was young, well-mannered and superbly handsome. Having made up her mind, she refused to rest until the matter was settled. The Regent's permission was somewhat grudgingly given and in the spring of the year 1816 Leopold and Charlotte were married. She had gained her freedom and he had fulfilled his ambitions; somewhat to their mutual surprise, they then proceeded to fall in love.

Leopold's marriage ushered in the one period of unalloyed happiness that he was ever to experience. Charlotte was an endearing creature, her lively, almost hoydenish personality making an excellent foil for his own conscientious Coburg nature. Before long, he was able to instill in her something of his own sense of purpose and awareness of royal duty. They had been granted £60,000 a year by the Government, and in order to ensure the privacy that Leopold considered so essential to domestic happiness, they left London and took up residence at Claremont House in Surrey. The simplicity and tranquillity of their life together here was, for the British public, a welcome change from the extravagance of the Prince Regent's court at Brighton and the turbulence of his estranged wife's cavortings about Europe. "In the house," noted a member of the Claremont suite, "reign harmony, peace and love—in short, everything that can promote domestic happiness. My master is the best of all husbands in all the five quarters of the globe; and his wife bears him an amount of love, the greatness of which can only be compared with the English national debt."

"Perfect happiness is by no means common," said Charlotte to a guest, "and I shall be delighted if you will often come and observe it at Claremont."

But what, perhaps, afforded Leopold the greatest satisfaction of all was that this charming wife, who by now loved him to the point of adoration, would one day wear a crown. It was a crown which she was more than willing to share. "I will not and cannot reign over England except upon the condition that he shall reign over England and myself ... ," she once declared fervently to Madame de Boigne. "Yes, he shall be King or I will never be Queen."

But it was not to be. By the spring of 1817 Charlotte, who had already had two miscarriages, was once more expecting a child. It was due to be born in mid-October, but November was already under way before her labor began. A healthy enough young woman, Charlotte, in the weeks before the birth, seems to have been considerably weakened by bleedings and dieting, and during her labor she manifested, says an eyewitness, "some symptoms of an alarming nature." On the evening of November 5, after protracted labor, she gave birth to a stillborn male child. Within six hours she herself was dead. It is generally believed that she died of exhaustion and hemorrhage.

Leopold, who had left her bedside for a few minutes, was not with her when she died. On being told the news, he hurried to her room and, kneeling by the bed, kissed her lifeless hands. He was desolate. "From the time of our marriage," he afterward told a friend, "we were almost inseparable ... we were always together in a state of unremitting happiness." And years later he was to admit to his niece, Queen Victoria, that he had never recaptured "the feeling of happiness" experienced during his short married life.

Prince Leopold had lost, at one blow, not only his chance of a throne, but his capacity for feeling really deeply about anything. It was the first of the disasters to strike a prince whose family, and dynasty, was to be curiously prone to disaster.

2

Count Otto von Bismarck, in years to come, was always to refer to the House of Coburg as "the stud farm of Europe." By that time the Coburgs would have married into almost every royal family on the Continent and not a few of them would be wearing crowns. It was due, very largely, to Prince Leopold's example and encouragement that this—for him—admirable state of affairs came about.

Determined that the Coburgs—poor, obscure and without influence—should leave their mark on the world, Prince Leopold set to work against almost overwhelming odds.

Although the marriage of his brother Ernest, Duke of Coburg, had added Gotha to the family domains, the Duchy still counted for very little and, with the exception of his sister Julie, who had married the brother of the Czar of Russia, none of Leopold's brothers and sisters had made a really brilliant marriage. With his own spectacular matrimonial achievement in ruins, Leopold was resolved to make good the loss.

Backing him up every inch of the way in these dynastic ambitions was his faithful adviser, Dr. Christian Frederick von Stockmar. This astute and conscientious Coburger had joined Prince Leopold's service before his marriage and, in the delicate maneuverings which lay ahead, was to prove himself a devoted champion of the Coburg cause.

The sudden death of Princess Charlotte, the Heiress Apparent, had thrown the British royal family into a quandary. While she had lived, it was confidently assumed that the crown would pass from her grandfather, the mad King George III, to her father, the Prince Regent, and then on to her and her heirs. But now, with her death, the Prince Regent's brothers were once more forced into the spotlight. Seldom has there been a less prepossessing line-up of possible successors. As Parliament would not hear of the Regent divorcing his bizarre wife, Princess Caroline, and marrying someone capable of producing an heir, it was up to the Regent's middle-aged bachelor brothers to do something about the succession. The Dukes of Clarence, Kent and Cambridge, turning their backs with extreme reluctance on the delights of their past lives, prepared to sacrifice themselves to the demands of the dynasty. As there was no lack of amenable Protestant princesses, it was simply a matter of choosing the most promising ones. The Duke of Clarence, aged fifty-three, chose Princess Adelaide of Saxe-Meiningen; the Duke of Kent, aged fifty-one, chose the widowed Princess Victoria Mary Louisa of Leiningen; the Duke of Cambridge, aged forty-four, chose Princess Augusta of Hesse-Cassel.

The second of these three matches, as far as Prince Leopold was concerned, was extremely gratifying, for the Duke of Kent's bride, the vivacious Princess Victoria Mary Louisa, was Leopold's sister. It was a match toward the achievement of which he had devoted himself since before Charlotte's death; now, with Charlotte gone, it became more significant still, for if Leopold had failed in his attempt to produce an heir, his sister might well be more successful. Killing two birds with one stone, the Dukes of Clarence and Kent were married at a double wedding on July 11, 1818 (the Duke of Cambridge had been married two months before), and the race to the cradle was on. It was with barely disguised triumph that Prince Leopold accompanied the Duke and Duchess of Kent to Claremont, where they spent not only their honeymoon, but their first year of married life.

The title at this time seemed to be running very strongly in Leopold's favor. In May 1819 the Duchess of Kent gave birth to a daughter. Leopold, who had been out of England at the time of her birth, saw to it that he was present at her christening in Kensington Palace. The baby princess was given the names of Alexandrina Victoria. Within a year both the baby's father, the Duke of Kent, and her grandfather, King George III, had died, bringing her two steps nearer the throne. The Prince Regent, crowned in almost oriental splendor, became King George IV, and his brother, the still childless Duke of Clarence, became his heir. That either of these two men would live for another seventeen years—by which time Leopold's niece, the baby Princess Victoria, would be of age—seemed highly unlikely. Leopold, who had seen his chance of becoming Prince Consort slip through his fingers, now began reaching out for a prize almost as brilliant: if Princess Victoria should succeed to the throne before coming of age, there seemed no reason why he, Leopold, should not become Regent. Unlike the royal dukes, he was young, popular, respectable and hard-working; after the profligacy, the extravagance and the idleness of the rest of the royal family, his advent would be as welcome as a breath of fresh air.

For the moment, however, he lay low. King George IV, his erstwhile father-in-law, could hardly bear the sight of him by now and it would not do for Leopold to flaunt his aspirations too openly. Always circumspect, he became even more so. In fact, during these years after Charlotte's death, Prince Leopold became as well known for his discretion as he did for his continuing good looks. It was not so much that his character was changing as that there was an intensification of his various characteristics. His prudence now began to smack of hypocrisy, his good manners of punctiliousness, his knowledge of pedantry. "His pomposity fatigues," complained that acidulous diarist Charles Greville, "and his avarice disgusts." It seems as if the once charming young officer was fast developing into a dignified and boring diplomat, old beyond his years. The passion for power—his one remaining passion—lay hidden behind a polite, inhuman facade, and it was only the most perspicacious who saw him for what he was. Although he retained the house at Claremont and accepted from the British Government a very handsome allowance, he thought it wiser to spend a great deal of his time abroad; "should my presence at home be deemed necessary," he wrote, significantly, to the Foreign Secretary, "I should be ready."

It was during these years of waiting that Prince Leopold became involved in a curious affair, if not exactly of the heart, then at least of the mind and the body. In addition to the Coburg thoroughness, Leopold had his full share of the Coburg lust, and there was never any lack of attractive young women to comfort the lonely widower. For the most part their comfortings left him untouched, but in the autumn of the year 1828, the sight of a young actress disporting herself as a Hottentot in a tiger skin, coral trinkets and colored feathers on the stage of the private theatre of the Neues Palais at Potsdam riveted his attention. "At the very first glance," he confessed to her delighted mother the following morning, "my heart inclined to her, because she looks so wondrously like my departed Charlotte." This carbon-copy of Leopold's late wife was a twenty-one-year-old girl by the name of Caroline Bauer who, besides looking like Princess

Charlotte, had something of Charlotte's wholesome, uncomplicated nature as well. The fact that she was a cousin of Leopold's adviser, Dr. Stockmar, was a further advantage. Leopold, with uncharacteristic impulsiveness, promptly proposed a morganatic marriage, and the young actress, overwhelmed by a blend of romance and ambition, accepted. With her triumphant mother by her side, Caroline followed Leopold to London. Here, housed in a charming villa in Regent's Park, Caroline prepared herself for what she imagined was to be a life of "ardently-longed-for bliss."

The realization fell far short of the expectation. Although she had never considered Leopold to be a particularly exciting person, there was about him a certain melancholy charm which Caroline had hitherto found attractive. Now, alone with him day after day, she found him deadly dull. He would arrive, each day, "in stiff, starched state, thickly encased in wrappings and formalities, and wearisome beyond endurance," and spend an hour or two in her company. She would play the piano or read from some ponderous book while he sat hunched over his drizzling-box. Drizzling—the art of reducing to powder the gold and silver threads from tassels, epaulets and frogging—was then the rage, and few society ladies gave themselves over to this unexacting pastime with more dedication than did Prince Leopold. During the year that he was associated with Caroline Bauer, in fact, Leopard drizzled enough silver to make a soup tureen. This, according to the frustrated Caroline, he then "solemnly presented to his young niece, the Princess Victoria of Kent."

When, after a month of this singular courtship in the Regent's Park villa, Leopold had still not married his actress, mother and daughter decided to force his hand. Either Leopold married Caroline immediately, they said to cousin Stockmar, or she returned to Germany. Leopold acquiesced and at a mock little ceremony on July 2, 1829, Caroline received a "modest allowance" and the title of Countess Montgomery. This act of marriage, meaningless as it was, seemed, momentarily, to rejuvenate the pedantic Leopold. The couple sang duets, played billiards, and even, says the amazed

Caroline, "took a walk in the twilight through the garden and counted the shooting stars."

"I am inclined to believe," she afterward wrote, "that these brief weeks in July dated the last expiring flush of romance in the life of the prince. It was the last youthful flicker of his burnt-out heart before it finally crumbled for ever into cold ashes."

This final flicker did not last long. Before the month was out Leopold, always obsessed with his health, went to Carlsbad to take the waters, and by the time Caroline saw him again, in November in Paris, he was once more armed with "the ominous drizzling-box." From here they returned to England; to a "lonely, desolate and mournful villa near Claremont House," where the days followed one another in doleful succession and mother and daughter sank into an ever deeper depression. By the summer of 1830 Caroline had reached the breaking point. The sight of this gloomy prince, perpetually muffled up against the weather, the sound of his ever present, never silent drizzling-box, the realization that she had thrown away almost two years of her life on such a heartless, dreary creature were almost too much for her to bear. Choking with rage, she one day burst into a stream of invective against the Prince, putting an end, once and for all, to their singular relationship. With the loyal and long-suffering Frau Bauer in tow, Caroline quit England and returned to the Continent. She never set eyes on Leopold again.

3

Prince Leopold, by the beginning of the year 1830, was thirty-nine years old. For all his burning ambition, he seemed no nearer a throne than he had ever been. Contrary to expectations, both the flamboyant King George IV and his heir and brother, the simple Duke of Clarence, were still alive, and within a mere seven years Prince Leopold's niece, Princess Victoria, would be of age. The possibility of a regency—if not for Leopold himself, then at least for his sister, the Duchess of Kent—seemed no more promising now than before. If

Leopold was one day to wield effective power, he had best make up his mind to do something about it. There was, in fact, an opportunity to hand. It was one which was plunging the cautious Prince into an agony of indecision.

In February that year the Greeks, having finally freed themselves from the domination of Turkey, were recognized as an independent nation. The next step was for them to find a king. Prince Leopold's name had already been bandied about at conference tables and, on the recognition of Greek independence, he became the official English candidate. "Leopold's election to the throne of Greece seems to be settled," noted Charles Greville in some amazement, "and while everyone has been wondering what could induce him to accept it, it turns out that he has been most anxious for it, and has moved heaven and earth to obtain it ... *il ne faut pas disputer des goûts.*" The prospect, in fact, seems to have fired Leopold's imagination. The idea of becoming King of Greece, of restoring that ravaged country to its former greatness, had, according to Stockmar, stirred "a certain vein of fancy and romance in his character." If his "burnt-out heart" could no longer kindle to the breath of love, it could still burst into flame at the possibility of reigning over that beautiful Aegean peninsula. Not quite all the romance had been drained from that once dashing young officer.

"I think it will be very pleasant," he enthused, "to breathe the balmy air, wandering in myrtle and orange groves, or resting under light blue silk tents, while beautiful Greek women dance their fantastic dances before me." He even opened discussions on the manufacture of these same light blue silk tents. Together with Stockmar, he pored over all available books on the country and opened an intimate correspondence with Count Capodistrias, President of the Provisional Greek Government. He blandly discussed with Caroline Bauer (who at that stage had not yet walked out on him) the choice of the future Queen of Greece. "All the princesses of Europe had to pass in review," she wrote bitterly, "and were analysed and criticized in an altogether business-like style."

Greece, Leopold felt sure, would satisfy "the poetic needs" of his soul.

But there was more to it than that. King George IV would not hear of Leopold's becoming King of Greece—or anywhere else, for that matter—and the Duke of Wellington's ardent championing of his candidature made Leopold suspect that the Government was eager to get him out of England. He was having second thoughts, too, on having to relinquish not only Claremont House, but his comforting £50,000-a-year allowance. Nor did the state of affairs in Greece itself seem too reassuring. The well-intentioned claims of Capodistrias that Leopold would be "leaving your fine palaces for little thatched ones—your sumptuous repasts to eat black bread" did not really match up with Leopold's dreams of Hellenic splendor. And as Greek territorial ambitions were still far from satisfied, Leopold, anxious to avoid taking over the country in its present unresolved state, hung back. Egged on by Capodistrias, he intimated that his final acceptance would depend on whether or not the Allied Powers met certain Greek demands. These the Powers refused to grant and at the same time Leopold learned that there was some opposition, in Greece itself, to his election. "It may end in a rupture," he confided to that old German patriot, Baron von Stein; "I care not. On this subject I am consistent with myself."

His dilemma was resolved in a most gratifying fashion. Toward the end of April 1830, George IV fell dangerously ill. As his death would leave only the elderly Duke of Clarence between the ten-year-old Victoria and the throne, Leopold's prospects of power nearer home suddenly brightened. In May, in a ponderous letter of renunciation, he finally declined the Greek throne. His elaborate reasons were greeted with considerable skepticism. "Instead of facing difficulties," accused the now disillusioned Baron von Stein, "instead of finishing what he had begun, he withdraws his hand like a coward from the plough, whilst he speculates on the changes which may supervene on the approaching death of George IV." Charles Greville was no less damning. "He is a poor creature, his intrigues about Greece were very despicable...."

George IV died on June 26, 1830, and the unpretentious Duke of Clarence, beside himself with excitement, became King William IV. The first act of his reign, according to that international gossip, Dorothea de Lieven, was to dismiss the late King's French cooks and replace them with English ones. Of almost more concern than the accession of this good-natured old man, however, was the question of who, in the event of his death, would become regent for the young Princess Victoria. The new King, who liked Leopold no better than had his late brother, favored the Duke of Wellington, and there was some talk of the regency's going to the new Queen—the kindly and self-effacing Adelaide. To counteract these possibilities, the Coburgs—brother and sister—began touting for support. "Prince Leopold and his sister," reported Madame de Lieven, "are exploring the provinces in pursuit of popularity. The Prince assumes the air of a presumptive heir. The regency question will in all probability be decided in favour of the Duchess of Kent...." The matter was finally settled by the passing of the Regency Act: in the event of the King's death, the Queen would act as regent to a child of her own, but if she remained childless, the Duchess of Kent would be regent during the minority of her daughter, Victoria.

This, to all intents and purposes, was what Leopold had wanted. But was it really enough? To be the power behind a regent's throne was not quite the same thing as sitting on a throne of one's own, particularly when there was a possibility that the regency might never materialize. To be the uncle of a queen would be very much second best to being a king in one's own right. Thirteen years before, when Leopold had married Charlotte, there had been a strong chance of his becoming King Consort; now he would have to content himself with becoming, at best, an *éminence grise* to a girl queen. The astute Greville claimed that Leopold "would do anything to be beking'd," and that in his anxiety to wear a crown, "He may think it 'better to reign in hell than serve in heaven.'...."

But Leopold did not have much longer to wait. Fulfillment was just around the corner.

4

On the night of August 25, 1830, there was being performed, at the Theatre de la Monnaie in Brussels, Auber's opera *La Muette de Portici*. Dealing with the Neapolitan rising against Spain, it was an emotional work and one which King Charles X of France (who had just been toppled from his throne) had always considered should not be played "too frequently." It seems, on this occasion, to have been played just once too often, for as the tenor launched into the famous aria *"Amor Sacré de la Patrie,"* the excited audience rose to a man and swept out into the street. Here their revolutionary fervor infected the crowds outside and before the night was out the entire city was in an uproar. Windows were smashed, houses sacked, gunsmiths looted and men shot dead in the streets. The Belgian revolution was under way.

It was against the Dutch masters of their country that this patriotic Belgian revolt was directed. Ever since the Congress of Vienna, in 1815, Belgium had been united with Holland under the Dutch King, William II. Belgium, which had briefly, under the rule of Napoleon, known some measure of contentment, bitterly resented its new subjugation to Holland. It was therefore to France that the Belgians looked for sympathy in their struggle against the Dutch King, and when, in July 1830, the French rose up in revolt against Charles X, the Belgians lost little time in following their lead. When the audience streamed out of the theatre that summer night, it was the French tricolor that was hoisted above the Hotel de Ville; it was only during the succeeding days that it was replaced by the red, yellow and black flag of Brabant and that the revolution resolved itself into an unequivocally national one. Almost simultaneously with the capital, the provinces rose in revolt and the movement gathered strength throughout the land.

The Dutch garrison, during that first aria-inspired night of revolution, had remained firmly in its barracks, leaving the Belgian bourgeoisie to form its own organizations for the maintenance of order. Nor, in the hectic days that followed, did the Dutch King show any eagerness to use force. "I have," he announced with commendable frankness, "a horror of bloodshed." The result was that those temporary citizens' organizations found themselves becoming more permanent, and their original aim of some measure of autonomy for Belgium hardened into a demand for complete independence. When the Dutch eventually marched 14,000 troops against Brussels, they were met by such determined opposition that they were forced to withdraw. The insurrection, to the amazement of everyone, not least of all the Belgians, had triumphed.

An elated Provisional Government, having declared total independence of Holland, now organized the election of a National Congress. The Congress, in turn, drew up a new constitution. The result, says Baron de Gruben, was "perhaps the purest specimen of the organization of a state according to principles of nineteenth-century liberalism." But lest so liberal a constitution alarm an already apprehensive Europe still further, they agreed that it should be headed by a monarch. It was to be a monarch, however, who would be chosen by the Congress and who would enjoy only very limited powers. "To declare a Republic meant hostility with all the world … ," declared Jean-Baptiste Nothomb in justification of this constitution. "There remained only one practical course, namely, to maintain independence, and to enter on negotiations for the establishment of a monarchy. Then alone might a new Belgium be established in old Europe."

Old Europe, in the form of the representatives of the various Great Powers, had already gathered together in London to keep an eye on the Belgian situation. The Northern Courts—Russia, Prussia and Austria—were all for stamping out the revolution; France, under its new King, Louis Philippe, was hoping to turn the muddled situation to its own advantage; Britain, inevitably, was playing a waiting game. When the Belgian National Congress proclaimed its independence, the London Conference, under the skillful guidance of Lord Palmerston, recognized the claim. It now remained for Belgium to elect its king.

The first choice of sovereign was the Duke de Nemours, son of King Louis Philippe. But Lord Palmerston, apprehensive of French territorial ambitions, would not hear of it. Nor did the name of Duke Augustus of Leuchtenberg or Prince Otto of Bavaria meet with general approval. Palmerston now began pushing the claims of his own favorite candidate—Prince Leopold of Saxe-Coburg-Gotha. Provided Leopold married a French princess, thereby conciliating France, he would, reckoned Palmerston, be a most suitable choice. The fact that the Belgian National Congress was none too enthusiastic about Leopold bothered Palmerston not at all; diplomatic coercion, combined with a national desire to get the business settled as soon as possible, forced the Congress to make up its mind. On April 20, 1831, a Belgian delegation arrived in England to offer Leopold the crown.

Before accepting what Greville called this "trumpery crown," Leopold wanted to make quite sure of his ground. Not without reason had the late King George IV referred to Leopold as the Marquis Peu-à-Peu, and he approached this Belgian offer with all his usual cat-like circumspection. The Belgian political situation, unstable since the revolution, had worsened considerably during the last few months; "anarchy," noted one eyewitness, "was rapidly spreading throughout Belgium." The Dutch King, William II, refusing to recognize Belgian independence, had overcome his initial distaste for bloodshed and was beginning to think of teaching his rebellious subjects a lesson. There was an abortive military rising in Ghent in favor of King William's son, the Prince of Orange. There was fresh talk about union with France and a growing inclination amongst some republicans to be done with the whole wretched question of king-making and to declare a republic. Nor were all Catholics happy at the prospect of being ruled by a Protestant king. And, most unsettling of all, the London Conference seemed unable to make up its mind about the exact boundaries of the new country. These frontiers would have to be decided upon and recognized, declared Leopold, before he could consider mounting the throne. "Belgium and her King must be in a position to be recognized by Europe," he said. "I could not accept the sovereignty of a State whose territory is disputed by all the Powers." And he wanted, as a further safeguard, to be elected to the throne by an overwhelming majority of the Congress. What the Austrian Baron von Wessenberg called Leopold's *"penchant décidé"* for a throne was still not powerful enough to eclipse his natural caution.

The negotiations dragged on for weeks. Not until June 4 did Leopold hear that he had been elected by 155 votes to 44. Still he hesitated. Only toward the end of June were matters finally wound up, and the Eighteen Articles, guaranteeing Belgium's independence, signed by the Powers. On the night of June 26, 1831, Prince Leopold finally accepted the crown of Belgium. "Human destiny," he said grandiloquently to the deputies assembled at Marlborough House in London, "offers no nobler or more useful task, than that of being called to uphold the independence of a nation and to consolidate its liberties."

The rhetoric done with, he sounded a note of warning. With an eye on the members of the London Conference, gratefully packing their bags, he declared that he accepted the throne "on the understanding that the Congress of the representatives of the nation will adopt those measures which alone can constitute the new State, and thereby secure for it the recognition of the States of Europe."

Three weeks later Prince Leopold set out for his new kingdom. Accompanied by an aide-de-camp, a secretary and the returning members of the Belgian delegation, he drove from London to Dover. The fact that he was "unaccompanied by any person of weight or consequence" caused, says Greville, considerable dismay. The situation in Belgium was still far from stable and Leopold seems to have been left, very largely, to fend for himself. The Russian

Ambassador is said to have gone on bended knees to Palmerston to get him to attach to Leopold someone "who would prevent him from getting into scrapes." But the Russian begged to no purpose. Leopold, says Greville, was "suffered to go alone and plunge his weakness, vanity and incapacity into the middle of [the Belgians'] turbulence, arrogance and folly." He would be back, reckoned Greville, before his debts were paid.

From Dover Leopold sailed on the *Crusader*, and as it came within sight of France, the guns of Fort Rouge thudded out a royal salute. At Calais he was greeted with all the honors due a crowned head and at six o'clock the following morning he set out by road for Belgium.

It was a day of brilliant sunshine. His open carriage, escorted by brightly uniformed French cuirassiers, went bowling along the coast road toward the frontier. Here the squadron of cuirassiers wheeled about and a platoon of Belgian Civic Guards, sporting black cockades, presented arms. At the frontier station of La Panne, in a modest, red-roofed inn standing on the seashore, Leopold was officially welcomed by the Count de Sauvage, Minister of the Interior, and Baron d'Hooghvorst, Commander-in-Chief of the Civic Guard. Then, with the flat fields of Flanders on his right, the North Sea a-dazzle on his left, and the vociferous cheers of his new subjects ringing in his ears, this pale, handsome, and cold-hearted King drove on into his kingdom.

As predicted, he was driving straight into trouble.

Leopold I
King Against Europe
1831-1865

Chapter One

1

"How is Leopold?" asked Lady Holland, turning, at dinner one evening, to Sylvain Van de Weyer, the new Belgian Ambassador.

"Does your Ladyship mean the King of the Belgians?" asked Van de Weyer.

"I have heard," she answered airily, "of Flemings, Hainaulters and Brabanters; but Belgians are new to me."

Nor was the outspoken Lady Holland alone in her skepticism about the newly established state. "There are no Belgians, never were any, and never will be any," was Talleyrand's bland comment. "There are French, Flemings or Dutch—the same thing—and Germans."

It was to this diversity of peoples that King Leopold now came to give cohesion. Their Catholicism had first brought to these particular inhabitants of the Low Countries some sort of unity but their provinces had hitherto always formed part of the Spanish, French or Austrian domains. Republican France had annexed Belgium in 1797 and it had been Napoleon who had welded the two main ethnic groups—Flemings in the north and Walloons in the south—into a lasting alliance. With the defeat of Napoleon at Waterloo, the victorious Allies, meeting at the Congress of Vienna, had been determined to use the Belgian provinces as a means of checking any future French expansion. The authoritative fashion in which Catholic Belgium was then tacked on to Protestant Holland further united Flemings and Walloons, and when the revolution erupted in 1830, the two peoples fought side by side against the Dutch. Having finally won their independence, they chose as their motto: *L'Union fait la Force*.

For all this newly professed unity, however, the Belgians still lacked any real national spirit. As a nation, they were as new to themselves as they were to Lady Holland. Not only was the flat, Flemish-speaking northwest of the country quite different from the undulating, French-speaking southeast, but long years of foreign domination had encouraged regional and communal loyalties, difficult to erase. People still tended to think of themselves as belonging to Bruges or Ghent or Liège or Antwerp rather than to Belgium. There remained, in fact, in this country which had just been given the most advanced constitution of its day, a great deal that was parochial, almost medieval. Leopold, fifteen years after his accession, was still to long for a "more robust national spirit," and his even more nationally ambitious son, Leopold II, was to complain that Belgium was a country of "small-minded people." And then, besides these linguistic, territorial and historical divisions, there was that great division characteristic of all nineteenth-century Europe—the animosity between Catholics and Liberals.

Undermining a sense of national identity still further was the fact that Belgium existed purely by the grace of the Great Powers. Wedged between France, Germany, Holland and—across a narrow strip of sea—England, it lay at the mercy of them all. It was an artificial state, dependent on the goodwill of its powerful neighbors, obliged to be always on its best behavior and with very little opportunity of asserting itself in European affairs. Pledged to permanent neutrality itself, it was looked upon as a convenient highway for the armies of other nations. It was to take all Leopold's celebrated dexterity to keep his country's various guarantors happy; no matter how strong the temptation, he must never step out of line. Hapsburg Austria looked upon Belgium as a dangerously radical state and upon cool, cautious Leopold as a hot-headed liberal; Prince Metternich, the Austrian Chancellor, was waiting with ill-disguised impatience for the whole revolutionary regime to collapse. As for Russia and Prussia, they refused to have anything to do with Belgium.

If Leopold was to retain the independence of his new country, it would have to be in defiance of almost every state in Europe.

Serious as many of these problems were to be, Leopold had hardly set foot in his kingdom before he had to face a problem more serious still. A few days after the new King had been proclaimed, the Dutch Army, defying the London Conference, marched into Belgium.

"See what I get by way of welcome," was Leopold's wry comment on hearing the news. The Belgian Constitution, which Leopold considered so limiting for the Sovereign ("Obviously, the Monarchy was not present to defend itself," he grumbled on first reading through the Constitution), nevertheless gave him supreme command of the army. It was a responsibility which he could happily have done without on this occasion. Realizing that the small Belgian Army was in no condition to face the disciplined Dutch troops, he reluctantly called upon England and France to honor their treaty obligations and defend his country. France lost no time in marching 50,000 men across the frontier, but at the last moment Leopold, coerced by his ministers, decided to halt the French advance and face the Dutch himself. It was a brave but, as far as Belgium was concerned, extremely foolish decision. The Belgians, still flushed with their success against the Dutch in the streets of Brussels the year before, now declared that it needed only *un baton et un sabot* to clear the enemy out of their country. Leopold, as Commander-in-Chief of the Army, issued a resounding address to the nation and went cantering off to Antwerp to join his men.

The campaign lasted for ten days and was an unmitigated disaster. The Belgians, routed by the superior Dutch forces, were obliged to swallow their pride and allow the French to advance after all. King William, who had no intention of fighting France as well as Belgium, beat a hasty retreat, abandoning all gains other than Antwerp. This fortress he resolutely refused to surrender, and the French forces, only too glad of an opportunity to entrench themselves on Belgian soil, laid siege to the city.

From out of the whole inglorious affair, King Leopold alone emerged with reputation enhanced. His calm, his courage and his common sense were an example to all. General Belliard, reporting to the Minister of Foreign Affairs on the Belgian retreat toward Louvain, had nothing but praise for the King's behavior; during all the chaos of the retreat, Leopold kept his head. "Without him, the Belgian Army would have been annihilated," declared Belliard. Even the Dutch general, Von Gahern, spoke of Leopold's "intrepidity and presence of mind" and of the *sang-froid* with which he exposed himself to danger. For a prince who had had very little experience of battle, this was no mean achievement. "I admire the King," confessed the somewhat astonished Lord Russell on arriving back from the seat of war. "I never gave him credit for what there is really in him. It seems it wants external causes to move his faculties into action."

But Leopold himself could draw no comfort from the disasters of the Ten Days War. "We suffer from that unfortunate campaign of 1831," he afterward declared. "It is a misfortune over which I groan daily." He would give anything, he once cried out, "to commence afresh the 2nd of August, 1831."

Nor was the humiliation of his Army his only trouble. The presence of French troops on Belgian soil had reawakened in the London Conference, once more assembled to consider this latest turn of events, all the old fear of French aggression. "That unfortunate campaign," reported Stockmar to his master, "has revived the old English principle that Holland must never be weakened." There was now, he noticed, a definite hardening of attitude toward Belgium. As a result of the Ten Days War, the Conference decided to replace the original Eighteen Articles by the Treaty of the Twenty-Four Articles. It was an agreement more favorable to Holland than to Belgium, for by this treaty parts of Limburg and Luxembourg, then in Belgium hands, were to go to Holland. Leopold was warned that as these decisions were "final and irrevocable," he had best accept them. Only the insistence of Stockmar stopped the disappointed Leopold from abdicating. Accepting it as one of the burdens of sovereignty and bringing into play all his powers of persuasion, Leopold got the Belgian Chambers to agree to the harsh treaty; "there is no dishonor," sighed one of the members, "in submitting to irresistible force."

If Belgium was prepared to abide by the Twenty-Four Articles, Holland was not. King William refused to evacuate Antwerp and in his stand he was supported by the Northern Courts. England now felt obliged to join France in opposing Holland; the British blockaded the Dutch coast while the French continued to besiege Antwerp. When the citadel finally fell to the French, the stubborn King William still refused to give up two of the forts, and in exasperation the Conference adjourned, leaving the business to be settled by a modus vivendi. King William retained the two Belgian forts and King Leopold hung onto those areas of Limburg and Luxembourg which had recently been ceded to Holland. It was an extremely unsatisfactory arrangement but one with which Leopold was to be saddled for the next half-dozen years. When, toward the end of the decade, King William finally decided to abide by the treaty, Belgium had become so accustomed to the two provinces that their surrender meant a considerable wrench.

Belgium's humiliating dependence on the goodwill of the Great Powers was further illustrated by the business of the abolition of the Barrier—the line of forts dividing France from Belgium. These had been built by the Allies after the defeat of Napoleon but were now of doubtful strategic value. As a gesture toward France, Leopold wanted to dismantle them but in this he came up against the opposition of the other Powers, particularly England. The Duke of Wellington, having had a hand in the erection of the forts, would not hear of their demolition and the Northern Courts, still championing Holland, accused Leopold of pro-French sympathies. Only by exercising all his ingenuity could Leopold get the Powers to demolish five of the forts. Even then the decision left France far from satisfied. "We are like shuttlecocks among the others," sighed the frustrated Leopold.

But in the same way that he had survived the debacle of the Ten Days War, so did he weather these more complicated diplomatic storms. There were few monarchs more capable of balancing on the knife-edge of European diplomacy than he. Raised in the atmosphere of the eighteenth century, matured in a Europe in which ruling families still treated their country as a personal heritage, Leopold delighted in the complex game of power politics. It was thus more in admiration than in disparagement that his subjects began calling him Monsieur *Tout-Doucement*. Having achieved his ambitions, Leopold now proceeded to show himself worthy of them, and those who had so confidently predicted that he would be back at Claremont before his debts were paid were to be proved very wrong. Considered by the greater number of Europe's monarchs as nothing more than a cardboard king of a cardboard kingdom, he would prove to be more durable than the lot of them. Long after the thrones of France, Germany, Austria and Russia had been tumbled in the dust, Leopold's descendants would still be seated on the throne which he, in the face of so much adversity, was to make safe for them.

Having survived this first round of difficulties, Leopold set about consolidating his position. He had established his kingdom; the next move would be to found his dynasty. "The heart," he was fond of saying, "plays a very useful part in political affairs." Now, in the spring of the year 1832, he decided to put his own arid heart to an eminently useful purpose. He set off, in May, for France in search of a bride.

2

Princess Louise d'Orléans was the eldest daughter of Louis Philippe, King of the French. She had been born in 1812 in Palermo in Sicily, the kingdom in which her Bourbon father had sought refuge during the Revolutionary and Napoleonic upheavals of the period. The defeat of Napoleon and the restoration of the Bourbons had allowed this younger branch of the family to return to France, but it was not until the carousel of French politics had brought her father to the throne that Princess Louise became a figure of some importance. As the eldest daughter of France's new if lackluster monarch, she was a very valuable pawn in the political game.

Hers was a limelight which she had done nothing to court. Like her father and mother—King Louis Philippe and Queen Marie Amélie—Princess Louise had very little appetite for the splendors of her position; her tastes were simple in the extreme. With her fair, corkscrew curls framing a pretty face and her blue eyes innocent of arrogance, she looked, indeed, more bourgeois than royal; only her Bourbon nose saved her face from vapidity. Gentle, pious and even-tempered, Louise was devoted to her family and self-sacrificing to a fault. She had been known, from babyhood, as "the good Louise"; it was a goodness that came, at times, very close to saintliness. And yet she was no milksop. She had a quick intellect, a certain independence of outlook and a strong sense of duty. Her kindness would always find a practical outlet and her sweetness was never cloying. For all her unobtrusiveness, Princess Louise would make someone a very good wife.

The choice of husband for this mild-mannered princess was rather limited. "The Orleans Princesses," observed the Duchess de Dino, "pleasant, well-mannered, well-dowered great ladies as they are, are nonetheless difficult to marry." Europe's long-established monarchies wanted nothing to do with what they considered a parvenu dynasty and all the more amenable princes tended to be non-Catholic. There was one suitor, however, who, except for the fact that he was a Protestant, was both suitable and willing, and this, of course, was King Leopold. A union between the royal houses of France and Belgium could bring nothing but satisfaction to both parties. Louis Philippe would be able to tuck Belgium even more deeply under his wing and Leopold would gain all the prestige and security he so ardently craved. His visit to Compiègne in May to ask for Louise's hand was eminently successful. He was greeted with all possible honors by King Louis Philippe, Queen Marie Amélie and the King's forceful sister, Mme. Adelaide, and the whole business of the marriage was thrashed out between them. "Portion, dower, expectations, all these questions he treated with perfect disinterestedness," notes one of his biographers, and Leopold raised no objection to his future children being Catholic. All that really mattered to him was that Louise was a daughter of the reigning House of France.

The French royal family, for their part, were no less pleased. "We are perfectly contented with King Leopold," wrote Mme. Adelaide to Talleyrand; the marriage was "so suitable from a political point of view." The date of the ceremony was fixed for August, and Leopold, highly gratified, returned to Brussels in triumph.

Only Princess Louise seemed less than happy. In the flurry of family discussions, she had barely been consulted. A cynical widower of forty-two, fast losing his once celebrated looks, was not really much of a match for a sweet-natured girl of twenty. Leopold's conventional declaration that it was on her "individual account more than any other reason" that he wished to marry her impressed Louise not at all; she understood the reasons for his eagerness only too well. He was as indifferent to her, she confided to a friend, "as a passer-by in the street." So devoted to France, her family and her friends, so happy in her familiar, tranquil day-to-day life, Louise was appalled at the prospect of marriage to Leopold. But this, said Mme. Adelaide breezily, "was only natural," and the arrangements went forward. On the day of the ceremony itself, when in a dress of Belgian lace Louise stood beside her new husband in the chapel at Compiègne, she seemed overwhelmed. And her melancholy appears to have affected the entire gathering. For all the richness of the setting, for all the brilliance of the ceremonial, for all the glitter of orders and the gleam of satins, "it was obvious," says one observer, "that everyone was sad."

"I have suffered cruelly these last few days ..." wrote Louise to a friend two days after the wedding. "Pity me, pray for me, though I am calm and resigned, for I have done my duty, and a duty done always brings calm and satisfaction. The goodness and tenderness of a husband for whom I still have done nothing are a promise of a tranquil future; but the present is sad, solemn and cruel. I feel all dizzy and overwhelmed."

When, at the end of their brief honeymoon, the royal couple crossed the border into Belgium, Louise burst into tears.

But, little by little, she came to accept the situation. Leopold might be indifferent but he was not cruel. Louise might complain that he did not fully appreciate the sacrifice she had made in leaving her family, but she had to admit that he was very kind. During those first few weeks at the country palace of Laeken, she came to realize how tactful, how considerate, how like herself in "his ideas and feelings" he was. By the end of the month she was writing to tell her mother of the "profound esteem" which she felt for her husband. "Every day adds to this esteem and affection, and to the serenity with which I foresee the future. If my heart had chosen for itself," she admitted, "it would not have chosen otherwise."

Life with this prudent, middle-aged man suited her gentle, self-effacing personality very well. Her days were not, after all, so very different from what they had been at her father's court. She rose late, heard Mass at ten, breakfasted alone with Leopold and then, accompanied by his dog, the two of them went out for a walk. In the afternoon, while the King attended to affairs of state, she would read, and toward four o'clock the two of them would again go walking or riding. Sometimes they dined alone, but if they had guests, Louise would spend the evening with the women, doing embroidery, while Leopold spoke to the men. His conversation over, they would retire to their private apartments. It was a calm, predictable, almost monotonous existence, but Louise, for all her youthfulness, was not really looking for excitement.

She was looking for a master and in Leopold she found exactly what she wanted. The more she knew him, the more she came to admire him. That he was not, in many ways, worthy of all this adulation was neither here nor there; her devotion to him was uncritical. "Deep affection," she wrote, "makes us always diffident and *very humble*. Those that we love stand so high in our own esteem, and are in our opinion so much above us and all others, that we naturally feel unworthy of them and unequal to the task of making them happy." All her wishes, she claimed ardently, "even the dearest, are subordinate to his."

All this masochistic self-abnegation was a pity; it merely encouraged the already egotistic Leopold. If Louise had been a more spirited and assertive personality, her solemn husband might have been forced to adapt himself and might, as a result, have developed into a less pompous and conceited old man. But gradually her own interests and independence were stifled until she lived for him alone. She became increasingly more self-effacing until, like a looking glass, she merely mirrored her husband's image and never originated one of her own.

And Leopold? It had been, as far as he was concerned, a *mariage de convenance* pure and simple, and as such, he was perfectly satisfied with it. In fact, he was rather more than satisfied. It would have been impossible, of course, to recapture the magic of his marriage to Charlotte, but he was older now and less romantic, and the devoted Louise suited him very well. Leopold was not one to be embarrassed by a surfeit of adulation. The somewhat honeyed description of her which he wrote to his niece, Princess Victoria, might well have owed more to tact than to truth, but it was not far from his real opinion. To General Goblet he was probably more frank. "I am delighted with my good little Queen: she is the sweetest creature you ever saw, and she has plenty of spirit," he wrote a week after the wedding, and then added the reassurance, hardly less important, that they had been received "with the most lively enthusiasm throughout the country."

Enthusiasm mounted higher still when in July 1833 Louise gave birth to a son. When the child died less than a year later, Leopold was almost broken by grief and disappointment. His first son, who would have been heir to the throne of England, had been stillborn; now his second son, heir to the throne of Belgium, died in infancy. The King, said a member of the household, was "crushed and afflicted to a degree which would touch the hardest heart." In a fit of black despair, Leopold decided to pass on the Belgian succession to his Coburg nephews. The announcement threw Europe—always suspicious of Leopold's motives—into a flurry. "They are annoyed about it at the Tuileries," reported the Duchess de Dino, and King Louis Philippe assured his son-in-law that he would "resist to the utmost everything that could possibly injure or *Germanize* Belgium...." Mme. Adelaide, always practical, could hardly believe that "King Leopold, who is only forty-three years of age, and with a young wife in perfect health, has allowed himself to be so carried away by grief at the loss of his child." The storm blew over, and in April 1835 Louise gave birth to another son. He was named Leopold and given the title of the Duke of Brabant. Less than two years later the delighted King Leopold was presented with yet another boy— Philip, Count of Flanders. And in June 1840, somewhat to the disappointment of the King, was born a daughter. Louise insisted that she be called Charlotte, as a tribute to Leopold's first wife.

Thus, by the tenth year of Leopold's reign, the succession seemed secure. Leopold, Duke of Brabant, and Philip, Count of Flanders, were growing up fast and Charlotte, now that the initial disappointment had worn off, was becoming her father's favorite child. They were all three, in their different ways, to develop strongly defined personalities: Leopold would become one of the world's most vilified monarchs, Philip one of its most studious princes, and Charlotte one of its most tragic empresses.

3

For all his anxiety to found a Belgian dynasty, King Leopold never let slip an opportunity of doing something for the dynasty from which he sprang—the Coburgs. Only by the aggrandizement of his family could he strengthen his position in a Europe which remained—for all his achievements—doggedly unsympathetic and unimpressed. His chief concern, of course, was for his sister's child, Princess Victoria. For years now his letters, heavily larded with advice, encouragement and protestations of affection, had been crossing the Channel to Kensington Palace, and to Laeken came Victoria's answers—appreciative, questioning and no less affectionate. No letter from dear Uncle Leopold, no matter how heavily pedantic or tediously instructive, was received with anything other than unfeigned gratitude; never did a teacher have a more willing pupil. "I am much obliged to you, dear Uncle, for the extract about Queen Anne," she wrote from St. Leonard's in the winter of 1834, "but must beg you, as you have sent me to show what a Queen *ought not* to be, that you will send me what a Queen *ought to be*." Dear Uncle needed no second bidding; the tutoring of future sovereigns was very much to his taste. This task, he answered joyously, "I will very conscientiously take upon myself on the first occasion which may offer itself...." And take it upon himself he did. As the young Princess neared her eighteenth birthday, so did the stream of Uncle Leopold's maxims, aphorisms and exhortations gather force; by the time King William IV died in 1837, it was in full flood. If King William had lived just long enough to rob Victoria's Coburg mother of the chance of the regency, her Coburg uncle was not going to let this lessen his influence one jot. One of the first letters Victoria wrote after her accession was to Uncle Leopold and he answered it, as usual, with reams of advice. Of the four points into which he divided this particular sermon, the last was undoubtedly the most significant. "Before you decide on anything important," he urged, "I should be glad if you would consult me...."

If the young Queen's answer was just a little less effusive on this occasion, Leopold seems not to have noticed it. His flow of instructions continued unabated. When Victoria seemed to be mentioning her Prime Minister, the charming Lord Melbourne, rather too frequently, Leopold countered by recommending Stockmar; when Victoria continued to praise Melbourne, Leopold very wisely changed tactics and began sending the Prime Minister his "kindest regards." A visit of Leopold, Louise and their eldest son to Windsor in the autumn of 1837 showed Victoria to be as affectionate as ever ("Oh! I feel very, very sad," she wrote on his departure) and, encouraged by this, Leopold decided to put their relationship to its first real test.

In 1838 Holland suddenly decided to accept the 1831 Treaty whereby she must evacuate those two Antwerp forts which she still held and reclaim those parts of Limburg and Luxembourg now held by Belgium. Belgium, having come to regard these two disputed territories as her own, was determined to hang on to them, and Leopold considered that the time was ripe for making a stand on the issue. In a rousing and vociferously applauded speech to the Belgian Chambers, he declared that the rights of his country would be defended "with courage and perseverance"; he was prepared, in short, for war. But once again he found the kingdoms of Europe ranged against him. Russia, Prussia and Austria openly supported Holland (Prussian troops were already massing on the frontier), and neither France nor England was prepared to back him up. Playing what he imagined to be his trump card, he wrote to Queen Victoria, asking her—in his oblique fashion — for support. Her attitude was as coolly constitutional as he himself had always urged that it should be. "The Treaty of November 1831 was perhaps not so advantageous to the Belgians as could have been wished," she answered primly. "This treaty having been ratified, it has become binding, and therefore it is almost impossible to consider it as otherwise."

The letter was, for all its polite phrasing, a slap in the face for Uncle Leopold, a sharp reminder that although Victoria was still his niece, she was the Queen of England first. Leopold, after having tried the last, face-saving solution of buying the disputed territory, was forced to climb down and accept the Treaty.

The incident brought home to him, as never before, his isolation in Europe. Both Austria and Prussia, seeing him abandoned by England and France, found excuses to break off diplomatic relations. With every mail bringing him a letter from King Louis Philippe chiding him for his defiant behavior, Leopold realized that he must, at all costs, keep in with his only real ally, Queen Victoria. Already the independent little Queen was behaving with marked coolness toward her mother. Would Victoria, in her satisfaction with her new life, and particularly with Lord Melbourne, gradually loosen all her Coburg ties? Lest this happen, Leopold now turned his full attention to another of his projects: the choosing of a husband for Victoria.

He did not have far to look. In fact, he did not have to look at all.

Leopold's eldest brother, the Duke of Coburg, had two sons; the elder was named Ernest and the younger Albert. It was on behalf of this second son, Albert, that Leopold had been busily scheming for the past few years. At the time of Victoria's coronation in June 1838, Albert was almost nineteen years of age and he seems, by all accounts, to have been a prince of exceptional physical beauty and of no less exceptional mental ability. He was, in fact, a not unfaithful copy of his Uncle Leopold at the same age. And not only did Albert resemble his uncle but he would, if he were to marry Victoria, find himself occupying exactly that position which the death of Princess Charlotte had denied to Leopold himself. It was almost as though the Coburgs were being given a second chance.

It was a chance which Leopold was determined not to lose. The young Coburg brothers had already paid one visit to England, and Victoria's reaction had been every bit as enthusiastic as Leopold had hoped it would be. "I must thank you, my beloved Uncle, for the prospect of *great* happiness you have contributed to give me, in the person of dear Albert. Allow me, then, my dearest Uncle, to tell you how delighted I am with him, and how much I like him in every way. He possesses every quality that could be desired to render me perfectly happy...."

So far, so good. But that particular outpouring had been penned in 1836, a year before Victoria's accession, and since then the young Queen had been revealing a particularly independent streak. She continued to show an interest in Albert's education (Leopold and Stockmar were cramming him with knowledge), but there was a slight cooling off in her attitude toward him. Eligible princes, moreover, had been flooding into England, and it must have been with some trepidation that Leopold watched the comings and goings of these hopeful young suitors. And then in the summer of 1839 Victoria dashed off an anxious letter in which she made clear to her uncle that she was determined not to be rushed into a marriage with Albert. "I can make *no final promise this year*, for, at the *very earliest*, any such event could not take place till *two or three years* hence....

"Though all the reports of Albert are most favourable, and though I have little doubt that I shall like him, still one can never answer beforehand for *feelings*, and I may not have the *feeling* for him which is requisite to ensure happiness. I may like him as a friend, and as a *cousin*, and as a *brother*, but not *more;* and should this be the case ... I am very anxious that it should be understood that I am not guilty of any breach of promise, for I *never gave any*...."

But Leopold was not known as the Marquis Peu-à-Peu for nothing; he knew better than to press his candidate's claim too strongly. Albert's grooming continued with Coburg thoroughness all through that autumn and in October 1839 the finished product was dispatched to Windsor for the Queen's inspection. One look was enough. "Albert's *beauty* is *most striking*, and he is so amiable and unaffected—in short, very fascinating; he is excessively admired here," wrote the enraptured young Queen a day or two after his arrival, and two days later she proposed marriage to him. "I *love* him *more* than I can say ... I do feel *very*, *very* happy," she confessed to her gratified uncle.

"My feelings are a *little* changed, I must say, since last Spring, when I said I couldn't *think* of marrying for *three or four years*," she admitted charmingly, "but seeing Albert has changed all this."

Nothing, wrote Leopold on the receipt of this delirious confession, could have given him greater pleasure, and he added, with refreshing candor, that he had "almost the feeling of old Zacharias— 'Now lettest Thou Thy servant depart in peace.'" The good-hearted Queen Louise, who seems to have been reduced to floods of tears on hearing the happy tidings, took the opportunity of passing on to Victoria a particularly characteristic piece of advice: "Feeling and acknowledging the superiority of those we love and must always love and respect, is a great satisfaction, and an increasing and everlasting one. You will feel it I am sure, as well as I do ..."

King Leopold had, indeed, every reason to be satisfied with his handiwork and when, on February 10, 1840, Victoria and Albert were married in great splendor, it was on King Leopold that a great deal of the reflected glory played.

Nor was this particular matrimonial triumph his only one. Coburg nephews and nieces were coming onto the marriage market by the dozen; no matter how unexpected the vacancy, Leopold always had a candidate to fill it. He had already arranged a marriage between his nephew, Prince Ferdinand of Coburg-Kohary, and the young, newly widowed Queen of Portugal, and now he negotiated two further dynastic alliances: his niece Princess Victoria of Saxe-Coburg-Kohary was married to Louis Philippe's son, the Duke de Nemours, and another nephew, Prince August of Saxe-Coburg, was married to the French King's daughter, Princess Clementine. By these matrimonial maneuverings Leopold allied the once obscure House of Coburg to the reigning houses of England, France and Portugal, and in 1846, when Europe became involved in a hunt for a husband for the young Queen Isabel II of Spain, Leopold had yet another candidate to hand. On this occasion, however, his move was checkmated, for he was brought up against a dynastic schemer no less astute than himself— his father-in-law, King Louis Philippe.

Leopold's choice of husband for the voluptuous young Queen of Spain was, of course, another nephew. This time it was Prince Leopold of Coburg, brother to the Coburg King of Portugal. In his choice Leopold had the enthusiastic support of Victoria and Albert who promptly accepted the Coburg prince as their own candidate. King Louis Philippe, on the other hand, wanted one of his own sons, preferably the Duke de Montpensier, to win the prize. At a meeting between Queen Victoria and King Louis Philippe, however, it was decided that neither France nor England would press her respective candidate. With one Coburg in Brussels, another in London and a third in Lisbon, protested Louis Philippe, he really must draw the line at Madrid. Queen Isabel would therefore be married to some Bourbon prince (provided that he was not a French Bourbon) and the marriage of Isabel's younger sister, Luisa, delayed until Isabel herself had married and produced children. This delay would insure that the crown did not pass to Luisa's descendants.

When Lord Palmerston, the British Foreign Secretary, airily and without instruction, later suggested that perhaps the Coburg prince might be the best candidate after all, King Louis Philippe took his chance. Contrary to the agreement, he said, England was pressing the candidature of the Coburg; therefore he felt free to disregard the agreement and to marry his son Montpensier, not to Queen Isabel herself, but to her sister Luisa. He did so, moreover, without waiting for Isabel to produce children, for the very good reason that the effeminate husband (the specified non-French Bourbon) whom they chose for Isabel was reckoned to be incapable of fathering any. Montpensier, therefore, stood a very good chance of one day becoming King Consort of Spain.

The duplicity of the French King infuriated Victoria. In letter after letter to King Leopold she berated the French Government for what she called their *"shabbily* dishonest" behavior. "This is *too* bad," she exclaimed, "for *we* were so honest as *almost to prevent* [Leopold's] marriage...." To anyone who cared to listen and to many who did not, she raved on and on about "this painful Spanish business." She even attacked poor Queen Louise on the subject. The Belgian Queen had been commissioned by her father to write Victoria a conciliatory letter, presenting the marriage as a purely family affair. *"Je veux seulement dire qu'il est impossible,"* answered Victoria tartly, *"de donner à cette affaire le cachet d'une simple affaire de famille...."*

Although King Leopold was disappointed at the failure of his nephew's candidature and although, privately, he agreed with Victoria on the dishonesty of Louis Philippe's conduct, he very wisely held his tongue. He was caught, as usual, between the devil and the deep blue sea. King Louis Philippe was his father-in-law and any trouble between England and France was bound to mean even more trouble for Belgium. It would serve Leopold's cause much better to try to calm his agitated niece and to effect a reconciliation between the two countries. He would act as mediator. It was a role for which he was becoming increasingly well qualified and one which he relished to the full. On this occasion, however, he could have saved himself the trouble. The surge of European events was soon to nullify King Louis Philippe's power and bring in their wake an infinitely more formidable personality to the throne of France.

4

"As regards Belgium," wrote King Leopold on one occasion, "the State means myself. I am the Atlas on whose shoulders rests our little Kingdom."

For all the characteristic complacency of the statement, it was nonetheless valid. On paper, and by the standards of the time, it was true that the Belgian Constitution allowed the monarch very little say. "All powers," it declared firmly, "come from the Nation." The King, who took an oath to the Constitution, could make no decision unless it be countersigned by a minister and although he could appoint ministers from outside Parliament, such ministers had to enjoy the confidence of the majority. On the death of the monarch, the succession of his heir was not automatic; to stress the sovereignty of Parliament, all authority was vested in the two Chambers until the new monarch had taken his oath before them and so obtained his constitutional powers. It was, in fact, essentially a republican constitution—headed by a monarch. When, however, that monarch was so shrewd a statesman as Leopold, the picture could be made to look rather different. By exercising his somewhat limited powers to the utmost, Leopold was able to control the destinies of his kingdom to an extent never visualized by the Constitution-makers of 1831.

This he did both by inclination and of necessity. It was his accession to the Belgian throne which had first given the revolutionary nation a semblance of respectability in the eyes of Europe's monarchs and from this position of strength (augmented by his almost immediate assumption of the supreme command of the army during the Ten Days War) Leopold was able to take over the direction of his country's foreign affairs. There were, in fact, few Belgian statesmen with either the taste or aptitude for the task; obsessed with the problems of domestic politics, successive governments allowed the King a free hand in diplomatic affairs. By a blend of firmness, flexibility, and at times downright cunning, King Leopold guided his kingdom through a series of international crises and established, beyond all possible doubt, the autonomy of Belgium in the concert of nations.

In domestic affairs his role was that of mediator and counselor; he was, after all, a constitutional monarch. His authority, however, was immense and in all national affairs he exercised a strong personal control. Where he could not get his way by constitutional means he resorted to other methods: he was a great believer, for instance, in calculated delays. In the struggle between the two political parties, Catholics and Liberals, Leopold remained scrupulously neutral. There were times, in fact, when he found their differences all but incomprehensible. "Here we have a quite superfluous struggle of Catholics and anti-Catholics," he reported with some cynicism to the Archduke John of Austria. "There is a good deal of childishness on both sides." It was the anti-Catholics—the Liberals—drawing their main support from the bourgeoisie of the cities, who dominated the country's political life for most of Leopold's reign, and the main bone of contention between them and the Catholics was the question of the relationship between Church and State. As neither of these opposing parties was anxious for a change of regime, however, King Leopold did not interfere. Only when there was some threat to curb his power did he make a move; no constitutional sovereign could have been more determined to preserve and strengthen his prerogatives.

Economically his reign marked a period of steady expansion: the population increased, the railways spread, the country developed into the workshop of the Continent. Karl Marx, busily writing his *Communist Manifesto*, described the country as "the paradise of capitalism." A less cognizant Austrian Archduke, visiting Belgium at about this time, was amazed at the evident prosperity of the country. "It is indeed the most lovely, blooming land that I have yet seen; a country possessing all the elements of prosperity and plenty; a fertile soil, rich cities crowded closely together, harbors, the sea, a well laid-out network of railways, commerce and factories. On all sides is manifest a feeling of well-being in which the traveller involuntarily shares; on all sides one sees happy friendly faces; the whole country is well cultivated; forests of factory chimneys, industrial establishments, on a scale which I have never seen before, cover whole stretches of the landscape. Belgium fully deserves the self-chosen name of a model country; this it undoubtedly owes in the first place to the prudent procedure of the King...."

But of more satisfaction to Leopold than the independence and prosperity of his country was his own mounting prestige among the sovereigns of Europe. Slowly, but very surely, he began to beat the Great Powers at their own game. Once over the humiliation of having to hand back those parts of Limburg and Luxembourg to Holland, Leopold began to go from strength to strength. The marriage of his nephew Albert to the Queen of England was a tremendous feather in his cap and earned him, if only superficially at first, the respect of many of his erstwhile belittlers. Hardly had this particular triumph been achieved than his handling of what was called the "Eastern Question"—a clash of interests between France and England in the Near East, with most of the countries of Europe taking sides—won him further acclaim. There is no doubt that his patient maneuverings averted a full-scale European conflict. And there were more triumphs to follow. He was offered, on one occasion, the crown of Poland by the insurgent Poles, and on another, the crown of the Confederation of German States. Flattered, but with commendable sagacity, he declined them both.

At no time, however, did his star shine brighter than during the revolutions that swept through Europe in the year 1848. While one country after another rose up in revolt against its rulers, and sovereigns, including his father-in-law Louis Philippe, fled for their lives, King Leopold remained firmly seated on his throne. "The ideas of the French revolution may go round the world," observed one Belgian politician calmly. "But in order to go round the world, they don't have to pass through Belgium." When, in the form of a trainload of French revolutionaries, these ideas did try to penetrate Belgium, the invaders were surrounded and sent packing.

"Curious enough that I, who in fact was desirous of retiring from politics, should be on the Continent the only sovereign who stood the storm," wrote Leopold to Queen Victoria. To this smug statement the Queen could only answer how "*truly* proud and delighted are we at the conduct of the Belgians, and at their loyalty and affection for you and yours, which I am sure must be a reward for all that you have done these seventeen years." Belgium, she wrote fervently, was "a bright star in the stormy night all around."

Leopold's self-satisfaction was given a further fillip when Prince Metternich, forced to flee the revolutionaries in Austria, took refuge in Brussels. One can appreciate with what gratification the King welcomed what he called "this proof of confidence" on the part of a statesman who had always considered Leopold to be nothing more than the parvenu sovereign of a parvenu state. Even now, however, the reactionary old statesman would not concede too much. "The manner in which Belgium behaves with a Constitution so badly drawn up," he muttered, "proves how easy the Belgians are to govern."

No such churlishness, however, could spoil Leopold's complacency. In his long struggle against European hostility, it was he who had come off best. While rulers scattered helter-skelter across the face of the Continent, he rode through the streets of Brussels, saluting the cheering crowds. That year's September festival, held to commemorate the gaining of independence, was particularly lavish. Floats, piled high with the agricultural and industrial products of each province and drawn by teams of twenty-four horses, passed in review before the King, and at night the Belgian capital was ablaze with light and gay with music. A vast pavilion, Moorish in style and capable of accommodating over 5,000 people, was erected in the market square and within it, it is claimed, "dancing and singing went on continuously." When the King distributed flags to the Civic Guard, the ovation was deafening. Standing with Queen Louise and their three children on a dais erected in front of the palace, he watched the colors dip before him, while all about the air was loud with the thunder of cannon and the roll of drums. "You have been surprised by a political crisis without parallel in history," he said in his speech to the Guard. "As yet you have passed through it gloriously—so gloriously that many a country has adopted your political organisation as a model; your name is everywhere respected and honoured, and you must feel it deserves to be. Let us know how to maintain this position, let us go on as we have gone hitherto, and so shall we insure ourselves an honourable name in history and a future full of glory."

By the middle of the century King Leopold was far and away the most highly respected monarch on the Continent, and men began to talk of him as the "Mentor of Europe" and the "Nestor of Sovereigns." And if Queen Victoria did once complain, in confidence, to Prince Albert that "dear Uncle is given to believe that he must rule the roast [sic] everywhere," such carpings never reached the ears of her vainglorious uncle himself.

Chapter Two

1

If Leopold had become Europe's leading king, Louise had certainly not become its leading queen. Her place was not so much at her husband's side as in his shadow. And this is where she wanted it to be. Queen Louise had nothing of her husband's ambition, vanity and taste for political intrigue; her horizons were purely domestic. When she did interest herself in public affairs, her interests tended to be charitable rather than political or social; hospitals, orphanages and schools were her particular concern. By this sincere interest in the poor, the sick and the unhappy, she came to enjoy immense popularity among her subjects. They called her *L'Ange des Belges* and even the sharp-tongued Madame de Lieven speaks of *"cette reine Louise, si adorée."*

Unlike her husband, she was deeply religious. His faith was a halfhearted Lutheranism, hers a passionate and unquestioning Catholicism. She spent several hours a day in prayer and there are few of her letters in which God, and her submissiveness to His decrees, is not mentioned. That she felt the need of spiritual comfort there is no doubt, for her private life was far from happy. Leopold, for all the apparent coldness of his temperament, was a man of powerful lusts. This was a side of his nature to which Louise, no matter how yielding, could not respond. So frail, so shy, so inhibited, she was incapable of satisfying his sexual needs; although still in her thirties, she felt too old for him. Her health, she protested, did not allow her to fulfill "her wifely duties." When Leopold began to seek sexual fulfillment elsewhere, it was with something akin to relief that she forgave him. In fact, she more than forgave him; she all but granted him her blessing. The fact that she had failed him, she once wrote, "only increases my adoration and gratitude."

Such self-abasement Leopold simply accepted as his due and continued to satisfy his lusts wherever and whenever he pleased. There was never, of course, any shortage of subjects willing to accede to their Sovereign's demands. "He loved a little here and there, without losing his heart to any," writes one of his biographers, and he always made some provision for the resulting illegitimate children. For the girls he would arrange marriages, for the boys commissions in the army or posts in the diplomatic corps. His most enduring mistress was a certain Arcadie Claret de Viescourt. Having decided that he wanted this beautiful young creature as a permanent mistress, Leopold cynically married her to one of his stewards—Von Eppinghoven—and then sent the husband packing. Once Arcadie, now Mme. Meyer Von Eppinghoven, had overcome a tendency to flaunt her position in public (an angry crowd once pelted her carriage with rotten vegetables), she settled down to the sort of bourgeois existence which Leopold preferred. Her drawing room became the meeting place for members of the Government and gave off an atmosphere hardly less respectable than that of the palace itself. Cheerful, intelligent and amusing, Mme. Meyer handled her royal lover with great tact and skill. Leopold loved music (he always complained of the Queen's lack of musical appreciation) and as his mistress was a very accomplished pianist, she was able, it is said, "to bring tears to his eyes and conjure up in his heart an irresistible longing for love and happiness." She bore him two sons and remained with him, growing more matronly and sedate each year, until the day he died.

Never a word of complaint about such infidelities escaped the lips of Queen Louise. She accepted them all as the mysterious movings of God. When her mother once asked whether, because of Leopold's prolonged absences, she did not feel neglected, Louise's answer was almost saintly in its humility. "If I know that Leopold is happy where he is, that's all I need. You should love those you love for themselves, not for yourself."

By way, perhaps, of compensation for her bleak marital life, Louise threw herself heart and soul into the affairs of her family. She could, when in the security of the family circle, be utterly charming—almost skittish. One gets a glimpse of her, laughing excitedly, as she encourages the young Victoria to try on some of her Paris dresses, and sees her, on another occasion, beating her niece at chess despite the hilariously conflicting advice being doled out by the onlookers. "My favourite Queen Louise is as nice as ever ... ," wrote Victoria's lady-in-waiting, Lady Lyttleton; "daily and hourly acts of kindness and modesty and peaceful dignity! There never was such a manner, I do think." Louise was a prodigious letter-writer and each day, from wherever the court happened to be in residence, her letters streamed out to the various members of her family. When Leopold was away from home, she wrote to him twice a day. Her letters were, for the most part, compilations of trivia—the comings and goings of her relations, the health of her children, family outings and journeys, detailed descriptions of dresses. When Queen Victoria once wrote asking whether there was anything she should know about the personal preferences of King Louis Philippe, who was about to pay a visit to Windsor, Louise answered with pages of advice, protesting all the while that her father was "most easy to please." He was *not* to have breakfast, he liked a horse-hair mattress with a plank of wood under it, he should not be allowed to act *le jeune homme*, he must not *"eat too much."*

With her own three children, Louise was every bit as solicitous. She watched over every detail of their upbringing. She supervised their clothes, their food, their games, their education and, above all, their religious instruction. She was present each month when they were examined by their tutors and she always presented a book to the one who had made the best progress. The eldest, Leopold, Duke of Brabant, seemed the least promising; he had a withdrawn, indifferent air and seemed incapable of sustained effort. "I was very upset to read the Colonel's report," wrote Louise to her eldest son on one occasion, "and find that you had again been lazy and that your dictations had been so bad and careless. This is not what you promised me ... your father was as grieved as I was to read your last report."

His father's remedy for such slackness was increased discipline. At the age of ten the young Prince Leopold started military training, and his tutors were constantly being exhorted to exercise greater firmness with the boy. "As I wish to inculcate ... the sentiment of duty—a sentiment which nowadays is growing weaker and only too often giving way to considerations of utility and convenience—everything must be made relevant to this sentiment," the King once wrote to Leopold's new tutor. The tutor obeyed, but the boy made little progress.

Coupled with the young Leopold's disappointing apathy was his no less disappointing appearance. He was tall but painfully thin, with a long, beak-like nose and a somewhat shifty look in his eye. His chest was said to be weak and he walked with a sciatic limp. No amount of rigorous military training seemed able to make him look anything other than a rather slovenly schoolboy; his uniform was usually creased and he seemed incapable of keeping his seat on a horse.

That this gangling, lethargic and crafty-looking boy was a disappointment to his ambitious father can be appreciated, but instead of giving him some encouragement, King Leopold withdrew yet further until he found himself incapable of taking the boy into his confidence and of teaching him the craft of kingship. "Leopold," said the King on one occasion, "is subtle and shy: he never takes a chance. The other day, when I was at Ardenne, I watched a fox which wanted to cross a stream unobserved: first of all he dipped a paw into the water to see how cold it was, then he lowered the paw carefully to see how deep it was, and then with a thousand precautions, very slowly made his way across. That is Leopold's way."

It was very much a matter of the pot calling the kettle black.

The King's second son, Philip, Count of Flanders, was a very different proposition. Two years younger than Leopold, he was a lively, quick-witted lad, much more attractive than his brother. *"Pas beau frère!"* the jealous young Leopold used to cry out in the months after his brother's birth, and the Queen's obvious delight in her second son merely strengthened this jealousy as the years went by. Philip was clearly the favorite and it was he who usually won his mother's book on examination days. Fair and solidly built, the Count of Flanders had his mother's pale blue eyes, but his health, too, was delicate and he was to suffer, in later years, from increasing deafness.

The training of this second, more favored son was no less severe than that of the heir. Both mother and father lectured them *ad nauseam* when they were home, and when they were not, their written instructions poured forth in a steady stream. "I forgot to tell you yesterday," wrote the Queen to a member of the household, "that the King allows the children to go down to see Charlotte if they have been good, on Thursdays and Sundays after their supper, and to pass part of the evening with her...."

It was this youngest child and only daughter, Charlotte, who was the apple of the King's eye. "Charlotte has become a great favourite with Leopold, as you prophesied she would," wrote Queen Louise to her mother, and it seemed, indeed, as though this little princess would be the only one of the children capable of achieving their father's high standards. When little more than a baby she began to show signs of what would one day be a remarkable beauty; her eyes were dark, her skin glowing, her hair lustrous. On her fourth birthday, her dark head "crowned with roses," she dined with her parents. "She will probably never have such a happy birthday as this!" exclaimed Queen Louise with some justification, for Charlotte's education, no less thorough than that of her brothers, was already awakening all the natural seriousness of her temperament. At the age of five she was able to read the Office for Holy Week "with an imperturbable air of sang-froid," and even her games were played with an unchildlike gravity.

"I have received the beautiful dolls' house you have been so kind as to send me, and I thank you very much for it," she wrote to Queen Victoria at the age of eight. "I am delighted with it; every morning I dress my doll and give her a good breakfast; and the day after her arrival she gave a great rout at which all my dolls were invited. Sometimes she plays at drafts on her pretty little draft board, and every evening I undress her and put her to bed.

"Be so good, my dearest Cousin, as to give my love to my dear little Cousins, and believe me always, your most affectionate Cousin, Charlotte."

Surely every inch a Coburg.

The year 1848 was a tragic one for Queen Louise. On the first day of January she heard that her aunt, the redoubtable Mme. Adelaide, had died. "The loss of my good, excellent, beloved Aunt is an *immense misfortune* for us *all*," she wrote to Queen Victoria, "and the most *dreadful blow* for my poor Father." Hardly had she recovered from his particular loss than her father, Louis Philippe himself, was toppled from his throne and forced to flee Paris. For thirty-six hours Louise had no idea whether he and her mother were alive or dead; the uncertainty, said Leopold, threw her into "a state of despair which is pitiful to behold." Death, she afterward claimed, "is not worse than what we endured during these horrible hours."

Her relief on hearing that the King and Queen had arrived safely in England was almost hysterical. "In the hours of agony we have gone through I asked God *only* to spare the *lives*, and I ask still *nothing else*," she wrote in a wild and rambling letter to her niece. "What has happened is *unaccountable, incomprehensible*, it appears to us like a *fearful* dream."

It was a dream from which she never really awoke. Although Louis Philippe himself—now settled with Queen Marie Amélie at Leopold's old home, Claremont House—seemed "wonderfully merry still and quite himself," Louise could not shake off her depression. Months after the revolution Queen Victoria was still inquiring anxiously after "poor, dear Louise," and not even Belgium's remarkable escape from the revolutionary flood could raise her spirits. It was at this time, too, that she finally realized that Leopold had very little interest in her as a wife. With her once powerful father now an exile and the French alliance in ruins, Louise had suddenly become less important to him, and it was now that he started his liaison with Mme. Meyer Von Eppinghoven. Although Louise, as always, was sublimely forgiving, she could not help feeling slighted. "What more could I ask on earth than to be your friend, to be your only friend?" she wrote to him early in 1849. "All my happiness I owe to you; all that is lacking from my happiness is my fault, alone, and I blame only myself for all that troubles me...."

In the spring of that year she fell ill (her chest was always weak) and her slow recovery was set back by the death, in August 1850, of her father at Claremont. Within a few weeks she herself was dying and in the hope that the sea air might improve her condition, they moved her to Ostend. Yet even now, in these last days of her life, her chief concern was that her husband should not be unduly troubled by her illness. "She is so contented, so cheerful, that the possibilities of danger appear to me impossible," wrote Leopold on the 7th of October. In the face of mounting public criticism the King had been shamed, says Madame de Lieven, into dispatching Madame Meyer *"avec enfant, meubles et bagages"* to Germany, but the gesture seems to have come too late. *"La situation du roi est bien mauvaise ... "* reported Madame de Lieven, *"l'irritation publique contre lui est bien grande."*

By now Louise's mother and her three brothers had hurried across from England to be with her, and on October 11, in the most terrible pain, the Queen died. She was thirty-eight years old.

Her body was carried on a funeral train from Ostend to Laeken. "It was the will of God," said Father Dechamps in his funeral oration, "that she should die at the extremity of the kingdom, in order that, carried as it were in the arms of the people across our provinces, she might leave, as she passed, on the hearts of all, the imprint of her holy life and holy death. Let us never forget that mourning procession, that funeral car, that covered crown, that blaze of lights, towards which turned every eye, passing through those multitudes that flocked together to kneel, to weep and to pray, as it passed...."

Queen Victoria was no less rhetorical. "*How* beautiful it must be to see that *your whole country* weeps and mourns *with* you!" she wrote to her uncle. And indeed, Belgium had cause to mourn, for in Queen Louise it had lost the one person still capable of introducing a breath of humanity into the cheerless court.

If Leopold, in his letters to his niece, seemed suitably heartbroken, his letters to his old confidante, the Archduke John, were probably more honest. He had lost, he explained to his friend in that chillingly self-obsessed fashion, "an infinitely devoted friend ... one who had no thought but for him, and existed only for him."

2

In the year of his wife's death, King Leopold of the Belgians turned sixty. Of the good looks which had once set so many feminine hearts aflutter not a vestige remained. Even the most flattering portraits reveal him as a cold and unattractive old man. Yet, as is the way with so many who have known beauty, he resolutely refused to admit its passing. The result was an almost grotesque parody of his younger self. In an age when all men were luxuriantly be-whiskered, King Leopold remained clean-shaven. His sunken, papery cheeks were brightly rouged, his ragged eyebrows darkly penciled. His bald head was covered by a jet-black stiffly ridged wig, combed forward in the wind-swept style of a half-century before, and looking, according to Lord Clarendon, exactly like a night cap. His mouth was a thin, downward-curving slit, his eyes dull behind their crepy lids, his pale skin cross-hatched with wrinkles. "He has the very face for the rôle he plays," said the Duchess de Dino, "parched rather than aged."

And hand in hand with his physical decline, there now set in a decline of his prestige. One of the chief reasons for this was the rise of a formidable rival in the country which had hitherto always been friendly—France.

To head the republic which had been proclaimed after the flight of King Louis Philippe, France elected a president. The successful candidate, by some five and a half million votes out of seven million, was Prince Louis Napoleon Bonaparte, nephew of the great Napoleon. His was a name to send shudders down the spines of Europe's monarchs but most of them comforted themselves with the belief that such an adventurer could not possibly last long in capricious France. It was left to Queen Victoria to show more perspicacity. "It will, however, perhaps be more difficult to get rid of him again than one at *first* may imagine," she wrote to King Leopold, and her uncle would have done better to have taken heed of her warning. In his dealings with the new Prince President, in fact, Leopold revealed for the first time an uncharacteristic clumsiness of touch. Forgetting that he himself had once been considered a parvenu, he was consistently highhanded with this brand-new Napoleon. It was an error which was to cause him a great deal of anxiety.

The Prince President's coup d'état of 1851, by which he extended his term of office with sovereign powers for another ten years, forced Leopold to take his new neighbor rather more seriously. Louis Napoleon's confiscation, the following year, of all the Orleans property in France, by which Leopold's children were deprived of their legal inheritance, further alarmed him. And when, later that year, Louis Napoleon, as a result of an overwhelmingly favorable plebiscite, was proclaimed Napoleon III, Emperor of the French, Leopold's worst fears seemed to have been realized. Little Belgium lay once more at the mercy of a Napoleon and found itself, said Leopold, "in the awkward position of persons in hot climates who find themselves in company, for instance in their beds, with a snake; they must *not move because that irritates* the creature, but they can hardly remain as they are, without a fair chance of being bitten."

Instead of trying to placate this venomous creature, however, Leopold thrashed about in an effort to form alliances against him. In letter after letter to his fellow sovereigns, he sounded dark warnings about the aggressive designs of the new Emperor. "Formerly I was the advance guard against confusion; now it is against ambition," he wrote to the Archduke John. "What the [Napoleonic] eagle meant in earlier times we know well, and so do Vienna, Berlin, Moscow and many other cities." When Louis Napoleon started looking for a bride, Leopold, for the first time in his life, offered no suggestion; in fact, he actively opposed the plan for a marriage between Napoleon III and one of Victoria's nieces, daughter of her half-sister, Feodora. By his shortsightedness Leopold lost the opportunity of associating himself with the most brilliant reign of the century. The Emperor married the beautiful and spirited Eugénie de Montijo and Leopold lost no time in letting Queen Victoria know that Napoleon had warned his young bride of all the dangers of her new position; *"le moyen sera peut-être la guerre,"* reported the King with obvious relish.

In the Emperor Napoleon III, however, King Leopold was brought face to face with a sovereign no less astute than himself. Anxious to avoid the rock upon which the first Napoleon's Empire had floundered, this new Napoleon was determined to form an alliance with England. And the road to London, he reckoned, ran by way of Brussels. He thus set himself out to be as courteous as possible to the suspicious King Leopold. He sent his cousin, Prince Jerome Napoleon (the surly Plon-Plon) to Brussels, and Leopold dispatched his nephew, the Duke of Saxe-Coburg-Gotha, on a return visit to Paris. "The Emperor has a *désir excessif* to be on good terms with me," said Leopold to Baron von Vrints. "It is very flattering, but his real aim is to place himself above me." He therefore remained polite but distant, and did very little toward fostering an Anglo-French entente.

But little by little he came to appreciate that Napoleon was managing to realize his aim without any help from him. Russian ambitions in Turkey were beginning to force England and France into an alliance, and Napoleon III was determined to make the most of the opportunity. A war in Crimea, with England and France supporting Turkey against Russia, seemed inevitable, and in spite of all King Leopold's frantic last-minute maneuverings, hostilities broke out in March 1854. Leopold, whom a contemporary news sheet likened to a fireman furiously extinguishing the blaze lest his own house be attacked by flames, tried to bring the war to a quick close. He even forced himself to visit Napoleon III at Boulogne. But it was all to no purpose. The war continued and Leopold retired in a huff to his house on Lake Como. Known as the Villa d'Este, the house had come to him through his first wife Charlotte, whose mother, the bizarre Queen Caroline, had bought it during her long years of wandering. Here, amidst its fairy-tale beauties, he found a little respite and was able to read, to listen to music and to go for those long walks which he enjoyed so much.

His peace of mind was short-lived. In spring the following year, while the Crimean War dragged on, Napoleon III visited Victoria. The visit was an immense success; the Queen was enchanted with the Imperial couple and in letter after letter to her uncle, with a wealth of underlinings, capitals and exclamations, she stressed the virtues of her guests. The Emperor was "fascinating"; the Empress had such "grace, elegance, sweetness, and *nature*"; the whole visit was "like a brilliant and most successful dream." The Emperor, she assured her doubtless cynically smiling uncle, "spoke very amiably of you." *"Le Roi,"* Napoleon is reported to have said, *"n'est pas seulement très-aimable, mais il a tant de bon sens."* When Victoria and Albert paid a return visit to Paris later in the year, King Leopold was left in no doubt that "the *complete* Union of the two countries is stamped and sealed in the most satisfactory manner, for it is not *only* a Union of the two Governments—the two Sovereigns—it is that of the *two Nations!"* Even old Stockmar was treated to a seemingly endless paean on the Emperor's overwhelming charm.

When the Crimean War ended with a victory for the Allies, it was in Paris that the Peace Congress was held. Conspicuously absent from the conference table was any representative of the one sovereign who had done his best to avert the war—King Leopold. The Emperor Napoleon III was the hero of the hour, and Belgium's star, which had gleamed so brightly in the troubled skies of 1848, was now eclipsed by the sun which shone with such brilliance in France.

3

A less prepossessing heir than Leopold, Duke of Brabant, would have been difficult to imagine. In April 1853 the Prince turned eighteen but looked, according to Lady Westmorland, more like sixteen. "A stick of asparagus, with a narrow chest and no suspicion of a beard," was her ladyship's description of him, and it was generally agreed that the only remarkable thing about Prince Leopold's face was the size of his nose. "It is such a nose," wrote Disraeli, "as a young prince has in a fairy tale, who has been banned by a malignant fairy, or as you see in the first scenes of a pantomime, or in the initial letter of a column of Punch." And not only was the young man gauche and unattractive, but he was known to suffer from a weak chest and a sciatic leg. Nor were these physical disabilities offset by any depth of intellect or charm of manner. Like his father, Prince Leopold was canny rather than clever, and although talkative, he talked, it was said, "like an old man." Queen Victoria considered him "very odd" and complained of his fondness for "saying disagreeable things to people."

It was with this unpromising material that King Leopold now set out to fashion a brilliant matrimonial alliance. As the once powerful Orleans family was of no more use to him and as he considered the Bonapartes to be of little dynastic consequence, Leopold began to look toward the older, more established royal houses. With the passing years he had become more and more conservative and it was with the illustrious but uncompromisingly reactionary Hapsburg dynasty that he now planned to ally his House. As usual, he prepared the ground very carefully. Through his old friend, the Archduke John, he sounded out the Emperor Franz Josef on the question of an

Austrian archduchess, and once permission had been obtained, he set off, with the compliant Duke of Brabant in tow, to visit Vienna. Here, amidst the splendors of the imperial capital, arrangements were finalized: Prince Leopold was to marry Marie Henriette, the daughter of the Archduke Josef, prince of Hungary and Bohemia. To the satisfaction of all concerned—other than the young couple themselves—the engagement was announced on May 18, 1853.

The Archduchess Marie Henriette was horrified at the prospect. Just sixteen years old, she was as unlike her future husband as she could possibly be. Where Prince Leopold was tall and thin and ugly, Marie Henriette was short and well-formed and pretty. Where he was sly and circumspect, she was noisily outspoken. Where he could hardly keep his seat on a horse, she was never happier than when galloping across the great plains of her native Hungary. Of the formalities and hypocrisies of courts she knew nothing; she was a boisterous, undisciplined creature with a raucous laugh and a taste for gypsy music. She had been brought up, noted Countess de Ficquelmont in some apprehension, "more as a boy than a girl." That such a fresh and hoydenish princess should be unwilling to ally herself to so pedantic and delicate a youth can be appreciated; there was even the inevitable gypsy warning against the match: "Beware of new kingdoms," a gypsy is said to have murmured as Marie Henriette was returning home from a walk one summer's evening. "From a throne you will dispense happiness unto others, but none will dispense any unto you." But it was too late now; Marie Henriette's tearful protestations went unheeded. The wedding date was fixed for August (there were to be two ceremonies—one in Vienna and one in Brussels) and father and son returned to Belgium. The coming *mésalliance* was summed up by Madame de Metternich as a marriage between a stable-boy and a nun. "And by nun," explained Madame de Metternich sharply, "I mean the Duke of Brabant."

The first ceremony, in Vienna on August 10, took place without the bridegroom. He was ill, in Brussels, with scarlet fever. Standing proxy for him was the Emperor's brother, the Archduke Charles. The ceremony over, Marie Henriette was obliged to go through the ridiculous ritual of being officially handed over to Belgium; etiquette forbade that she simply travel by train from Vienna to Brussels and there go through the second marriage ceremony. She and her bridegroom must meet on neutral ground, and as no such ground was available, it must needs be created. A wealthy Belgian countess, living close to the German border, offered her home as the royal meeting place and her estate was duly declared to be neutral territory. A special station was erected on the property and the two royal trains, one from Vienna and the other from Brussels, stood puffing in nearby stations, waiting for the signal which would ensure that they converge simultaneously on the temporary station. When, after a thirty-minute delay, the Belgian train had still not received its signal to move forward, the anxious King Leopold sent an aide-de-camp to find out what was happening. It appears that the boy responsible for receiving the signal had ambled off to listen to the band and that the signal bell had been shrilling away unheeded. By the time that the apologetic Belgian royalties tumbled out of their train on the flag-bedecked temporary station, the Archduchess Marie Henriette had been kept waiting for over half an hour.

The couple were married, for the second time, at the cathedral of Sainte Gudule in Brussels, on August 22. The match forged the first link in the chain which was to bind Coburgs and Hapsburgs in tragic alliance; no marriage between the two royal houses was to bring anything but heartbreak. For poor tomboyish Marie Henriette, marriage to the sarcastic-tongued and sexually insatiable Duke of Brabant had all the quality of a nightmare.

"If God hears my prayers," she wrote in anguish to a friend a few weeks after the ceremony, "I shall not go on living much longer."

4

An even more illustrious match, from King Leopold's point of view, was that of his only daughter, Princess Charlotte.

Of his three children, Charlotte was the only one in whom he took an unalloyed delight. Industrious, intelligent and beautiful, Charlotte was a Coburg to the very tips of her fingers. No lecture from her father, no matter how wordy, was listened to with anything other than serious appreciation; no problem, no matter how intricate, was laid aside until it had been mastered; no social obligation, no matter how tedious, was ever shirked. At thirteen, Plutarch was her favorite author. At fourteen she could report that her governess would find her "completely changed both physically and mentally, since I am now working better and have grown a great deal and am less awkward than before." At fifteen she considered the music favored by her brother's wife, Marie Henriette, to be far too light. "Marie is very kind," she wrote, "but her education is so poor that she has not developed a taste for more serious things."

And yet, for all her precocity, Charlotte was no prig. She loved dancing, she had a tremendous zest for life and she had a melting charm of manner. Slim, elegant and dark-eyed, she was already remarkably pretty. "I think she will be the most beautiful princess in Europe," claimed her proud father. "If only it might bring her happiness."

The best way to secure her this happiness, he reckoned, was to arrange a good marriage. He already had two suitors in mind. The one was the nineteen-year-old Portuguese King, Pedro V, whose late father was one of Leopold's Coburg nephews. The other was the twenty-four-year-old Prince George of Saxony. Queen Victoria, on being asked for an opinion, was all for King Pedro. "He is out and out *the* most distinguished young Prince there is, and besides that, good, excellent, and steady according to one's heart's desire, and as one could wish for an *only and beloved daughter*. For Portugal, too, an *amiable*, well-educated Queen would be an immense blessing, for there *never* has been one. I am sure you would be more likely to secure Charlotte's happiness if you gave her to Pedro than to one of those innumerable Archdukes, or to Prince George of Saxony." Pedro, she repeated a few weeks later, "is full of resource—fond of music, fond of drawing, of languages, of natural history and literature, in all of which Charlotte would suit him, and would be a *real* benefit to the country." The Queen would give Pedro one of her own daughters, she declared, were he not a Catholic.

But it was not to be. There visited Brussels, in the summer of 1856, the Archduke Maximilian, brother of the Emperor Franz Josef of Austria. With his tall figure, his good looks, his exquisite manners and his very real intelligence, the Archduke Maximilian was everything that Charlotte could have wished for. Although she was not yet sixteen, she was immediately attracted to the fair-haired young Archduke. It was an attraction which was enthusiastically reciprocated.

The Archduke Maximilian had come on to Belgium from France where he had been the guest of the Emperor Napoleon III and the Empress Eugénie. What struck him immediately on his arrival in Belgium was the contrast between the French Emperor's parvenu court and the undeniably regal atmosphere surrounding the Belgian King. "The Court is well ordered," he reported to Franz Josef with more than a touch of patronage, "a certain dignity is to be noticed in everything, a *ton de bonne compagnie* and the accustomed formality of a Court; and by comparison with Paris I was impressed here with a comfortable sensation of being once more among my own kind, for Brussels has for me that pleasant feeling which I missed in France, of well-bred existence and of being at home."

Maximilian might appreciate the tone of Leopold's court but he had to admit that the King himself was deadly dull. They had hardly finished dinner that first evening before Leopold trapped him in a window embrasure and there subjected him to a seemingly endless sermon on current politics. The monologue ended by Leopold offering to continue the lecture the next day; it was an offer, confessed his guest, "which I received yawning in spirit." But there was no escape. As promised, Leopold appeared in Maximilian's apartments the following morning, and so carried away was he by his own eloquence that the household was obliged to have luncheon an hour late. The Archduke had to admit that for all his host's verbosity, he had some "very shrewd, if not quite novel ideas." How far he could be trusted he did not know, for "in everything he says and does, the fox peeps out unmistakably."

The father might be tedious but the daughter was enchanting. Thus, when Maximilian got back to Vienna, he made a formal request for Charlotte's hand. Although Leopold would have preferred Pedro (Pedro was, after all, a king), he revealed a surprising depth of understanding in this matter of his daughter's future husband. "My object is and was," he told Queen Victoria, "that Charlotte should decide as *she* likes it, and uninfluenced by what I might prefer … the Archduke has made a favourable impression on Charlotte; I saw that long before any question of engagement had taken place." And in spite of all Victoria's objections ("The Austrian society is *médisante* and profligate and worthless—and the Italian possessions very shaky"), he let Charlotte make up her own mind. Once it was made up, Leopold granted his permission and Maximilian returned to Belgium to pay another visit to his betrothed.

During the months between Maximilian's two visits, Belgium celebrated the twenty-fifth anniversary of the King's inauguration. On July 21, 1856, King Leopold, with the Duke of Brabant on his right, the Count of Flanders on his left and his brilliantly uniformed staff following behind, rode out in blazing sunshine through the streets of his capital. Through a surging mass of people he made his way to the very spot where, in 1831, he had taken the constitutional oath. Here he mounted a broad flight of stairs to take his place on a great dais, canopied in crimson and supported by gigantic figures in gold. Baron de Gerlache, the same statesman who twenty-five years earlier had invited him to ascend the throne, then treated the vast assembly to a paean on their Sovereign's virtues. "It only remains for us now, Sire," he cried out in conclusion, "to give thanks in the country's name to Heaven, praying at the same time for a prolongation for years to come of your Majesty's precious life and glorious reign...." As the King listened to this heartfelt address from his old colleague, his eyes, they say, were wet with tears.

Sir Henry Drummond Wolff, visiting Brussels with the British envoy, was immensely impressed by the scene. "The brightness of the day—calling to mind a southern climate—the whiteness of the buildings, the vivid tints of the verdure, the enthusiasm of the crowd, the music of the orchestras, combined to produce a scene which will perhaps never be rivalled."

"Never," he declared, "was a King so popular, or a people so ready to celebrate the virtues of their sovereign."

For three days Brussels was *en fête* and throughout the summer and autumn of that year Leopold and his sons visited the various cities and provinces of the country. The Archduke Maximilian, arriving in December, caught the tail end of the national festivities. Although he was greatly impressed by the prosperity achieved by Belgium under Leopold's rule, Maximilian was rather more critical of the celebrations themselves. He found himself unable to stomach the self-congratulatory pomposity of either Sovereign or statesmen. At a New Year's Day reception he complained of having to listen to "the hackneyed phrases ground out to each other by the constitutional ruler and the various authorities and corporate bodies." He thought the King too glib and the deputations decidedly comic. "The whole affair," noted the Archduke, "was calculated to inspire the unprejudiced observer with a profound disgust for constitutional shams." But then Maximilian, as a Hapsburg, was hardly unprejudiced. What he dismissed as "a constitutional Court ball" on January 6 pleased him no better. So ill-defined were the rules for presentation at court, he grumbled, "that the higher nobility of the land rubs shoulders with its own tailors and cobblers; all the English shop-keepers who have retired to Brussels on grounds of economy have access to the ball with their respective families. The crowd is enormous...."

With the lovely Charlotte, however, he had no fault to find, nor she with him. "The Archduke is charming in every way," she confessed, "and you may imagine how happy I am to have him here for the past week. Physically I find him more handsome and morally there is nothing further to be desired." They sat together for hours talking about their future. Maximilian's romanticism, his professed liberalism, his yearning to be of some service to mankind delighted Charlotte and struck an answering chord in her own enlightened nature. He let her read the diaries which he had kept during his years in the Austrian Navy, and as he was a writer of some talent, she was enchanted by them. He told her all about his plans for building a castle on a rocky promontory above the sea near Trieste; he would call it Miramare and he promised her a chapel in which she could hear Mass every day. Since their last meeting, his brother, the Emperor Franz Josef, had given Maximilian the position of Viceroy for the Austrian provinces of Lombardy and Venezia, and the prospect of queening it in Milan was one which Charlotte found irresistible. Here, surely, was an opportunity for the two of them to put their talents to good use. "However," she noted conscientiously, "it will be a difficult undertaking. It is a mission of good which we must fulfill. I can feel the thorns already, but I can also foresee the satisfaction to be derived from doing something good."

Just before the end of this second visit, Maximilian tackled Leopold on the question of Charlotte's dowry. The cautious King promised to "do something" but would name no sum. Once back in Austria, Maximilian dispatched an envoy to continue negotiations; only after prolonged argument was the matter satisfactorily settled. "I was rather pleased with myself," reported Maximilian to his brother, "for having at last wrung from the old miser something of which he has most at heart."

Charlotte and Maximilian were married in the Royal Palace in Brussels on July 27, 1857. It was an occasion of great splendor. She, in heavy gold-embroidered white satin with a veil of Brussels lace, looked radiant; he, in his dark-blue Vice-Admiral's uniform, all aglitter with gold, looked strikingly handsome. "At *this* very *moment* the marriage is going on," wrote Queen Victoria to Leopold on the day of the wedding (a visit by Maximilian the month before had swept away all her earlier reservations), "the *Knot* is being tied which binds your lovely sweet child to a thoroughly worthy husband—and I am sure you will be much moved. May every blessing attend her!"

Unable to be present at the wedding herself, Victoria had insisted that Albert go. He was able to report that King Leopold was indeed much moved, that Brussels was in a state of great excitement and that feeling amongst the people was excellent. For three days the newly married couple were fêted in the Belgian capital and then traveled south, by way of Vienna, to Italy. At Trieste they spent a week in Maximilian's little villa on the Miramare estate. It was, enthused Charlotte, "a perfect jewel set in this magnificent southern climate, facing one of the most beautiful gulfs in the world. In the north one has no idea of a really blue sea, and when I first saw it I was enchanted." But the beauties of the gulf of Trieste paled beside her first sight of Venice. "I do not believe that there is a finer sight anywhere in the world than the entrance to the canals," she wrote. "Venice, with its present full of poetry, its past full of memories, its half-oriental character, its majestic calm, its canals, churches and palaces, and its indescribable charm, has made the deepest impression on me."

In this flushed, intoxicated state, she journeyed on to Milan. On September 6, 1857, the Archducal couple made their state entry into the city. If Austria's Italian subjects were something less than vociferous in their welcome of the new Viceroy and his beautiful bride, Charlotte either did not notice it or chose not to. She was so deeply in love with her husband and so confident that together—by their tact, their liberalism and the very goodness of their intentions—they would win the hearts of their subjects, that she could see "no shadow on the picture."

"I could not be happier," she wrote to a friend after ten days in Milan. "Max is perfect in every way, so good, so devoted, so gentle. I am experiencing the most perfect happiness. As you can imagine, my former life holds no regrets for me. This life has everything heart and soul could desire...."

It was all so brilliant, so full of promise, this springtime of Charlotte's life.

Chapter Three

1

The year 1859 found Leopold again in his role of fireman, desperately trying to save his house from the flames. His neighbor, the Emperor Napoleon III, was about to set Europe ablaze once more. At a secret meeting the year before between the French Emperor and Count Cavour, the Sardinian Prime Minister, Napoleon III had promised to help Sardinia overthrow Austrian rule and free Italy from "the Alps to the Adriatic." King Leopold, who quite early on suspected that France was planning to liberate northern Italy, was thoroughly alarmed at the prospect. A French triumph would mean nothing but trouble for Belgium. Austria, with whom Leopold had been allying himself more and more closely in recent years, would be humiliated; Charlotte and Maximilian would be forced to abdicate their position in Lombardy-Venezia; France, rendered more powerful still, might well seek aggrandizement on its northern border and re-open the question of a Rhine frontier.

Leopold, in his efforts to preserve peace, was more tireless than ever. His advice—to England, to France, to Austria, to Prussia—poured forth in a steady stream. He urged Austria to ally herself with Prussia, and Prussia to ally herself with Austria; he advised England to remain on friendly terms with France but to build up her navy. "Heaven knows what dance our Emperor *Napoleon Troisième de nom* will lead us," he confessed in anguish to Queen Victoria.

But the days when Leopold had been looked upon as the Nestor of Sovereigns were over. No one was prepared to pay much attention to him and he found himself face to face once more with an unsympathetic and indifferent Europe. The Emperor Franz Josef, considering his brother Maximilian far too soft and idealistic for the job of keeping the Italian provinces in order, had him recalled and then ordered Sardinia to disarm. By these two foolish moves, Austria played directly into the hands of the French: the Italian provinces lost a sympathetic governor and, by ignoring the Austrian ultimatum, Sardinia cast Austria in the role of aggressor. Austria crossed the Sardinian frontier and Napoleon III marched his troops into Italy. There, by a large measure of good fortune, the French won two battles. Fearing that he might not win a third and alarmed at reports of Prussian mobilization on the Rhine, Napoleon III met the Emperor Franz Josef and concluded a hasty peace. Although he had not, as promised, freed Italy to the Adriatic, Napoleon III returned home the victor and King Leopold was forced to accept the mortifying situation. More than that, he felt obliged to make some sort of conciliatory move toward the Emperor. Swallowing his pride, he visited Napoleon and Eugénie at Biarritz that autumn. The visit was one, reported the imperial doctor, of "infinite boredom to our Majesties"; Napoleon, as was his way, listened to everything that Leopold had to say but volunteered very little information himself. Such comment as he did offer, however, was calculated to please the Austrian Emperor, to whom he knew Leopold was bound to repeat it. When the Belgian King, in an excess of diplomatic zeal, suggested that Belgium support France in a punitive expedition to the Far East, Napoleon very wisely ignored the offer. King and Emperor parted on what seemed like the best of terms and Leopold announced that he was quite *"satisfait."* Exactly what he was so *satisfait* about, remarked Disraeli, no one seemed to know and before long it was quite obvious that the two monarchs were working against each other as actively as ever.

In the winter of 1861 King Leopold suffered a further loss of influence. On December 14 of that year the Prince Consort died and his death was a severe blow to Leopold. The King had, in his way, been fond of his nephew, but it was the political loss which he felt more keenly. However devoted to her uncle the Queen might be, the link between the British and Belgian Coburgs was bound to be weakened. Losing no time, Leopold hurried to Osborne to comfort his heartbroken niece. He had hardly arrived, however, before he himself fell ill; he suffered a painful attack of gallstones. A combination of vanity and prudence caused him to hide the real nature of his illness from the public and it was given out that he was suffering from the vagaries of the English climate. Of Victoria, wallowing in grief, he saw very little, and when he went up to London to spend a day or two at Buckingham Palace, a fresh attack forced him to remain there for a fortnight. While at the Palace he sent for Lord Clarendon and subjected him to one of his customary monologues. He talked, said Clarendon, about every subject under the sun, and "though he kept me for an hour and three-quarters, I am not aware that I brought away anything that could be considered a fair equivalent for my railway ticket." The King assured Clarendon that the Queen, contrary to growing suspicion, was in "a healthy state of mind."

With Leopold, in the so-called Belgium Suite of the Palace, was his long-standing mistress, Madame Meyer Von Eppinghoven. Now that the initial flame of their passion had burnt itself out, she remained beside him as "a self-sacrificing, very tactful, and tender-hearted friend." It was she who nursed him through this particular illness. When they returned to Belgium in February, the King's health worsened; he was forced to undergo so much medical treatment that he began to grumble about the doctors "making money" out of him. When, at one stage, he seemed to be on the point of death, Madame Meyer was again bundled off to Germany lest her presence at his death-bed provoke public antagonism. She went, protesting bitterly, but was back at Laeken as soon as his health improved. During the long weeks of his convalescence, in fact, the King would allow only Madame Meyer into his sickroom; even the members of his family were kept at bay. When he did finally give audiences, he would receive his visitors, reports Baron von Hügel, with his face "painted in all the colors of health and youth." In spite of the fact that he had twice, the night before, fainted from pain, he assured even his lifelong associate, Count Conway, that he felt "remarkably well," and when the Archduke Albrecht saw him in August, the visitor reported that the King had the greatest difficulty in standing erect and that his remarks "were of no value whatsoever."

In one way only could the aging King still exert his influence and this was the way which still lay closest to his heart—the aggrandizement of his family. It was with good reason that a disgruntled Hapsburg Archduke could complain that "the Coburgs gain throne after throne and spread their growing power abroad over the whole earth." Already in 1858, King Leopold had had the satisfaction of seeing Queen Victoria's eldest daughter, the Princess Royal, marry the Crown Prince of Prussia. It was Leopold, in his anxiety to have a Coburg at the Prussian Court, who had all along urged the match. Now, in 1862, he was able to chalk up a further triumph. In September Queen Victoria came to Laeken to inspect the young woman whom Leopold had helped choose as a bride for her eldest son, the Prince of Wales. She was Princess Alexandra, daughter of the future King of Denmark. The Princess passed the intimidating test with flying colors ("Alexandra is lovely, such a beautiful refined profile, and quiet ladylike manner") and on September 9, with his mother's permission, the Prince of Wales proposed to her. That night the entire royal party, with the exception of Queen Victoria, who had already left on her pilgrimage to the scenes of her late husband's childhood at Coburg, dined with the gratified King Leopold at Laeken.

One of the family's most spectacular triumphs, however, still lay ahead. It concerned the King's favorite child—Princess Charlotte.

2

The Duke of Brabant, claimed Queen Victoria, "was considered as *unfit*, *idle* and unpromising an Heir Apparent as *ever was known*." It was a harsh judgment and one which was not entirely justified. If Prince Leopold seemed ineffectual, it was because he was denied any opportunity of proving himself otherwise. The King might be too racked with pain to stand upright and too haggard to show himself, unpainted, to even his closest associates, but he refused to delegate one iota of responsibility to his son. Any suggestion of a regency—even a temporary one—was waved aside as unthinkable. The father, attended by his mistress, would lie for months on end in his sickroom while his son was left, very largely, to his own devices. Exactly what these devices were was only gradually becoming apparent.

As predicted, his marriage to the hoydenish Marie Henriette was a disaster. It was a disaster which he had not made the slightest effort to avert. "If Leopold is not happy with her," declared his sister, Princess Charlotte, "it is because he is determined not to be." He neither understood, nor tried to understand her. He found her freshness, her naïveté and her noisy spontaneity embarrassing; he treated her, in private and in public, with thinly veiled contempt. Even on their honeymoon their opposing personalities caused an unseemly clash in public. While in Venice, Marie Henriette was all for taking a second ride in a gondola; Leopold forbade it and, ignoring her tears, dismissed the musicians and boats already hired for the evening.

On another occasion, during an interminable and pompous speech made by some old man to the assembled royal family, Marie Henriette started giggling. The more she tried to control it, the worse it became. So infectious was her merriment that first those near her, then the entire court and finally the slightly bewildered old man himself were convulsed with laughter. Only the King and the Duke of Brabant remained sternly unaffected.

If her husband found Marie Henriette irritating, others, however, considered her charming. Whereas the best that anyone could find to say about Prince Leopold was that he resembled his father and was a confident talker, she was often highly praised. "The Duchess of Brabant," reported Queen Victoria's maid of honor, the Hon. Eleanor Stanley, to her mother, "seems very nice looking ... she is neither tall nor short, fair, rather fat, with pretty eyes and a brilliant color." When King Leopold once sent the pair of them to Paris, Marie Henriette was an immediate success. Napoleon III made a great fuss over her, and the Austrian Ambassador, Count Hübner, considered her "charming in her simplicity, in her frank, childish little manners, in her bearing and, when she talks, in her spontaneity." She had none of that "forced banality, or the tediousness produced by it which is the curse of courts." She even went so far as to teach her hosts a card game in which the winners blackened the faces of the losers with burnt cork. It was a game which seems to have been rapturously taken up by the imperial circle.

For the more serious-minded Prince Leopold, such boisterous behavior, no matter how amusing, would simply not do. He had, in any case, a very poor opinion of women—especially one who laughed so uproariously at court functions, who bred and broke her own horses, and who was even known to join in cavalry charges on maneuvers. Slowly, but very surely, he began to break her spirit. As his father before him had stifled the youthful gaiety of his wife, Queen Louise, so did Prince Leopold—by his sarcasm, his indifference and his blatant unfaithfulness—embitter this far more vital personality. Hardly was their honeymoon over before he took up with the celebrated actress, Aimée Desclée. To justify his behavior, he started a rumor to the effect that Marie Henriette was enamored of her handsome coachman. Hurt and bewildered, Marie Henriette dismissed the coachman and left Brussels. The Archbishop of Malines was dispatched, posthaste, to bring her back; in her position, explained the prelate smoothly to the anguished bride, she must learn to suffer without protesting. It was simply another of her royal duties. Marie Henriette returned, and Leopold, unconcerned, continued his liaison with the actress.

During the first ten years of marriage, Marie Henriette dutifully presented her husband with three children. A daughter, Louise, was born in 1858; a son, Leopold Count of Hainaut, was born in 1859, and a second daughter, Stephanie, in 1864. The birth of a son afforded Leopold immense satisfaction; like his father the King, the

Duke of Brabant had a strong sense of dynasty. He concentrated what little affection he had to give on this son and heir, leaving his wife and daughters all but disregarded. "He had very little inclination for family life," wrote one of these daughters in later years, "and I find it distressing to think how these two, my father and my mother, on whom Providence had bestowed so many advantages, might have lived a harmonious family life and have made a happy home for themselves and one another. Alas, they were unable to do so. One pursued the course of indifference, injustice, unfaithfulness, the other that of self-sacrificing aloofness."

Prince Leopold's real interests lay far from hearth and home. They lay in ways and means of amassing money and using it for the strengthening of his dynasty and the enrichment of his realm. For Prince Leopold, despite his gaucherie and his pedantry, was a man of formidable ambitions. His passions—or rather his lusts—were on a grand scale, and whether sexual, financial or territorial, they were lusts which even in these early days he was impatient to satisfy. His most cherished dream was to convert humble little Belgium into a rich, important country. He wanted to drive wide boulevards through her cramped medieval towns; he wanted her ships to sail the oceans and her merchandise to find its way to the far corners of the earth; he wanted her to colonize and civilize and found an empire; he wanted her people to throw off their timidity and to lead significant, heroic lives. His father had enhanced his position by means of diplomatic achievements and illustrious marriages. Leopold wanted to do it by the glorification of his country. He wanted, one day, to be the great sovereign of a great people.

It was during the course of his many travels that his first vague yearnings developed into an overpowering obsession. At the age of nineteen, on his honeymoon journey, he visited Egypt. Here he watched the building of the Nile dam, listened to the Khedive's talk about the projected Suez Canal, and spent a great deal of his time in the company of Blondeel, the Belgian consul who dreamed of establishing Belgian influence in Africa. From Egypt he went to the

Levant. There was fuel here, too, for his mounting flame of imperialism, for in Palestine were the graves of those two Belgian crusaders, first of a line of Belgian Kings of Jerusalem—Godfrey de Bouillon and Baudouin. The year 1860 found him in Eastern Europe, where he sailed down the Danube on a Turkish warship to spend three weeks with the Sultan in Constantinople. From Athens, which he visited on the way home, he sent the Belgian Minister of Finance a piece of marble from the Acropolis. On it, encircling a relief portrait of himself, was cut the blunt message: *Il faut à la Belgique une Colonie*. Two years later he visited Spain and then traveled slowly along the coast of North Africa to Egypt where he was now able to watch the excavating of the Suez Canal. And at the end of 1864 he undertook his longest and most significant journey yet: he sailed to the Far East. The sight of these fruitful lands, so ripe for exploitation, excited his already fevered imagination; here indeed was an opportunity for Belgium to grow rich and powerful.

Exactly how she should set about it was still uncertain. At first he envisaged the establishment of foreign trading posts, supplied and protected by Belgium. Then he began considering colonies. He thought first of West Africa, then of China or Japan ("the only way to civilize and moralize these idle and corrupted populations of the Far East") and then of South America. Wherever such colonies might be, however, he considered that a system of forced labor would guarantee the quickest returns. If the native populations picked up a little civilization on the way, well and good, but his sole aim was the quick and easy aggrandizement of his country.

If the Duke of Brabant was almost beside himself with colonial ambitions, his countrymen remained cheerfully unresponsive. His father, the King, was too old and too ill to think in terms of colonization; he had his hands full just keeping Belgium intact, and his tentative attempts at overseas settlement in Guatemala and West Africa had been disastrous. Nor were any of the Belgian ministries, be they Liberal or Catholic, anxious to embark on what they considered a wildcat scheme of colonial expansion. And as for the Belgian people, nothing seemed able to shake them out of their national apathy. The complacency, the thrift, the pettiness of the Belgians infuriated young Leopold; they were far too satisfied with things as they were. *"Petit gens, petit pays"* was his oft-repeated opinion of the Belgians and their country. "Belgium doesn't exploit the world," complained Prince Leopold to one of his assistants in 1863, "it's a taste we have got to make her learn." And so, almost single-handed, he set about teaching her. In conversations, in letters, in pamphlets and in speeches, he exhorted his future subjects to widen their horizons and to "show the world that they also are an imperial people capable of dominating and teaching others."

"The time has come for us to expand abroad," he cried out in an impassioned speech in the Chambers. "I hold that there is no time to be lost unless we wish to see all the best positions, already scarce, occupied successively by more enterprising nations than ourselves...."

But he was baying at the moon. "The territorial and psychological limits of his small country were too narrow for the vaulting intelligence and imperious character that he possessed," says the Baron de Gruben, and there was nothing for him to do but wait until he was in a position to force, or even trick, his fellow Belgians into a colonial adventure. In the year 1865 he celebrated his thirtieth birthday; he did not have much longer to wait.

3

Ever since the Emperor Franz Josef had recalled them from Milan before the Italian War of Liberation, Maximilian and Charlotte had been living quietly at Trieste. Disillusioned by the turn of events, Maximilian had withdrawn from public affairs and had devoted himself to writing and to the completing of his castle of Miramare. White-walled, crenelated and many-windowed, it rose on a rocky outcrop above the blue Adriatic. At its foot lay a small, sheltered harbor; behind stretched a magnificent park. With its high-ceilinged rooms, its stained-glass windows and its damasked walls, it gave off an atmosphere at once melancholy and romantic; it was an atmosphere which suited, very nicely, the present mood of its owners. "We have relegated past grandeurs to our memories and we are calmly enjoying what the present has to offer," confided Charlotte to a friend. "Providence has done so much for us that in taking away some of her gifts she has left us enough to be happy in another and perhaps more lasting manner."

Late in 1859 Maximilian, in search of "the peace which excited Europe can no longer give the troubled soul," sailed away on a visit to Brazil. The journey seems to have awakened all his interest in life and to have thrown open tantalizing new vistas. He explored, he inspected, he made copious notes; everything in this vast country seemed to excite and stimulate him. Surely here, in the New World, was the opportunity for fresh beginnings. It was, he wrote, a haven "for those who have come to a resolution to break with the stormy past and to work their way to a blameless future." That he himself was coming to such a resolution there is no doubt, although he did not think that Brazil, for all its attractions, was the answer to his still unchanneled yearnings. He had, he wrote, "the feeling that I had not yet arrived at my ultimate destination."

Back at Miramare he and Charlotte played host to the Empress Elizabeth, wife of the Emperor Franz Josef. This beautiful and highly-strung creature, tottering on the brink of a nervous breakdown, had fled Vienna to spend five months on the island of Madeira. The change appears to have done her good, for when she arrived at Miramare, en route home, she seemed happier and more relaxed. Although Elizabeth was enchanted with the beauties of Miramare, there seems to have been little love lost between her and her sister-in-law, Charlotte. "It was impossible," noted one witness, "for those two beautiful women to shine in the same firmament." To the practical, ambitious Charlotte, a true daughter of King Leopold, the Austrian Empress seemed thoroughly spoiled and far too ready to shirk her imperial duties. No sooner, in fact, had Elizabeth reached

Vienna than it was suddenly announced that she was leaving it again. Within a fortnight she was back in Trieste, and Maximilian was obliged to accompany her to Corfu where she spent the rest of the summer. In this fashion began the Empress Elizabeth's years of wandering; distraught, restless and neurotic, she seemed incapable of remaining by her husband's side for more than a few weeks at a time. And the Emperor Franz Josef, one of the most unimaginative of men, simply did not understand it. He loved her to distraction but he could not hold her interest.

How idyllic, by contrast, did the married life of Maximilian and Charlotte appear to the outside world. He, tall, handsome, luxuriantly bearded, and she, slender, elegant, and strikingly beautiful, made an ideal couple; they seemed to be blissfully happy in each other's company. The appearance, however, was deceptive. Although they had been married for four years, they still had no children; some said the fault lay with Charlotte, others that it was Maximilian who was to blame. Whichever it was, it was a fact that they no longer cohabited. On a trip to Vienna, Maximilian had contracted a venereal disease from a prostitute, and had passed it on to his wife. From the time of this discovery, Charlotte had decided to put an end to their sexual relationship. "Although their mutual attitude before the world remained affectionate and loving," noted Antonio Grill, Maximilian's valet, "privately there was no such affection or confidence."

Nor did life at Miramare satisfy Charlotte. Maximilian, with his deep interest in botany, was often happy enough improving and embellishing the park, but she was too much of a Coburg to be content with so limited an existence. She wrote, she painted, she bathed, she sailed, but all the time she longed for some more significant employment. "I believe the day will come—and this without any ambitious notions on my part—when the Archduke will again occupy a prominent position," she wrote to her friend Countess Hulst. "By this I mean a position where he will govern, for he was made for that and blessed by Providence with everything necessary to make a people happy, and it seems impossible to me that these gifts should be buried forever after shining for a brief three years."

His gifts were not to be buried much longer. The New World, whose call he had considered all but irresistible two years before, now called him with a more insistent voice still: he was asked to become the Emperor of Mexico.

In the year 1861 France, in alliance with England and Spain, had invaded the Mexican Republic in order to force that unstable country into settling its foreign debts. On realizing the complications to which armed intervention in Mexican affairs might lead, England and Spain had hastily withdrawn from the enterprise, leaving France to carry on alone. Napoleon III, glad of the opportunity to win a measure of glory for his regime, poured reinforcements into Mexico and the French, having defeated the inferior Republican forces, occupied the capital. Here a self-styled national assembly, made up of die-hard conservatives and bigoted clericals, proclaimed a monarchy and offered the crown of Mexico to the Archduke Maximilian.

It seems to have been Eugénie, Empress of the French, who first suggested that Maximilian might be interested in accepting the Mexican crown. She was, in fact, one of the main driving forces behind the enterprise; *"une très haute pensée politique et civilisatrice"* was her somewhat emotional description of the proposed adventure. Napoleon III, a little less idealistic, was anxious for a *rapprochement* with Austria, and the offer of a crown to Franz Josef's brother seemed a very good way of achieving it. What was needed in Mexico, reckoned Napoleon, was a liberal Catholic monarch, and the Archduke Maximilian seemed to answer the need exactly. Maximilian, on first hearing of the proposal, was immediately interested. It was an interest which was more than shared by his wife. In fact, at the prospect of becoming an empress, Charlotte's imagination took fire, and throughout the tortuous and often seemingly hopeless negotiations which followed this first tentative proposal, she remained resolute in her determination to see the business through.

Her first move was to consult "our dear wise father," King Leopold. He advised caution and, remembering his own dilemma thirty years before, suggested that, without rejecting the proposition, they first learn the opinion of the Mexican people. This was easier said than done. The only opinions that they were likely to hear were those of the Mexican monarchist emigrés and of the French-protected conservatives in Mexico itself. The Emperor Franz Josef gave his qualified consent (the Empress Elizabeth thought them mad to want to exchange the freedom of Miramare for the restrictions of Mexico) but Britain, whose sanction Maximilian was very eager to obtain, remained lukewarm. In an effort to win British support, Charlotte visited Brussels and there begged her father to approach Queen Victoria on the matter. Like so many Continental royalties, Charlotte could never quite appreciate the extent to which Victoria was a constitutional monarch, and she still tended to look upon such matters as purely family affairs. Leopold, who knew better, promised to do what he could, but seemed rather doubtful of success. His own reservations, by this time, seem to have been swept away completely. It might be that he had been infected by Charlotte's enthusiasm or that he was simply incapable of letting so glittering a prize slip through his fingers. For his daughter to become the Empress of Mexico would be a dynastic achievement indeed! He gave her a great deal of sound advice on minor matters but never once suggested that she actually turn down the Mexican offer. "The undertaking is a perilous one," he admitted to Queen Victoria, "but if it succeeds it will be one of the greatest and most useful of our time." Charlotte, he assured his niece, "is very venturesome and would go with Max to the end of the world; she will be of the greatest use to him; and, if success there is to be, much will be owing to her."

Gratifying as the prospect of a Coburg empress might be to old King Leopold, his gratification was as nothing when set against the enthusiasm of his eldest son, the Duke of Brabant. The prospect had, for the ambitious Prince Leopold, all the quality of a dream come true. "It's a magnificent country, where there is plenty of good to be done," he informed Charlotte with his customary blend of pseudo-philanthropy and avarice. "If I had a son of the right age, I would try to get him made King of Mexico. Every brave heart must long to devote himself to that land. In America, there are so many great works to be done. I want the Coburgs to claim that task!"

On October 3, 1863, the deputation bringing the offer of the Mexican crown arrived at Miramare. Maximilian welcomed them, thanked them, but still did not accept. He was not yet satisfied that the "whole nation expressing freely its will" wanted him or that he should rely on French support alone. Nor was he getting much encouragement from his brother Franz Josef. By this time, however, Napoleon III was getting impatient. Threatening Maximilian with a rival candidate, he now got him to accept the crown, subject to certain guarantees from Napoleon himself. These the French Emperor promised to grant and invited Maximilian and Charlotte to Paris to finalize things. A week of festivities in the French capital, during which Napoleon promised Maximilian that "France should never fail the new Empire," stilled Maximilian's fears and led to the signing of a formal agreement between the French Emperor and himself. He and Charlotte then went on to England, where Victoria was kind but noncommittal and where their visit to Charlotte's grandmother, the aged Queen Marie Amélie, was spoiled by the old lady shouting out: "They will be murdered! They will be murdered!"

Just as the negotiations reached their final stage, the Emperor Franz Josef dropped a bombshell. He informed his brother that his acceptance of the Mexican crown would mean the renunciation of all his rights as a member of the House of Hapsburg. He would lose his rights both of succession and of inheritance. This Maximilian refused to contemplate and promptly announced his decision to decline the offer of the Mexican throne. The news infuriated the French Emperor, but nothing that he could do would make either Maximilian or Franz Josef change his mind. There was nothing for it but for Maximilian to break his signed agreement with Napoleon and for him to give up the prospect of the crown.

It was at this stage that Charlotte came into her own. From now on, while Maximilian floundered about in a swamp of uncertainty, she took matters into her own hands. Armed with a letter from her husband, she made for Vienna and there sought an interview with the Emperor Franz Josef. For three hours she harangued her brother-in-law, forcing him to "abandon all his arguments," but not, unfortunately, to abandon the idea of depriving Maximilian of his inheritance. To back up her impassioned arguments there now came a torrent of advice from King Leopold in Brussels; the Coburgs, father and daughter, were prepared to fight every inch of the way to get what they wanted. "Give up nothing," commanded Leopold. "Do not consent to any proposal of the kind." She must insist on Maximilian's retaining his rights. This she did with considerable vehemence throughout the next interview but the result was the same: Maximilian must either renounce his rights or remain in Austria. With all the stubbornness of the unimaginative, Franz Josef stood his ground. "Must one choose renunciation or compromise?" wired Charlotte to her father, and he, anxious now lest her unyielding stand on the rights of succession lose her the crown altogether, advised compromise. His message seems to have decided her; there was nothing for it but to accept Franz Josef's terms. "Nothing obtained from Vienna," she wired. "Max cannot leave Austria without renunciation."

The business settled, Franz Josef traveled down to Miramare. There, in the presence of a galaxy of Austrian Archdukes, Maximilian signed away his inheritance. On the following day he formally accepted the Mexican crown. Looking pale and edgy, he made a short speech of acceptance to the Mexican delegation and then swore the oath which made him Emperor of Mexico. The imperial Mexican flag was run up on the castle tower and the guns of the Austrian and French frigates *Bellona* and *Themis* fired salutes. "Max has accepted," was Charlotte's final message to her father. "Give us your blessing."

It was Maximilian who needed the blessing more than she. That evening, physically and emotionally exhausted, he escaped to the little villa in the park. Here his doctor found him slumped over a table. "If someone were to tell me that the whole thing was broken off," he cried, "I should jump for joy. But Carlota?"

Carlota—for Charlotte now adopted the Spanish version of her name—was in her element. During the days prior to their departure, while Maximilian remained shut up in the villa, she played her new role for all it was worth. She received deputations, she presided at banquets, she made all arrangements for the journey to Mexico. When her husband drafted what she considered an unsatisfactory letter in reply to the Emperor Napoleon III's congratulatory telegram, she rewrote it in her own hand.

By April 14 Maximilian was considered well enough to embark. While he spent the day mooning about the castle and taking a final look at his beloved gardens, Carlota was attending to all the last-minute details. At two o'clock in the afternoon, in the presence of a vast crowd of well-wishers, the imperial couple walked slowly down the marble steps to the little harbor. Here they boarded the small boat, canopied in red and gold and flying the red, white and green flag of Mexico, which was to carry them to the *Novara*—the warship which would take them to Mexico. As the boat slipped away, the sound of cannon—from the ships lying at anchor and from the guns on the castle terrace—filled the afternoon air. Side by side in the prow of the boat stood the new Emperor and Empress of Mexico, both wearing dark colors and she with a white veil streaming in the sea breeze. On its rocky promontory, growing smaller and smaller as the boat drew nearer the *Novara*, rose Miramare castle, its battlements all beflagged, its white walls glinting in the sunlight.

"Look," said Carlota quietly to one of her ladies. "Look at poor Max. How he is crying!"

4

"You see an old man who has suffered long and severely," said King Leopold one day in the spring of 1863 to Henry Thompson, the renowned British urologist. The King, by this time, was once more dangerously ill and Thompson had been summoned to Laeken to examine him.

"I found," wrote the doctor in his diary, "a tall fine-looking man ... whose long warm quilted dressing-gown covering him from the shoulders to within a few inches of the ground made him look taller even than he was." For the past fortnight, the King told Thompson, the pain of the stone had prevented him from lying in bed and he had been obliged to sleep standing up. Two thick horse-hair mattresses had been set on end, at right angles to the wall, and in the narrow space between them, the King would stand himself, each mattress supporting him under the armpits. His head would rest against the wall on a soft, folded napkin. Wedged upright in this fashion, the King would try to get some sleep.

The clumsy ministerings of a string of doctors had made Leopold loath to be examined, but the combination of Queen Victoria's urgings and Henry Thompson's reputation overcame his reservations and he put himself in the surgeon's hands. On June 6, the stone was found and crushed, and the operation pronounced a success. Thompson was much fêted (the operation was looked upon as the climax of his career) and the delighted Leopold seems to have paid the huge bill without a murmur. When, in the spring of the following year, the King visited Queen Victoria, he sent for Thompson and assured him that he was brimful of energy and on his feet for six hours a day. He had walked for four hours one night, he boasted, in order to watch a fire brigade at work.

Lord Clarendon, who saw Leopold on this same visit to England, endorsed this opinion. He claimed that the King "looks wonderfully well and says he has got rid of all his ailments." The King had also, it seems, treated himself to a new wig; it had, says Clarendon, "a dandy little curl à la Normanby in the centre of his forehead which shows *qu'il a encore des prétentions*."

But he could not keep them up much longer. The respite was short-lived. He might still shuffle along the promenade at Ostend, focusing his binoculars on every pretty face; he might still go shooting at his castle in the Ardennes; he might still impress his ministers by "the old uprightness, the old firmness and nobility of attitude, the old kingly bearing," but he was in his seventies now and sinking fast. First he suffered a slight stroke, then he developed bronchitis; his feet swelled and his sight began failing. With that parchment skin and that impassive manner he already looked half-dead; he seemed, noted Baron Beyens, "to have nothing human or living about him except the eyes."

And yet his interest in politics remained as strong as ever. "He had still the vigour of his character and all the freshness of his mind," wrote Charles Faider, his one-time Minister of Justice. It was a mind which now, as always, was concerned with ways and means of safeguarding Belgium's position in a turbulent Europe. His whole reign, he once declared, "had been entirely dedicated to the existence of the country" and now, in his sunset years, that existence seemed to be menaced as never before. To the south, France (for Leopold did not live to see the eclipse of Napoleon III) seemed as aggressive as ever and, to the east, Germany, under the iron guidance of Bismarck, was becoming daily more powerful. Wedged between these two giants, Belgium was in a dangerously vulnerable position (unknown to Leopold, the two countries were about to open discussions on the partitioning of Belgium) but nothing that the King could say seemed able to shake his ministers out of their complacency.

"I beg you to remember," he once exhorted them, "that the least invasion of the country by foreign forces would not only cost it hundreds of millions but, what is still more precious, it might cost its *political existence*." More and more his mind reverted to the Ten Days War at the beginning of his reign. "1831 must never be forgotten!" he said. "A country could not *twice* expose itself to such a danger *without perishing*." For thirty-five years, by skillful diplomacy, he had defied Europe; would a less adroit successor do as well? He wanted to build up the army, to strengthen the country's defenses, to back up the "rampart of parchment" of Belgium's neutrality with a less ephemeral system of defense. He was thinking in terms of converting Antwerp into a great national fortress, of making it into a refuge for the dynasty and the Government—a place of final defiance. This vision of a last-ditch stand against the invader was strangely prophetic; exactly fifty years later Leopold's grandson, King Albert, was to be forced into making just such a stand.

But his scheme did not get very far. His countrymen seemed to him too pacifist, too selfish, too absorbed in their petty squabbles and their ideological differences to pay any attention to the security of the country. Neither his ministers nor the citizens of Antwerp showed any enthusiasm for their monarch's grandiose plan. Concerned about the increase in taxes to which such fortification was bound to lead, a deputation from the Antwerp Council presented the King with a petition against the scheme. Leopold received them in full dress uniform and having read through the petition, thrust it back into the burgomaster's hands and stalked out of the room without saying a word.

"You, gentlemen," he advised his ministers bitterly on another occasion, "devote yourselves to your ideals. I have to look after the State."

He could not, however, look after it much longer. All through the year 1865 his health worsened. In August, hoping that the sea air might help him, he spent a few weeks at Ostend. Here Queen Victoria visited him for the last time. During the autumn he went as usual to the Ardennes, but by the end of November he was back at Laeken and could no longer leave his bed. The palace by now was beginning to fill up, but the dying King refused to see anyone other than Madame Meyer and his valet. On December 9 his daughter-in-law, Marie Henriette, who had once promised that she would tell him when the end was near, braved the presence of Madame Meyer and came in to keep her promise. There was always the chance, moreover, that she might be able to achieve a death-bed conversion of the Protestant King to the Catholic faith.

"Do you regret the sins you have committed, Sire?" she asked.

"Yes," answered the King.

"In the name of the love you bear for the Queen's memory," she urged, "will you not be converted to her religion so that you may meet her again in heaven?"

The King, however, was not quite so far gone as Marie Henriette imagined.

"Nein," he said firmly.

The following day, in a room jam-packed with relations, friends, ministers, doctors and servants, King Leopold died. His last coherent word had been "Charlotte," but whether he meant his long-dead wife Charlotte who was to have been Queen of England, or his daughter Charlotte who was now the Empress of Mexico, no one knew.

The funeral was a magnificent affair, with kings and princes following the body to the vault at Laeken, but it was not what King Leopold had wanted. He had asked to be buried beside Princess Charlotte at Windsor but neither his son, the new King, nor his ministers would allow it. Queen Victoria had to content herself with erecting a monument in his honor in St. George's Chapel and with giving vent to her feelings in a letter to her daughter, the Princess Royal.

"All you tell me of the Funeral is very painful and caused by that atrocious Catholic Clergy!" she wrote. " 'Nasty Beggahs' as Brown would say...."

Leopold II
King Against The World
1865–1909

Chapter Four

1

On December 17, 1865, the thirty-year-old King Leopold II made his *Joyeuse Entrée* into Brussels. Mounted on a great black horse and trailing an impressive array of foreign princes and envoys extraordinary, he rode from the palace of Laeken to the triumphal gate of the capital. Here, in his reply to the welcoming burgomaster, he lost no time in drawing attention to the inadequacies of the city through which he was about to ride. He was anxious, he told the assembled citizens firmly, for "new embellishments" to the capital in order that it might become a more impressive city than it was at present. What he wanted, in fact, was a fitting capital for the sort of country into which he was planning to mold Belgium. Having sounded that note of warning, he rode on amidst the dutiful cheers of his new subjects to the Palais de la Nation for his inauguration.

There is no doubt that Leopold II would dearly have loved a coronation. Although personally unostentatious, he probably felt that the pomp and solemnity of such a ceremony would have emphasized its significance. The slow pacing up the aisle of a sumptuously decorated cathedral, the to-ings and fro-ings of the gold-vestmented priests, the gleam and flash of crown jewels in the candlelight—all this would have been in full accord with his notions of sovereignty. The simplicity of this inauguration seemed, by comparison, almost embarrassing. But *faute de mieux*, he was determined to make the most of it. The original suggestion that he and his family enter the Chamber together and sit grouped in bourgeois respectability on the dais, he dismissed out of hand. Not only did he enter the Chamber alone, but he insisted that Queen Marie Henriette and the children be put at the side of the hall, well away from the throne. Only thus, he reckoned, could he inject a little majesty into the lackluster occasion and forestall the patronizing smiles of visiting royalties.

The result, in fact, was not unimpressive. Tall, manfully bearded and attended by his uniformed staff officers, Leopold looked undeniably royal. His bearing was lordly and his speech was considered excellent—just the right blend of personal humility and public defiance. Only once, during the admirable address, did he hint at his own plans for the future. "Gentlemen," he said, "during the first twenty-five years Belgium has seen the accomplishment of things which, in a country the extent of ours, are seldom realized by one generation. But the edifice, whose foundations were laid by Congress, can, and will, raise itself higher still." The full implication of the words was lost amongst the applause, the *bravos* and the cries of *"Vive le Roi!"*

While King Leopold II was busily making oblique references to future schemes for heightening the Belgian edifice, his neighbors were discussing, with even greater secrecy, their plans for bringing it down. A few months after Leopold II's accession, Napoleon III offered Bismarck a secret treaty whereby France, with Prussian connivance, would annex Belgium whenever she felt so inclined. Bismarck, far too astute either to agree to or to reject the outrageous proposal, put the draft treaty carefully away. Not until four years later, and then with devastating effect, did he bring it out of his drawer and publish it.

The Belgian King, blissfully unaware of these nefarious negotiations, now turned his hand to a little land-grabbing himself. The loss of North Limburg and Luxembourg to Holland in 1839 was something which Belgium had never ceased to resent. Now, in this first year of his reign, Leopold imagined that he might be able to make good the loss. Luxembourg was about to come onto the market once more. The Prussian victory over Austria at Sadowa in 1866 left France feeling very apprehensive about the growing might of Germany and, as a sop to Napoleon III, Bismarck suggested that France offer to buy Luxembourg from Holland; *"Politique des pourboires"* was how Bismarck dismissed this particular sort of compensation. The offer was made, and caused, as Bismarck possibly hoped it would, an uproar in Europe. Leopold II, imagining that the time was now ripe for claiming the disputed territory himself, started a series of surreptitious moves toward achieving his aim. He encouraged a fiery press campaign in which Belgium demanded her "natural frontiers"; he allowed the romantic old Liberal, Charles Rogier, to test reactions to a Belgian scheme for buying Luxembourg. One of the King's supporters was even rumored to have entered the country with a crate-full of proclamations and Belgian flags.

But the Belgian claim caused hardly less of a furor than the French claim had done and in the end Luxembourg was declared an independent Duchy. The King, having burned his fingers without implicating himself too publicly, was forced to retire.

Leopold II was never to forget this first diplomatic defeat. For years afterward he was to assert that "only fear prevented us from getting Luxembourg in 1867." The fracas was not, however, without its significance. It provided the first example of the King's clandestine methods and forced him to look beyond Belgium's borders for further territorial gains. In years to come he would blandly claim that his unashamed exploitation of distant colonies was only to be expected in view of the loss, in 1839, of North Limburg and Luxembourg.

2

Mexico had proved to be no bed of roses for the zealous Carlota. Hardly had she and Maximilian set foot in their new country before their troubles started. At the port of Vera Cruz where they landed on May 24, 1864, their welcome was distinctly cool, and on the long, uncomfortable drive to the capital, Mexico City, they passed through country which was undeniably hostile. Although the occupying French forces saw to it that the imperial couple were given an ostensibly loyal reception in Mexico City itself, the Mexicans were obviously not so well disposed toward them as they had been led to believe. The Palacio Nacional, their home in the capital, turned out to be a shabby, barracks-like building, both unimpressive to look at and uncomfortable to live in. Carlota's drawing room, reported one of her ladies, looked more like a tastelessly decorated hotel room than the receiving salon of an empress. Within a week they had moved out to the castle of Chapultepec which, although beautifully situated on a crest above a spacious park, was in a state of squalid disrepair. On their first night in this new home they were so badly bitten by bugs that the Empress kept asking for insect powder while the Emperor was forced to sleep on a billiard table.

Nor were the less personal aspects of their position any more encouraging. The position itself was such an extraordinarily difficult one. As a liberally minded monarch depending on conservative support, Maximilian was to have his hands full trying to please all, or indeed any, of his subjects. The conservatives wanted an authoritarian government, Maximilian wanted a liberal government, and the liberals, by and large, did not want Maximilian at all. Ignoring the susceptibilities of those who had put him into power, Maximilian raked together a predominantly liberal cabinet and set to work to win the trust of his new subjects.

Almost immediately, he came up against the Church. The previous regime—the Republic headed by that ardent liberal, Benito Juárez—had passed a law for the secularization of Church property; Maximilian, instead of reversing the law as expected by the clericals, was all for seeing it efficiently carried out. He was likewise in favor of complete freedom of worship. His attitude horrified the newly appointed Papal Nuncio, and when the two of them could come to no agreement (the Emperor was hoping to find the basis for a concordat), Maximilian got Carlota to speak to the Nuncio. She, for all her renowned forcefulness, was no more successful than her husband had been. "Everything slid off the Nuncio as though off polished marble," she complained bitterly. There was nothing for it, she said, but to throw the stubborn Nuncio out of the window. And this, in a manner of speaking, is what they did. Maximilian published an imperial decree confirming the principle of freedom of worship and the nationalization of Church property, and the Nuncio, supported up to the hilt by the Pope, left the country. Thus, in the spring of 1865, by the withdrawal of Vatican support the Mexican Empire lost one of its stoutest props.

It was at this time, too, that the Civil War ended in the United States. It was due, very largely, to the fact that Mexico's powerful northern neighbor was embroiled in this civil strife that the Mexican Empire had been established in the first place. Now, with the war at an end, the United States could turn its full attention to what was considered a French violation of the Monroe Doctrine. Maximilian's hopes that the United States might recognize his regime were short-lived. The American Secretary of State informed the Emperor Napoleon III's that his country had no intention of recognizing the Mexican Empire, and the United States continued to credit its representative to the government of President Juarez. The French Emperor was asked, politely but firmly, to withdraw his forces from Mexico.

These same forces were not, in fact, having much success. Not only was the pacification of the country still unaccomplished; it seemed unlikely that it ever would be accomplished. The so-called Juarist rebels were everywhere. The cumbersome French army was simply no match for these guerrilla bands. Even the most spectacular-seeming French successes proved ephemeral; the Juarists merely retreated, re-formed and turned up somewhere else. There were occasions when even the Court was in danger. To complicate matters still further, there was considerable ill feeling between the Emperor Maximilian and François Bazaine, Commander-in-Chief of the French forces. Maximilian felt that Bazaine was not trying nearly hard enough to defeat the enemy, and Bazaine accused the Emperor of not giving enough attention to serious matters of State. Both sent long letters of complaint to the Emperor Napoleon III and by the end of the year 1865 there was little doubt as to whose complaints were winning more sympathy. "The Emperor Maximilian must understand," wrote Napoleon III ominously to Bazaine, "that we cannot stay in Mexico forever."

And yet, in spite of all this—in spite of the opposition, the disappointments and the very real dangers—Maximilian and Carlota remained determinedly cheerful. They were resolved on making a success of their mission. "Our task is great for there is everything to be done," wrote Carlota confidently. "However, progress is already considerable and the country is with us. I feel perfectly happy here, and so does Max. A life of action suits us; we were too young to do nothing." Claiming, with romantic effusion, that from now on every drop of his blood was Mexican, the Emperor flung himself into his new role with gusto. He rode about wearing the colorful native charro costume, he went out of his way to charm and win over his opponents, he toured the country in an effort to find things out for himself, he encouraged local scholars, artists, actors and architects. No Mexican, he declared, "loves the country and has its advancement at heart so much as I and ... I am working for this in all sincerity and with the best intentions." Seldom, indeed, has a hell been paved with better intentions.

Carlota, if anything, was working even harder than he. Although she had nothing like her husband's personal magnetism, she had the more valuable traits of tenacity and level-headedness. Where he was sometimes weak and impractical, she was always unyielding and adroit; where he was always open to persuasion, she was didactic. Sara Yorke, a young American who was often at Maximilian's court, compared the Empress's hauteur unfavorably with the Emperor's easy charm but claimed that Carlota's "determined expression impressed one with the feeling that she was the better equipped of the two to cope intelligently with the difficulties of practical life."

Although Carlota always fulfilled her social obligations conscientiously, it was in affairs of state that her real interests lay. Taking the energetic Empress Eugénie as her example (and making sure that Eugénie appreciated the fact) Carlota began to concern herself more and more with the workings of the government. During Maximilian's tours of the country she acted as regent, deputizing for him on all occasions and never hesitating to air her views at the council table. Late in 1865 she herself paid a state visit to the peninsula of Yucatan. The journey was a great success. "Everyone acclaimed me," she reported to Maximilian, "and threw flowers at my carriage." Here her confidence was given an added fillip by hearing the name of her father, King Leopold I, loudly acclaimed "by populations that know not even the name of the country he ruled."

Protesting that her only concern was to save her husband from doing too much and that her work was merely that of a *chef de cabinet*, she took it upon herself not only to advise the Emperor, but to draft his official papers. These he would then dutifully sign. When Matthew Maury, an American whom Maximilian had made councillor in his civil cabinet, submitted a series of extremely critical reports on the state of the country to the Emperor, Carlota was the only official personage to escape his censure. The Empress, said Maury, was "very clever, practical and business-like." Once, when he told her that he thought she would be able to do more business in a day than all the other ministers lumped together could do in a week, her reply was disarmingly frank. "I believe I could," she said.

It was inevitable that Carlota's well-meant activities should be misrepresented. When she came to hear that she was being talked of in Europe as a virago, she was extremely offended. "Possibly I am ambitious to do good," she explained in a letter to her grandmother, Queen Marie Amélie, "but not in order that it should be talked about, simply to see that it is done...."

There were times, however, in the midst of all the political uncertainties, when life at the imperial court seemed happy enough. On Monday evenings (again emulating the Empress Eugénie) Carlota would give a reception at Chapultepec Castle; there would be singing and dancing, and from the terrace the guests could admire the view which Carlota claimed to be one of the finest in the world. As often as they could, the imperial couple would escape from the formalities of Mexico City to savor the rustic delights of La Borda, their villa at Cuernavaca. "In this happy valley, a few hours from the capital," wrote Maximilian to a friend, "we live in a pleasant unpretentious villa set in the midst of a luxuriant garden ... on the terrace running the length of our rooms and shaded by a veranda hang our fine hammocks, and with the song of gaily-coloured birds in our ears we lull ourselves to sweet dreams. Here at Cuernavaca for the first time we lead a real tropical life." Wearing a blue charro suit with silver ornaments and a shady sombrero, Maximilian would stroll through the gardens, deep in conversation with some visiting cleric or general or botanist, while Carlota, in a simple white dress with a bunch of fresh flowers at the waist, would be leading her ladies in a hectic butterfly chase.

And there were diversions less naive than this. There was a rumor that Maximilian had started a liaison with the wife of the gardener at La Borda—a seventeen-year-old girl by the name of Concepción Sedano y Leguizano. It was afterward proved that she had borne him a son—a boy who was to have a curious future. There seems to have been a secret garden door which led into the bathroom of Maximilian's apartment, and through this door, according to the Emperor's valet, Antonio Grill, passed not only the lovely Concepción, but several other young women as well. Nor did Maximilian confine his amorous adventures to the seclusion of La Borda. At the Palacio Nacional in Mexico City and at Chapultepec he seems to have been no less active. "The Emperor's bedroom was visited many times by ladies of the Court," reported Grill, "who slipped in and out so mysteriously that only I saw them, and frequently without knowing who they were. How many of them, who no one would believe capable of it, yielded to His Majesty's desires!"

With his wife, the beautiful twenty-five-year-old Carlota, Maximilian continued to have no sexual relationship whatsoever. "For neither in Puebla, nor in Mexico City in the palace, nor at Chapultepec," wrote José Blasio, the Emperor's secretary, "did they ever sleep together." Once, during a state visit to Puebla, Maximilian feigned great delight on being shown the richly canopied double bed which his host had prepared for him and Carlota. No sooner had the gratified host bowed himself out of the room, however, than Maximilian, displaying an uncharacteristic brusqueness, ordered his servants to set up his traveling bed in a room far removed from this seductively furnished chamber.

This was no way, of course, to produce an heir. Even those who were unaware of their Sovereign's private life were beginning to realize that if, after almost ten years of marriage, there was still no child, it was unlikely that there would ever be one. Determined to establish the succession, Maximilian began to look elsewhere.

Some forty-five years before, soon after Mexico had freed itself of Spanish domination, a patriot by the name of Augustin Iturbide had proclaimed himself Emperor of Mexico. His reign had been short and bloody and had ended in his execution. He had been survived, however, by three sons and a daughter, and it was the infant male child of one of these sons that the Emperor Maximilian now proposed to adopt as his heir. As the child's father (Iturbide's second son) was already dead, Maximilian came to an agreement with the mother and the two uncles whereby, for a generous allowance, they would quit the country, leaving the infant Augustin to become Crown Prince of Mexico. He would be cared for not only by Maximilian and Carlota, but by his aunt, the late Emperor Augustin Iturbide's only daughter, Josefa. No sooner had the boy's mother signed the agreement and set about leaving Mexico than she had second thoughts on the matter. She came back, brokenhearted, to the capital to demand the return of her son. But Maximilian was having none of her. She was escorted to Vera Cruz and forcibly put aboard a steamer. From here she sailed, by way of the United States, to France, leaving in her wake a very convincing story of how the Emperor Maximilian had robbed her of her only child. What had at first seemed to Maximilian like an excellent way to continue the dynasty now turned into a source of acute embarrassment. His scheme was considered at best foolish, and at worst inhuman, and the fact of Carlota's childlessness was brought sharply home to all the world.

At this point, moreover, it was beginning to seem unlikely that the Empire would ever need an heir. Militarily, things were going from bad to worse. Marshal Bazaine's somewhat half-hearted attempts to stamp out the revolutionaries were having even less effect than before; everywhere the Juarists were gaining ground. The province of Michoacán, a few miles west of the capital, was already in republican hands and the main road from Mexico City to the coast was becoming increasingly unsafe for travelers. Early in 1866 the Belgian mission which had come to Mexico to announce the accession of Carlota's brother, King Leopold II, was attacked on the road near Puebla. Baron Huart, aide-de-camp to the Count of Flanders, was killed and three of his men wounded. The incident was a poor advertisement for the stability of the new Mexican regime.

If the French troops were proving ineffectual, Maximilian's Mexican army was proving even more so. Bazaine refused to interest himself in the raising of local units ("The French marshal has worked day and night by endless intrigues, by orders and counter-orders, to render a good and final organization of our brave troops impossible," complained the Emperor) and with the state tottering on the brink of bankruptcy, there was no way of paying such units. In the spring of 1866 the President of the Council of State informed Maximilian that as all foreign loans were now exhausted, the Mexican army could no longer be paid and would have to be disbanded. And in the same year came the most devastating blow of all. The Emperor Napoleon III informed Maximilian that as his Chamber had refused him any more money for the maintenance of the army in Mexico, the French would have to put an end to their occupation. The withdrawal would begin that autumn and be completed by the following year.

Now desperate, Maximilian sent a galaxy of envoys to Europe to plead his cause. But it was all to no purpose. No one—not the Pope in Rome, or Napoleon III in Paris, or Leopold II in Brussels—was prepared to help him. When his brother, the Emperor Franz Josef, did agree to dispatch some troops, a strongly worded protest from the United States forced him to change his mind and cancel the sailings. There was obviously nothing more that Maximilian could do. Regretfully, he decided to announce his abdication and leave the country.

It was now that the resolute Carlota took matters once more into her own hands. She was too much of a Coburg to relinquish so hard-won a crown. Leaving her husband in no doubt as to what she thought of his spineless behavior, she lectured him on the sacred duties of a sovereign. "Emperors do not give themselves up," she exclaimed. "So long as there is an emperor here, there will be an empire, even if no more than six feet of earth belong to him. The Empire is nothing but the Emperor. It is not a sufficient objection that he has no money. One will get it if one has credit, but credit can only be got by success, and success is won by effort." He must remain at his post and she herself would go to Europe to confront both Napoleon and the Pope. She would leave by the next steamer.

She set off from Mexico City for the coast on the morning of July 9, 1866. It was a hazardous journey. Besides the constant threat of *guerrilleros* (on one occasion her carriage mules were stolen), torrential rain made the road all but impassable. Expressing what to her companions seemed the unaccountable fear that the steamer would not wait for her, Carlota left her carriage and accomplished a great deal of the journey on horseback at night. She was, says one of the party, "a truly glorious vision ... on her splendid thoroughbred charger lit by the silvery rays of the moon."

At Puebla, about halfway to Vera Cruz, a strange thing happened. At midnight the Empress, who had retired some time before, suddenly emerged from her room and ordered a carriage. She then drove to the deserted house of a Señor Esteva who had entertained her with a banquet some months before. Waking the caretaker, she walked through the dark empty rooms until she reached the dining room. Here, she explained to her bemused companions, was where the banquet had been held. She then returned to her lodgings.

Three days later she reached Vera Cruz and at six that evening she sailed for Europe on the *Empress Eugénie*.

3

Very much odd-man-out amongst his active, ambitious, keenly political relations was the late King Leopold's second son, Philip, Count of Flanders. Thirty years old in 1867, his life had been remarkable chiefly for its unobtrusiveness. King Leopold I's one and only scheme to elevate the young man—by putting forward his name as a possible ruler for the Danubian principalities (now Rumania)—had come to nothing. The Prince had refused the position, it was said, with "no more ceremony than if he had been negotiating the offer of a bale of cotton." Since then, increasing deafness had made any future aggrandizement unlikely. It was a state of affairs which suited the Count admirably. From his mother, Queen Louise, he had inherited—along with her blue eyes and fair coloring—her simple tastes and lack of personal ambition. He was a quiet, studious, somewhat abstracted young man, never happier than when shut away in his great library. The "good Philip," reported Queen Victoria to her daughter the Princess Royal, "is always kind and amiable and clever." That there was little affinity between him and his hard-headed brother, King Leopold II, can be appreciated; they "seldom agreed upon any topic [and] were continually disputing," reported one observer. To his brother's children, however, the company of this easy-going uncle was a delight. "I was very fond of my uncle," wrote Leopold's second daughter, Stephanie. "His lovely blue eyes, his frank expression of countenance, his well-modulated voice, his cheerful laughter, his kindly manner, exerted an irresistible attraction for me.

The dynasty was still too precariously rooted, however, for the Count of Flanders to be allowed to evade his royal duties. Even if he was not prepared to play a more active part in public life, he must at least do his bit toward enlarging the royal family. His continuing bachelorhood was proving a source of some concern to his matchmaking cousin, Queen Victoria; together with Queen Augusta of Prussia, she now engineered an engagement between the good Philip and Princess Marie of Hohenzollern-Sigmaringen. A princess of the Catholic branch of the Prussian royal family, with two slightly exotic, Napoleonic-tinctured grandmothers—one a Beauharnais and the other a Murat—Princess Marie was an excellent choice. Like her future husband, she was a woman of retiring disposition and deep cultural interests, with very little taste for court life. They were duly married in Berlin in the spring of 1867.

For the first time in almost half a century, Belgium was now treated to the spectacle of a happy royal household. In their palace in the Rue de la Régence and at the Château des Amerois in the Ardennes, the Count and Countess of Flanders lived a life of admirable domesticity. They entertained very rarely and confined their contact with King Leopold II to regular Sunday dinner. In the year after their marriage the Countess gave birth to a son. He was named Baudouin, in honor of that Belgian crusader who had been King of Jerusalem. His birth was followed by that of two daughters, Henriette and Josephine, and a son, Albert. They were, it is said, a devoted family. "One could not but admire the cordial family life which prevailed in their palace," noted a member of the court, "could not but appreciate the veneration and trust the children showed for their father and mother." Its warmth and its tranquility were a far cry from the home life of King Leopold II.

4

In few palaces in Europe was life more austere than in the palace of Laeken. At six each morning, having risen from his hard camp bed, King Leopold II would have four buckets of cold sea water dashed over his body and then, dressing quickly, would sit down to a solitary breakfast. During the meal he would read through the morning papers (they had to be ironed flat, as a safeguard against germs, before being presented to him), discuss the day's program with the officer on duty and inspect the menu for that evening's dinner. After breakfast, and at intervals throughout the day, he would drink a cup of hot water. With the aide-decamp trotting by his side, he would then stride swiftly through the palace grounds, breaking the long silences with an occasional acrimonious comment on the behavior of some minister or with the sudden order: "*Monsieur l'officier*, take down!" The officer would hurriedly bring out a notebook and pencil and take down his Sovereign's precise and emphatic dictation. Sometimes the King would stop to inspect the progress of improvements to Laeken which he had put in hand soon after his inauguration, or else he would tour his greenhouses. These greenhouses, on which he was spending many millions of francs, were one of his main preoccupations. Beneath immense glass domes there grew, in lush profusion, palms and ferns, orchids, azaleas, camellias, rhododendrons and lilac. In his espalier orchards hung fruit of almost unreal size and perfection, the progress of each peach or pear or bunch of grapes being carefully noted. Once when his eldest daughter Louise, then eleven years of age, picked and ate a peach without permission, she was subjected to a formal inquiry and punished severely. One did not lightly tamper with King Leopold's property. When, in a rare moment of effusion, the King once presented her with a gardenia from one of the hothouses, the gesture so bemused Louise that she never forgot it.

On his return from his walk, the King retired to his study. This was a huge room, the walls lined with books, and the King's desk so vast that it seemed to his children "a world in itself." No on as allowed to touch this desk; the King dusted it himself once a week. Here he would sit reading, rereading and making notes on every official document; nothing was signed without careful consideration. At other times he would pace, stork-like, to and fro across the carpet while from the walls there gazed down, in mute detachment, the portraits of King Leopold I and Queen Louise.

The King would lunch with Queen Marie Henriette and the children. At exactly twenty minutes past twelve the three children—Louise, Leopold Count of Hainaut, and Stephanie—would be taken by a governess to the Queen's drawing room. The Queen would then ask the governess for a report on their behavior; any misdemeanor, no matter how trifling, would be reported and punished.

This pre-luncheon inquisition over, the Queen would lead the children to their father's study to fetch him for the meal. The girls would curtsey and kiss his hand and he would touch their foreheads. That was all. "Not a kindly word, not a sign of welcome escaped his lips," says Stephanie; his wife he would greet with a stiff wave of the hand. Then, in an unbroken and oppressive silence, the royal family would eat their luncheon. The meal over, they would retire to the King's study where Leopold would smoke a cigar while Marie Henriette read the newspapers and the children stood by the window, whispering together. "When we were at length given our dismissal," says one of them, "we hurried through the passages and down the stairs, rejoicing in the prospect that we should be freed from our chains, from the presence of our parents, for hours to come."

In the afternoon the King might go to his palace in Brussels for consultation with his ministers. In this he was tireless. When some exhausted minister left him after an audience of nearly three hours, Leopold would summon the next one without a pause. One never knew what to expect of him. He could be charming, he could be arrogant, he could be sarcastic. He delighted in cornering his interviewees by first assuming a most disarming innocence and then asking some sharp question. But harsh or sly, he was always the King. "Leopold? Do you want me to sum him up in a word?" asked Fernand Neuray, the Belgian journalist. "Majesty!" It was a quality of which the King himself was very conscious. Once, in conversation, when a minister was incautious enough to cry out, "Your Majesty must—" Leopold was furious. "The King gives orders," he answered icily, "he does not accept advice from anyone."

A great deal of his time was taken up with schemes for the laying out of the capital. Just as he was enlarging and beautifying Laeken, so was he transforming Brussels. Not for nothing was he known as Leopold the Builder. He himself drew up plans for parks, monuments, palaces and triumphal roads. He was determined, in spite of parsimonious ministries, to change Brussels from a quiet medieval town into a spacious, imperial capital—a patriotic center for the Belgian nation. "It is not sufficient that public service be regulated, that industry be prosperous, the people content," he once said to Charles Rogier. "It is necessary still in some way to gild." His views on gilding were very much in tune with contemporary—mid-nineteenth century—taste. He had no time for the slender, delicate Gothic traceries of so much of Belgium's architecture; whatever was massive, ornate, pillared, pedimented and domed, he loved. Something of a Renaissance prince himself, he warmed to the grandiose style of the Renaissance. It was due almost entirely to King Leopold's ideas on town planning that Brussels came to be known as Paris *en miniature*.

While the King was planning future glories, the Queen would be amusing herself in a very different fashion. By now the royal couple lived almost entirely separate lives. Neither intellectually, emotionally nor physically was there any bond between them. "With regard to his attitude towards the Queen," wrote Princess Louise of her father, "as far back as I can remember I always see him as the same self-centred and taciturn man in his relations with her." Louise could not recall "a single act of kindness or tenderness on his part towards my mother." The result was that the once insouciant Marie Henriette developed into something of a busybody, finding consolation in ceaseless daily activity and in the discipline of religion. However, she was not without a certain breezy charm and even her daughters, toward whom her manner was often that of a martinet, spoke of her "generous and expansive nature."

Horses were her passion. A visit to the great stables at Laeken was one of her chief delights. She would groom her horses herself and spend weeks teaching them tricks. It was nothing unusual, they said, to see a horse calmly ascend the grand staircase of the palace, enter the Queen's rooms and then make his way down again. She could ride and drive like a champion. "The little carriage and fine horses that she drove herself, with faultless elegance and supreme skill, used to give her a picturesque popularity in Brussels," remembered one observer. As she went bowling along the Avenue Louise, the gentlemen would doff their hats and the ladies bow under their parasols. But more to the Queen's taste than these sedate urban outings was a drive across country. With a team of wild Hungarian horses which had been refreshed with champagne or bread dipped in red wine, she would go careering along the flat Belgian roads and for a while this embittered, unhappy Queen could imagine herself back on the plains of her native Hungary.

Music was another of her passions. She herself played the piano and the harp and was said to be fond of "composing fantasias on motifs borrowed from her favourite operas." She even once wrote an opera called *Wanda*. She was often to be seen at the Theatre de la Monnaie and did a great deal toward furthering the careers of singers, musicians and actors. The great Melba always claimed that Queen Marie Henriette was "very good and clever about music" and that she had been particularly kind to her during her season in Brussels. "She rarely missed one of my evenings," said Melba to a friend, "and whenever she came to the Opera she used to send for me to come to the royal box and talk with her."

This was yet another of her interests that the King could not bring himself to share. In the same way that he disliked hunting and riding so was he bored by music and musicians. He considered music "the most expensive of all noises" and was once seen to be yawning his head off at a gala performance of *Faust*. Even the "Brabançonne"— the Belgian National Anthem—left him unmoved. "You seem to like the 'Brabançonne,'" he once remarked to a nephew. "Anyone who can stand that can stand anything!"

As a mother, Marie Henriette was strict and unsentimental. The children were brought up, says Princess Louise, "after the English fashion." This meant sleeping on hard beds, living in sparsely furnished rooms and washing in ice-cold water. She interested herself mainly in their religious instruction and in the administering of their punishments. Princess Stephanie complains of being forced to kneel with bare knees on parched peas, and of being shut up for hours or even entire days in the dark narrow space between double doors. "Neither sighs nor tears nor promises of amendment would make my mother show forbearance and free me from this terrible duress," she says.

There were occasions, however, when the children found their mother enchanting. Sometimes, in a surge of nostalgia, she would regale them with stories of her own childhood. With tears in her eyes she would tell them about her life in Hungary. "She described the wide plains, which were golden and sun-drenched in harvest-time, and the boundless steppes of the Pussta. A land of freedom, of dreams and of music!" writes one of her daughters. "She never tired of playing the melancholy and ardent airs of the gypsies, and of singing songs in her mother tongue." If the King and Queen were attending some state function in the evening, Marie Henriette would send for her daughters to allow them to see her in full evening dress. In her sumptuous velvets and sparkling jewels she seemed, to these unspoiled and uncritical girls, almost ethereal. "I shall never forget what a radiant picture she made," wrote Stephanie in later years. "Dumb with astonishment, I could not tear my eyes away. She was then in her prime. Her chestnut hair with golden glints in it, her beautifully formed neck, her white shoulders and arms, her lovely figure, entranced me. I was proud to have so lovely a mother."

The only child in whom both parents took an uncritical delight was their son, the Count of Hainaut. King Leopold, in his awkward and unsmiling way, doted on the little prince. This was as much for what the boy—as his heir—represented, as for what he was. The King's sense of dynasty was so strong, in fact, that he was determined to shower his son with every possible benefit. He saw no reason, for instance, why his two daughters should enjoy the same rights of inheritance as the heir. For a king to divide his legacy among all his children, regardless of sex, simply meant the weakening of the main dynastic stem, argued Leopold; sons should divide the inheritance and the daughters be paid temporary allowances until they were married off. "My system would favor the male line of descent from the King, in other words, the Belgian dynasty," announced a memorandum, generally attributed to Leopold. "It seems to be unnecessary to put money into the pockets of archdukes yet unborn." It was a system which, although contrary to Belgian law, he would fight tooth and nail to implement.

The young Count of Hainaut seems, by all accounts, to have been a charming little boy. His sister Louise, a year older than he, calls him "handsome, sweet, sincere, tender and intelligent," and his sister Stephanie speaks of his extreme sensitivity. When he had outgrown his love of dolls (his favorite was a Hungarian doll called "Irma"), he laid out and tended a little garden, but his chief joy was his Shetland pony called "Kiss-me-quick." In the year 1868, when he was nine years old, the Prince fell into a pond and caught pneumonia. This led, in turn, to a heart complication and for several months the boy lay dangerously ill. The King, broken with worry, was able, nevertheless, to send the Chambers a characteristically double-edged reply on receiving their wishes for the Prince's recovery. "Say to the Chambers that to the life of our son are attached, not only our tenderness and our solicitude, but also the hope of the services which he might render the country by consecrating to it, as we have done, all his devotion."

On January 22, 1869, in a room crowded with priests and relations, the boy died. His death almost broke King Leopold's heart. No one had ever seen, or was ever again to see, the King so moved. The funeral was held on a day of glacial cold. Leaning on the arm of his brother, the Count of Flanders, the King followed the little coffin to the chapel at Laeken. Behind, in the funeral procession, walked the now riderless "Kiss-me-quick." As the body was about to be lowered into the crypt, the King, sobbing bitterly, fell to his knees and leaned his head on the coffin. The terrible sound of his crying could be heard throughout the hushed stillness of the church.

The death of the Count of Hainaut was a blow from which King Leopold II never recovered. An ambitious and dedicated dynast, he had lost his son and heir; it was almost as though his life had been robbed of its raison d'être. Over thirty years later, when King Leopold pulled off some particularly shrewd and profitable deal, a collaborator congratulated him, saying:

"The King is very lucky."

"Lucky," scoffed Leopold bitterly. "I have lost my son."

His grief was not quite so overwhelming, however, as to make him forget to arrange, through a special law, for the funeral expenses of 70,000 francs to be defrayed by the state.

Chapter Five

1

On August 8, 1866, the *Empress Eugénie*, bringing the Empress Carlota from Mexico to Europe, steamed into the harbor of St. Nazaire in France. Seldom has a state visitor been less welcome. This was to be one of the few occasions, in fact, on which the Emperor and Empress of the French did not overwhelm a royal guest with their renowned hospitality. Indeed, they tried their best to avoid her altogether. When Carlota stepped ashore at St. Nazaire there was no representative of the imperial government to meet her, no guard of honor to present arms and no military escort to accompany her through the town. She was even obliged to walk some distance to find a cab to take her to the station. Before entering the train she sent the French Emperor a short telegram warning him of her imminent arrival and an even shorter one to her brother, King Leopold II, informing him that the unsympathetic attitude of the Belgian government toward Mexico made it impossible for her to visit Brussels.

During the train journey to Paris she received an answer from the Emperor Napoleon telling her that he was ill but that as he imagined she was going first to Belgium, he hoped to be recovered by the time she visited Paris. Her reply was very much to the point: she was continuing on to Paris at once. In the French capital, as at St. Nazaire, there was no sign of an official welcome and Carlota was obliged to leave the station with no more ceremony than an ordinary traveler. Once again she had to hire a carriage to take her to a hotel. Napoleon had, in fact, sent an aide-de-camp to meet her with the court carriages but—typical of the Second Empire—he had gone to the wrong station.

Unable to ignore his imperial visitor completely, Napoleon sent Eugénie to visit her the following afternoon. Although the French Empress did her best to avoid the one topic that Carlota was determined to discuss—France's obligation toward the Mexican Empire—Carlota would not be side-tracked. She insisted on reminding Eugénie of that obligation and pressed her to tackle Napoleon himself on the subject. If the Emperor refused to see her, said Carlota to the somewhat startled Eugenie, "I will break in upon him." Realizing that this was no idle threat, Eugénie arranged that Carlota should visit the Emperor at noon the next day. Ill, unhappy and apprehensive, Napoleon braced himself for the interview.

It was every bit as unpleasant as he feared it would be. Carlota, looking especially elegant in a black silk crinoline and a new white hat, wasted no time on pleasantries. With characteristic vigor and admirable logic she outlined the desperate situation in Mexico, reminded Napoleon of his promises and suggested a way out of the impasse. It was not long before she had reduced the French Emperor to tears and the Empress, who was made of sterner stuff, to silence. Taking refuge behind the Constitution, Napoleon protested that there was nothing that he, personally, could do, but promised to have a word with his ministers about it. Carlota promptly offered to see and convince the various ministers herself. In the course of this long and heartrending interview a footman suddenly entered the room with a tray of orangeade. Carlota, having at first refused a glass, was finally persuaded by the Empress to drink one, and the incident was later to give rise to the absurd story that the Emperor and Empress had tried to poison their guest.

For Carlota, the following ten days had all the quality of a nightmare. One after another Napoleon's ministers refused to be won round by her impassioned pleas. She had another interview with the Emperor and although he "wept more the second time than the first" there was still no promise of support. Confronted on that occasion by the ministers of Finance and War, Carlota worked herself up into such a frenzy that she fell, sobbing hysterically, into an armchair. On the following day the Council of Ministers unanimously decided to abandon the Mexican enterprise and recall Bazaine; when Carlota was informed of the decision, she refused to credit it. She was prepared, she said, to deal only with Napoleon and not with his government. Plucking up courage for a third interview, the Emperor arrived at Carlota's hotel and told her, unequivocally, that Mexico could expect no further help from France. Two days later he reaffirmed the decision in writing. He advised Maximilian to abdicate, to summon a representative assembly and to have a government elected. It was "no longer possible to lull ourselves with illusions," he wrote, "and the Mexican question, so far as it concerns France, must be settled once and for all."

It was at this stage that Carlota's mind definitely began to give way. Already, during the last few weeks, her close companions had noticed a certain strangeness of behavior, but in her letter to Maximilian, written on receipt of Napoleon's final message, there were unmistakable signs of mental derangement. To her fevered imagination Napoleon had become the Devil incarnate; she referred to him throughout the long, incoherent letter as "He." "He wants to commit a long-premeditated evil deed," she wrote, "because He is the evil principle upon earth and wants to get rid of the good."

With nothing more to be gained in Paris, Carlota traveled to Miramare, there to await Maximilian's instructions. Her behavior on her journey through Italy seems to have been normal enough; only when staying at her late father's villa on Lake Como did she show some signs of persecution mania. Once when out driving she suddenly urged the driver to go faster and then, pointing to an old peasant by the roadside, told her lady-in-waiting that she had recognized him as a hired assassin. She hurriedly changed places and covered her face with a handkerchief for the rest of the journey.

At Miramare she received young José Blasio, her husband's secretary, who had just arrived from Mexico. He brought news of the rapidly deteriorating situation in the country and a letter from Maximilian asking Carlota to go and plead their cause with the Pope.

Blasio was somewhat puzzled at the Empress's exaggerated suspicions that his dispatches had been tampered with. "I am always afraid of Napoleon who is our mortal enemy," she explained darkly. She set off for Rome during the third week of September.

It was while in Rome that Carlota's reason finally gave way. The Pope's refusal to try to influence Napoleon III on her behalf was probably the last straw. The audience itself seems to have passed off without incident and the Pope's return visit to her hotel was likewise unremarkable. Two days later, however, very early in the morning, the Empress suddenly burst in on the startled Pontiff and, flinging herself at his feet, cried out that the members of her suite were trying to poison her. Plunging her fingers into a cup of chocolate on the Pope's breakfast tray, she exclaimed: "This at least is not poisoned. Everything they give me is drugged and I am starving, literally starving." When the Pontiff, understandably alarmed at having his visitor dip her fingers into his cup of chocolate, offered to send for a cup of her own, she refused vehemently. "No, no! They would poison it, knowing it was for me," she cried out. "No thank you! I prefer sharing Your Holiness's cup." Licking her fingers appreciatively, she assured the Pope how good it was and asked whether he used any antidotes against poison. "Yes," answered His Holiness with just a hint of sharpness, "the rosary and prayer."

Carlota, determined not to leave what she considered the safety of the Vatican, spent the morning in the Library and, having invited herself to luncheon, would eat nothing but the food off her lady-in-waiting's plate. In the afternoon, taking a goblet from the Pope's private apartment, she drove to the Fountain of Trevi and there drank some water. Returning to the Vatican that evening, she announced her intention of spending the night there.

The Pope, with admirable tolerance and in the face of considerable consternation among the members of his entourage, let her have her way. Two beds, one for the Empress and one for her lady, were set up in the Library and for the first time in recorded history, a woman spent the night in the Vatican. "Everything comes our way in the end," sighed the Pope with sublime resignation. "Till now the only thing that hadn't happened was for a woman to go crazy in the Vatican!"

But by the following morning His Holiness, for all his forbearance, had had enough. Carlota, who was planning to attend mass in his private chapel, was told that the Pope would not be leaving his rooms. In an effort to get the suspicious Empress out of the building, his entourage devised a scheme whereby the Mother Superior of the Convent of St. Vincent de Paul would invite Carlota to visit the orphanage. The ruse was successful and the Empress agreed to go. Cowering in a corner of the carriage, with her face hidden by a handkerchief, Carlota drove to the convent. Here, to the astonishment of her companions, she made a perfectly lucid and charming speech to the welcoming orphans.

The respite did not last long. On being shown the kitchens where the orphans' food was being prepared, the Empress suddenly thrust her hand into a cauldron of boiling stew and pulled out a piece of meat. "I felt so hungry," she explained to the Mother Superior, biting at the meat, "and they can't have poisoned this morsel."

When the pain of her burned hand caused her to faint, her attendants took advantage of the situation to hustle her into a carriage and take her back to the hotel. The Pope, in the meantime, had sent a telegram to Carlota's family in Brussels, and her brother Philip, the mild-mannered Count of Flanders, was already on his way to Rome. During the days before his arrival, Carlota remained shut up in her hotel bedroom. She dismissed several members of her suite on the grounds that they were conspiring against her. Refusing to eat any food which had not been prepared in her presence, she kept live chickens tied to the table legs in her room; these were then killed and cooked by her maid. When she was thirsty she took the Pope's goblet and drove to various public fountains where she drank her fill.

The Count of Flanders arrived on October 8, and a few days later took her back to Miramare. Here she was installed in the little villa in the park. As a result of regular food and exercise, she regained her health and her beauty but her mind remained as clouded as ever. When she spoke of Maximilian, it was usually in the most extravagant context. At times she imagined that he, too, was trying to poison her; at others that he was the "Lord of the Earth" and the "Sovereign of the Universe." She once claimed that Napoleon III had died and that Maximilian was about to become Emperor of France, Spain and Portugal. Such ravings, thought the Count of Flanders, were the result of her own burning desire to wear a crown. It was a desire which, having been realized and then frustrated, had led on to her madness.

It was, perhaps, as well that she was living in a world of dreams: the reality was so very grave. After toying with the idea of following Napoleon's advice to abdicate, Maximilian decided to stay on. At dawn on February 5, 1867, with bands blaring and flags flying, the French troops marched out of Mexico City, bound for home. As they moved out, so did the Juarist troops close in. Taking the advice of his now wholly conservative adherents, Maximilian moved to Querétaro—a town of proved Catholic and imperial sympathies about one hundred and seventy miles from Mexico City. Here, with unruffled good humor, Maximilian settled down while the enemy slowly encircled the town. By the beginning of March, Querétaro was in a state of siege. The siege, marked by several unsuccessful sorties, lasted some two and a half months and ended with the fall of the town and the capture of the Emperor. On instructions from Juárez, Maximilian was tried by a military court on charges of promoting invasion and usurping supreme power. He was found guilty and sentenced to death. Early on the morning of June 19, 1867, on a hilltop outside Querétaro, this brave, chivalrous and well-meaning prince was executed. It was the end of the Mexican Empire.

Of all this, poor demented Carlota knew nothing. Maximilian's death did, however, raise the whole question of her future. Under the terms of the late King Leopold I's will, Carlota was a very wealthy woman and Leopold II was not likely to let such a prize fall into the hands of the Emperor Franz Josef. He sent his aide-de-camp, Baron

Goffinet, to Vienna to discuss the matter and, after a great deal of haggling, it was agreed that Leopold should take charge of his sister.

The matter settled, Queen Marie Henriette traveled to Miramare to fetch Carlota. Leaving off mourning lest her sister-in-law suspect Maximilian's death, Marie Henriette managed to coax Carlota away without too much trouble. "You would never believe the barbaric and heathen surroundings from which we had to tear poor Charlotte away," she afterward reported. "I don't imagine there has ever been in history a case of a young woman who has been so deserted as this unfortunate Empress."

For a few months after her arrival back in Belgium, Carlota seemed to be improving and was able to live with the royal family at Laeken. José Blasio, visiting Brussels, once caught a glimpse of the Empress as she walked between two ladies in the park. Pressing himself against the railings, he watched the black-clad figure advancing toward him. "She was strolling along slowly, dressed and groomed with extreme elegance and care," he noted. "Her gentle and kind face was profoundly sad. Her large eyes, so black and beautiful, appeared even larger and more beautiful under their purple lids. But they stared vacantly, as though questioning her destiny." Moved almost to tears, young Blasio wanted to cry out to her; he wanted to assure her that he, at least, had remained loyal and devoted to the Empire. But the three ladies turned and, taking another path, disappeared into the shadows of the trees.

During the summer of 1868 Carlota's condition deteriorated and she had to be moved to the Château de Tervueren. By June her behavior was so violent that the family expected her death at any moment.

But she did not die. For year after year in the Château de Tervueren, in a room crowded with a bizarre assortment of souvenirs, the beautiful Empress of Mexico lived on. Sometimes laughing, sometimes crying, talking for hours on end to a life-sized doll dressed in imperial robes, Carlota spent her days in almost complete unawareness of life about her. And she was to live, in this twilight world, for another sixty years.

2

In the summer of 1870 the Spanish throne, recently made vacant, was offered to Prince Leopold of Hohenzollern-Sigmaringen, brother-in-law of the Count of Flanders. Bismarck, who had been longing to go to war against France (a war with France was necessary to complete his unification of Germany), and knowing that a German king on the Spanish throne would infuriate the French, championed Prince Leopold's candidature. As expected, the announcement brought an hysterical protest from the French. The Count of Flanders, on instructions from King Leopold, who feared for Belgium's neutrality, begged his brother-in-law to withdraw his candidature. Prince Leopold, somewhat startled at the hornet's nest which his acceptance had stirred up, complied. But it was too late. France insisted on a guarantee from the King of Prussia that the candidacy would never be proposed again, and this the King refused to give. The delighted Bismarck published a shortened, more abrupt-sounding version of his royal master's report to him on the matter, and France, considering herself insulted, declared war.

The prospect sent King Leopold into a flurry of anxious preparations. The Banque Nationale shifted its bullion from Brussels to Antwerp; the King asked permission to send his valuables to England; the army, in a state of pitiful unpreparedness, was rushed to the borders. A letter from Napoleon III promising to respect Belgium's neutrality brought an immediate assurance from Leopold that he had "already taken the most energetic means" to ensure that neutrality. Hardly had these polite assurances been exchanged, however, than Bismarck pulled Napoleon's four-year-old draft treaty on the proposed French annexation of Belgium out of his drawer and sent it to the London *Times*. The effect was electric. This threat to the existence of Britain's godchild—Belgium—opened English eyes to

French duplicity and to their own duty toward Belgium. A treaty was drawn up in which Britain, in the event of either France or Prussia's violating Belgian territory, promised to help the opposing side expel the intruder. Prussia signed the treaty immediately and France not until August 9.

"Belgium has been through more than one perilous trial," said King Leopold at the opening of the hastily assembled Chambers on August 8. "None has been so grave as she is undergoing today. By her prudence, by her loyalty, by her steady patriotism, she will show herself worthy of herself." She showed her worthiness, in fact, by sitting tight and hoping for the best. Not until Napoleon III had been beaten and taken prisoner at Sedan early the following month could King Leopold breathe freely again. When the French Emperor finally did cross Belgian territory it was in a train on his way to captivity in Germany. On the station platform at Verviers, just before crossing the border into Germany, the fallen Emperor heard a newsboy yelling: *"Chute de l'Empire! Fuite de l'Impératrice!"*

In a way, the fall of the Second Empire was a victory for Belgium as well as for Germany. France ceased to be a danger; Belgium's neutrality had been reaffirmed; a wave of self-confidence swept through the country. With what the late King Leopold I used to dismiss as the "rampart of parchment" of Belgium's neutrality having proved effective, his son's ministers began thinking in terms of disarmament once more. In this they came up against the iron resolve of their Sovereign. Although by no stretch of the imagination a military man (he was more interested in dividends and balance sheets than in military maneuvers), King Leopold was a practical one. He knew that the only way to protect his crown and his money was by protecting Belgium. "We are not an island," he said to his Prime Minister, "we cannot escape the repercussions of events taking place on our doorstep and which have not nearly finished, and you must know that as far as I am concerned, I am determined to do anything rather than govern in conditions which would endanger our national security."

But they refused to listen. Try as he might, the King—like his father before him—could not get his fellow countrymen to understand that a well-armed neutrality was a relatively assured neutrality. While he spoke in terms of arms and armies, they spoke in terms of rates and taxes. The danger, they said, was over. They now wanted to enjoy the fruits of peace. With the once mighty France lying helpless at their feet, they did not think to look behind them where an even mightier Germany was standing upright and beginning to stretch its limbs.

3

Fighting down their mutual distaste for the sake of the dynasty, King Leopold and Queen Marie Henriette resumed, for no longer than was strictly necessary, their intimate marital relations. The result of this loveless mating was yet another girl. Born in the year 1872, she was named Clementine. "The King," says Princess Louise, "was furious and thenceforth refused to have anything to do with his admirable wife to whom God had refused a son." And yet Princess Clementine, whose birth had proved such a bitter disappointment to the King, was to be the only one of his three daughters on whom he would one day bestow a somewhat grudging affection.

The eldest, Louise, at fifteen years of age, he now considered ripe for marriage. Louise was a strange girl: mercurial, emotional, a compulsive liar who felt very keenly the neglect of her parents. She claimed, in later life, that her father had once discovered her, at the age of ten, carrying a love letter to her mother from an admirer; as a result of her refusing to give up the note, the King had withdrawn his affection from her. It is unlikely that the incident ever took place (Leopold, had he been interested enough, would simply have wrenched the note from her), but it does furnish Louise with an excuse for her parents' coldness toward her—the Queen was too busy with her lovers and the King resented this act of defiance on the part of his daughter.

It was one of the Queen's lovers, Louise afterward claimed, who was now chosen as her husband. If the wild accusation was true, then it does not say much for Queen Marie Henriette's taste. Prince Philip of Saxe-Coburg, Louise's future husband, was a squat, myopic, coarse-natured creature, fourteen years older than his intended bride. He was also her cousin. It was not for Princess Louise, however, to question her parents' choice; hardly more than a child, she was almost as excited about going into long dresses as she was about getting engaged. "I gave my whole soul to my approaching marriage without troubling myself what marriage might mean," she says. The ill-assorted couple were officially engaged in March 1874, and for the following year the immature young Princess gave herself over to a whirlwind of preparations. "Loaded with jewels, I soared higher and higher, flattered by homage, congratulations and good wishes," run the breathless phrases. "I was praised on all sides in verse and in prose, with or without music, and it seemed that I was a 'flower of radiant beauty.'"

She was brought to earth with a thud. Marie Henriette, despite the horrors and humiliation of her own wedding night, had done nothing to prepare the highly-strung Louise for what was expected of her. She had merely been instructed to submit to her husband's wishes. She went to the altar on February 18, 1875, utterly ignorant of what these particular wishes might be. "I am not, I am sure," Louise afterward wrote, "the first woman who having lived in the clouds during her engagement, has been as suddenly hurled to the ground on her marriage night, and who, bruised and mangled in her soul, has fled from humanity in tears."

It was, more accurately, from her husband that Louise fled. Before dawn on the day after her wedding, when Prince Philip had left the room for a moment, the anguished Louise threw a cloak over her nightgown and ran out into the park at Laeken. She hid herself among the camellias in one of her father's greenhouses. A sentry, having recognized her scurrying across the wet lawn, reported her presence and she was led back to the palace. Here Marie Henriette took her in hand. "I listened to her scolding me, coaxing me and telling me of duties which it was imperative for me to understand," says Louise. "I dared not object to these on the grounds that they were totally different from those which I had been led to expect."

If Louise is to be believed, it was her dissolute husband who first initiated her into the sort of unconventional behavior for which she was afterward to become notorious. In the Coburg palace in Vienna, where the couple settled down after their wedding, the Prince, "from the standpoint of his superior age," began her training. He taught her to drink, he gave her spicy books to read, he encouraged her in a certain liberty of speech and behavior, he even showed her pieces in his art collection "which a young woman could not look at without blushing." And although Louise never grew to like her husband or to share his perverted tastes, she seems to have responded to what she calls his "Bacchic regime." As she matured, so did she begin to enjoy herself. She learned to make the most of her looks ("the golden ears of corn are not more golden than was once my golden hair"), she spent vast sums of money on clothes, she became the center of a somewhat risqué and outspoken circle. When she paid her first visit to Brussels after her marriage, her sister Stephanie was amazed at the transformation. "My sister Louise was no longer the same!" she exclaimed. "Other interests had claimed her attention. She was now a young wife, admired and fêted. She had become more beautiful than ever, looked extremely elegant, and wore charming dresses." The goose, in fact, had become a swan. Crown Prince Rudolf, only son of the Emperor Franz Josef, delighted in her vivacity. Kaiser Wilhelm II admired her figure; she would make, he told her approvingly, "a fine Prussian grenadier." He even commissioned her to choose his wife's clothes. The Tsar of Bulgaria, Louise's brother-in-law Ferdinand of Coburg, once offered to lay his kingdom, himself included, at her feet.

Starved of affection during her childhood, Louise was intoxicated by all this flattering attention. In a city noted for the lightheartedness of its women, none was more so than she. Even the birth of her two children—Leopold in 1878 and Dorothea (Dora) three years later—made very little difference to the rush and glitter of her life. She was accused, in fact, of not taking the slightest interest in the children. When her son Leopold's tutor fell in love with and married her daughter Dora's governess, the couple were allowed to remain at their posts with the result that little Princess Dora, sharing a room with her governess, remained extremely ignorant except for a great deal of "worldly knowledge she would have been better without." Princess Louise was far more concerned, declared another royal governess, with her own looks than with her children's upbringing. She was known to sit for hours on end in the garden with a looking glass in her hand, gazing at her reflection from every possible angle. "Narcissus himself," says the governess, "could not have shown greater reluctance to leave the beloved image." And when Louise was not admiring her looks, she would be repeating the most scurrilous gossip; she had, it was said, a "vulgar mind."

Flamboyant, extravagant and indiscreet, Princess Louise was soon the talk of all Vienna. Theodor Herzl, the future Zionist leader, seeing her all a-sparkle in her box at the opera, turned to a companion and whispered: "Eve after the Fall!"

4

"I have no other desire," King Leopold II once said to his close associate Baron Lambermont, "than to leave Belgium greater, stronger and more beautiful." It was, indeed, no mean desire nor was it one which Leopold was likely to leave unsatisfied. He had already, by the tenth year of his reign, started making his country more beautiful, but he had not yet succeeded in making it either greater or stronger. But then he was not a man to rush his fences. The Coburgs, it was said, matured late; the Orleans family, on the other hand, knew how to play a waiting game. As a combination of the two, King Leopold was just about ready to make his first move.

In the area of domestic politics Leopold II, like his father before him, showed very little skill. His reign was to see a long and bitter battle between Catholics and Liberals, the rise of Socialism, the extension of the franchise and a series of grave economic crises, but throughout these upheavals the King would play a somewhat negative—if never negligent—role. The Belgian Constitution was far too restricting and Belgium's internal politics far too parochial for a man of his overweening ambition. One of his rare, and characteristic, attempts to intervene in domestic affairs—his demand that he be allowed to call referenda—was firmly nipped in the bud by an apprehensive government. No, it was beyond his country's borders that he must look for the means whereby he could glorify his realm.

Almost since boyhood King Leopold had dreamed of founding an empire but to date, says one of his biographers, "his ambition roamed shelterless over the globe; his imperialism had as yet no address." Now, in the autumn of 1875, he felt that he had discovered that address. "I intend to find out discreetly," he wrote to Baron Lambermont, "whether there may not be anything to be done in Africa."

In this tentative-sounding fashion did Leopold give notice of the scheme which was finally to satisfy his aspirations. "In general," he once complained, "we are too timid and we miss our chance to get the good pieces of cake." Now, by something which looked very like timidity, he was to get hold of a piece of a 900,000-square-mile cake almost eighty times larger than the country down whose unwilling throat he was one day to ram it. And the Machiavellian cunning with which he managed it was to make even his artful father look like a bumbling amateur.

In September 1876 King Leopold invited a collection of explorers, geographers and philanthropists to a conference in the Royal Palace in Brussels. They were assembled to discuss—so the King assured them in his opening address—how best they could open up the "Dark Continent" of Africa to the blessings and benefits of civilization. He would like them to think of their task, he said, as a latter-day crusade. "Do I need tell you," he continued "that in calling you together in Brussels, I have not been guided by egotistical motives? No, gentlemen, if Belgium is small, she is happy and contented with her lot. I have no other ambition than to serve her well." His tone was so modest, so benevolent, that the delegates, wary of any political entanglements, responded with enthusiasm to his ideas. His dream, he said, was to abolish the slave trade and to set up research stations in the heart of Africa. An organization, to be known as the *Association Internationale Africaine*, or simply AIA, was thereupon formed and King Leopold elected as the first chairman of the international committee. Aglow with good intentions, the delegates dispersed. Their enthusiasm, however, was short-lived. Meeting with very little encouragement from the governments of their respective more nationally minded countries, they soon lost interest. The international committee met only once the following year and then it, too, faded into oblivion. All that was now left of the once impressive AIA was its name. But this, in fact, was all that King Leopold needed. Under cover of the innocuous-sounding organization (which he had done nothing toward keeping alive) Leopold could put his plan into operation. The flag of the AIA—a gold star on a sky-blue field—was planted for the first time on African soil, and no one dreamed that this fresh, reassuring-looking banner was to all intents and purposes the personal standard of the King of the Belgians.

The AIA had given Leopold the means to found his empire; he must now find the way to do so. He did not have to wait long. In August 1877 there re-emerged into a world which had almost given him up for dead the African explorer, Henry Morton Stanley. He had re-emerged, moreover, at the mouth of the Congo River, having crossed the continent of Africa from east to west. Almost alone in Europe, King Leopold realized not merely the significance of this fact, but the use to which it could be put. It was toward the basin of the Congo River that King Leopold's rapacious gaze had for some time been directed; now Stanley, after three and a half years of almost incredible hardship, had traced the course of the river. When the explorer arrived at Marseilles on his way back from Africa to England, there were two representatives of the Belgian King to meet him. They had come to ask him whether he was prepared to help King Leopold with his great civilizing mission in Africa. Stanley, anxious for England to reap the harvest of his discoveries, at first declined the Belgian offer. It was only on encountering extreme British indifference toward his achievement that he accepted. An organization with the inoffensive name of *Comité d'Etudes du Haut-Congo*, generally assumed to be an offshoot of the AIA, was formed in Brussels, and Stanley, hardly conscious of the fact that beneath the velvet glove of the AIA was the iron hand of territorial ambition, sailed off to Africa once more.

Here, in his thorough and ruthless fashion, he set about erecting "stations" along the Congo River. Each station, other than serving as a center from which civilization was to be spread to the heathen, would in time—so ran Leopold's honeyed explanation—form the nucleus of a series of "Free Negro Republics." It was a prospect to warm the heart of the most skeptical humanitarian.

Although Stanley worked well he worked slowly. The sudden appearance of a French explorer on the north shore of Stanley Pool (the Congo river basin on which Brazzaville was later established) threatened to upset all Leopold's carefully laid plans. If he wanted to keep France out of the Congo he would have to acquire sovereign rights over the territory. And the only way to do this was through treaties signed by the various African chieftains. Stanley was now urged to get as many chiefs signed up as possible; that the majority of them had not the slightest idea of what it was that they were signing mattered not at all. By the end of 1883 over three hundred chiefs, in exchange for bottles of gin and bolts of cloth, had signed away their independence and placed themselves under the dubious protection of the gold and blue flag.

The same flag, however, no longer represented the long defunct AIA or even its off-shoot, the *Comité d'Etudes*. King Leopold, in a move known only to his closest associates, had dissolved the *Comité* by first alarming the shareholders with talk of bankruptcy and by then offering to reimburse them with their original investments. That accomplished, he formed an entirely new company known as the *Association Internationale du Congo*. This was shortened to AIC, and the fact that Leopold was the only subscriber and that he now had sole control of the entire Congo operation was never really appreciated. With the AIC sounding so like the AIA, it was generally assumed that it was all the same philanthropic and civilizing project, and that a disinterested King Leopold was merely carrying out the resolutions of those well-meaning geographers and missionaries whom he had assembled in Brussels seven years before.

Hardly had Leopold checked French encroachment by the hurried signing-up and "confederating" of the chiefs under the AIC flag than Portugal entered the arena. Backed up by Britain (who also feared French expansion in Africa) Portugal now laid claim to the Congo mouth. It was a nasty moment for King Leopold. Unless he had an outlet to the sea, his years of patient maneuvering would have been in vain. While Britain and Portugal prepared to sign a treaty giving the Portuguese sovereignty over both banks of the Congo estuary, Leopold thrashed about for some way to save himself. As usual, he found it.

His only hope would be to play the Great Powers off against each other. Rather than let any one of the Powers gain control of the Congo basin, the others would willingly support some weak, uncommitted regime, and this was exactly how Leopold planned to present his AIC. By using his very weakness as strength, he set about defying the world. The first thing to do would be to get diplomatic recognition for the AIC; the so-called "Federation of Free Negro Republics" would have to be granted statehood.

It was to the United States that he turned first. By laying heavy stress on both the humanitarian aspects and the commercial advantages of a series of "free" states in the Congo, Leopold won American support. President Arthur had nothing but praise for the impeccable principles of what he still called the AIA, and both houses of Congress recommended diplomatic recognition of what they imagined to be a collection of states. That achieved, Leopold now turned to France. By offering her a "right of preference" in event of his ever wishing to dispose of his Congo possessions, Leopold gained first a French promise of friendly neutrality and then full recognition. This immediately alarmed Britain and Germany. Lest France, in fact, inherit the Congo from the Association, they must needs keep the Association alive and happy. Bismarck gave the idea of AIC statehood immediate support and German recognition followed in November 1884. A week later Germany and France jointly convoked a conference to clear up the question of the Congo once and for all. As a result of the Conference, Britain was obliged to repudiate her treaty with Portugal and Leopold retained his outlet to the sea. The Portuguese, faced with an ultimatum from the other Powers, were forced to climb down. The Association was recognized by all the States represented and at the close of the Conference, Bismarck, as chairman, welcomed the "new Congo State" into being. In his final speech he praised "the noble efforts of the King of the Belgians, the founder of a work which will confer most important benefits on mankind." His private opinion of the Belgian King was a little different. In the margin of one of Leopold's documents dealing with the evils of the slave trade, Bismarck had scrawled one word: *"Schwindel!"*

Leopold could now safely slough off the fake skin of internationalism. The Congo—all 920,000 square miles of it—belonged to him alone. As Belgium wanted no truck with it whatsoever ("Belgians are not drawn toward overseas enterprises," explained the Prime Minister dryly), he would have to take full control of it himself. And the best way of doing this, he reckoned, would be to make himself King of the Congo. On the strict understanding that they themselves would never be saddled with his new kingdom, the members of the Belgian Parliament were persuaded into giving him the necessary permission for accepting a second, crown. To those members who feared that Leopold might be torn between obeying his Belgian or his Congolese Parliaments, he explained that the question would never arise as he intended to be an absolute king in his new kingdom.

On August 1, 1885, King Leopold, in a lordly note to the Powers of Europe, announced that "His Majesty, in accord with the International Association, has taken the title of Sovereign of the Independent State of the Congo." By a duplicity seldom equaled in international politics King Leopold had made his dream come true. Almost overnight little Belgium's constitutional monarch had emerged as the absolute sovereign of a country the size of Western Europe. The world stood amazed at his success; it was soon to stand appalled at the use to which he was to put it.

Chapter Six

1

Princess Stephanie, King Leopold's second daughter, was no beauty. It was a fact of which she herself seems to have been serenely unaware. Her hair, which she referred to as her "chief adornment," was tow-colored and inclined to be frizzy; her eyes were small and set close together; her nose, like her father's, was too long, and from her mother she inherited her pursed and sulky-looking mouth. Her cheeks were plump, her movements graceless and her clothes, or what she calls her "beautiful dresses," in the worst possible taste. She was known, she asserts blandly, as the "Rose of Brabant."

Naive yet self-assured, sentimental without being sensitive, stubborn rather than strong-willed, Princess Stephanie had her full share of the Coburg conceit. At the age of fifteen, in her frilled, draped, beribboned and be-flowered dresses, she was paraded before Duke Ernest of Saxe-Coburg-Gotha, doyen of the Coburgs, who had come to assess her chances of landing a good husband. She passed the test, she says, with flying colors. "I was not shy or embarrassed, and could congratulate myself afterward on having behaved modestly and naturally."

"Your little girl is extremely well-bred," Uncle Ernest is reported to have said, "so you have every reason to be satisfied with her and happy about her."

Judgment pronounced, the family set about finding her a husband. King Leopold was resolved on nothing less than a reigning sovereign or an heir to a throne. He had enough money; what he wanted now was a brilliant connection. There was some talk of a marriage between Stephanie and young King Alfonso XII of Spain, but toward the end of the year 1879 a still more alluring prospect began to take shape: the twenty-one-year-old Crown Prince Rudolf of Austria-Hungary, heir to the Emperor Franz Josef, was looking for a bride. Eligible Catholic princesses were a bit thin on the ground that season. Having already rejected a Saxon princess and a Spanish infanta, Prince Rudolf was obliged to think in terms of Belgium. This possible alliance was not one which was contemplated with much enthusiasm by the Court of Vienna: Hapsburg and Coburg had never been a happy combination. "Is Charlotte such a success that we have to have another Coburg in the family?" asked the Empress Elizabeth of her husband on one occasion, and the unhappiness of Queen Marie Henriette's married life was no secret. And then, by Franz Josef's standards, the Coburgs were still very much a parvenu dynasty. But the Emperor was anxious for his son to get married as soon as possible and, *faute de mieux*, Rudolf was packed off to Brussels to pay court to Princess Stephanie. They say that there traveled with him in the imperial train, as consolation for the onerous task which lay ahead, a charming Viennese actress.

Crown Prince Rudolf of Austria-Hungary was very much his mother's son. Like the beautiful Empress Elizabeth, he was a mercurial, imaginative, self-obsessed young man, and like her, utterly at odds with the stolid and conscientious Franz Josef. And yet there was no bond between mother and son. Elizabeth was too absorbed in her own frenetic search for distraction to bother herself with her son, and he, rebuffed and largely ignored by both parents, amused himself as best he could. That these amusements took the form, more and more, of love affairs with assorted Viennese ladies was one of the reasons why the Emperor Franz Josef was so eager to get the boy married.

There was more to the Crown Prince Rudolf, however, than met the eye. He might appear, to a casual acquaintance, as nothing more than a charming and capricious young man, but he was no fool. He had a very real intelligence which could come close, at times, to brilliance, and a deep interest in the political affairs of his country. "I soon recognized that I had no ordinary person before me," wrote someone who came to know him well. "His is a rich mind, impetuous and impulsive, with a warm heart and a noble character, developed far beyond his years."

What this brilliant young man needed was a sympathetic and intelligent wife; what he got was smug and silly Stephanie.

On the afternoon of Friday, March 5, 1880, Princess Stephanie was sent for by her parents. As she entered the room, King Leopold rose to his feet and told her, in his sonorous fashion, that Crown Prince Rudolf had come to Brussels to ask for her hand in marriage. "Your mother and I are very much in favor of the marriage," he said. "It is our desire that you should be the future Empress of Austria and Queen of Hungary. You can withdraw now, think over this plan, and give us your answer tomorrow."

There was, of course, no thinking-over to be done. The answer was a foregone conclusion. Stephanie, nevertheless, hurried about the palace, asking the advice of this one and that, and they were all, she says, of the same opinion: she ought not to reject the offer. "You have, my child," she alleges Queen Marie Henriette to have said, "all the qualities calculated to make of you a beloved and honored ruler, like myself. Your assured religious convictions, your docile, upright character, your kindliness, your quickness of apprehension, your talents, and your outward appearance furnish you with the requisites for a great career. Your charm will win all hearts!" A pearl, surely, beyond all price.

Stephanie's own prettily expressed doubts at marrying a man on whom she had never set eyes were a mere sop to convention; not for a second did she think of refusing the offer. She managed to clothe her burning ambition, however, in the usual cloak of Coburg sanctimoniousness. "A new world presented itself alluringly to my imagination—a splendid world, one in which I should have an exalted mission.... The thought of this lofty mission—to love my people, to care for its welfare, to alleviate its sufferings, to dry its tears—filled me with yearning! As we in Belgium lived with the people, so, in fancy, did I picture my relationship to the spirit of my new country."

While Stephanie was busily making up her mind, her father was calmly going ahead with arrangements for the betrothal dinner that evening. No sooner, in fact, had Stephanie told her parents of her acceptance ("beaming with joy they embraced me affectionately") than she had to hurry off to dress. Half an hour before dinner, wearing pale blue, Stephanie joined her parents and her uncle and aunt, the Count and Countess of Flanders, in one of the Queen's reception rooms. It was then that she saw her future husband for the first time. Rudolf, in his colonel's uniform aglitter with orders, seems to have been at his most charming. Stephanie, however, was not allowing herself to be overawed. "He could not be called handsome," she says airily, "but I found his appearance by no means unpleasing." Having been presented to her, Rudolf kissed her hand and, addressing her in German, spoke about her sister Louise, for whom he had "the greatest regard." He then asked her to marry him. She accepted and, arm in arm, the young couple crossed to her parents to ask for their sanction. This was readily given and onto one of Stephanie's stumpy fingers Rudolf pushed a sapphire-and-diamond ring.

The Empress Elizabeth, Rudolf's mother, was in England at the time, having just returned from a season's hunting in Ireland. When she received the telegram telling her of her son's betrothal, she turned so pale that her lady-in-waiting imagined some catastrophe to have happened. In a tremulous voice, the Empress told her of Rudolf's engagement.

"Thank God it's not news of some disaster," said her companion in relief.

"Let us pray," answered Elizabeth quietly, "that it does not turn out to be one."

The Crown Prince seems to have suffered no such premonition. He was, on the contrary, basking in the attention he was receiving at the Belgian court. With his own father tending to treat him as little more than *ein Plauscher*—a talker—he was extremely flattered by the friendship of the Belgian King. "I am on a very good footing with the King," he reported to a friend. "We talk a great deal together." He even, so expansive was his present mood, imagined himself in love with his fiancée. "In Stephanie I have found a real angel," he wrote, "a sweet and faithful being who loves me, a charming and tactful companion who will help me and stand by me in my difficult life." He was not to hold the opinion long.

The Empress Elizabeth, fighting down her distaste for court life and for Coburg court life in particular, arrived in Brussels from London to meet her prospective daughter-in-law. The sight of his mother, looking exquisitely young in her blue sable-trimmed costume as she stepped down from the train, so enchanted Rudolf that he threw his arms about her and kissed her again and again. For the gauche and dowdy Stephanie standing by his side it could have been an awkward moment, but she was never one for self-criticism. Indeed, she claims that she was "young, good-looking and greatly admired." When she had to make the three customary curtseys to the "whole official world" on the occasion of her formal betrothal in the palace chapel, her elegant performance so delighted the Crown Prince that he cried out: "Stephanie, you did that splendidly."

Elizabeth, bored to tears at Laeken, got away as soon as she decently could. Rudolf, still aglow from being the center of attention, left soon afterward. The wedding was scheduled for December 1880, by which time it was hoped that the Princess would be what she called "sufficiently developed"; the truth was that she had not yet menstruated.

Nor by the end of the year had she begun to do so, and the ceremony had to be postponed until the following May. In that year between betrothal and marriage, Stephanie was subjected to a course of rigorous training. Somehow out of this sow's ear of a Belgian princess must be made the silk purse of an Austrian empress. She was lectured on religion, philosophy, literature and politics; she was taught to speak Hungarian and was given talks on Hungarian history; she had lessons in dancing and deportment and public speaking; she was photographed, painted and fitted out with a trousseau which was to be as "costly as possible."

"Nothing," she ways, "was omitted that might enhance my accomplishments and prepare me thoroughly for the position I was to fill."

Early in May 1881, accompanied by King Leopold and Queen Marie Henriette, she left Brussels for Vienna. The three-hour drive from the palace to the station seems, according to Stephanie, to have been a triumph. "I do not think I exaggerate," she says, "when I declare that seldom, if ever, has a princess departed from her own country attended by so extravagant an outburst of farewell good wishes as I."

In Vienna things seem to have been no less enthusiastic. The imperial capital was *en fête* for a week and even Stephanie appears to have been somewhat overwhelmed by the splendor of it all. Although the flowers decorating the royal palaces "did not show the same profusion to which I was accustomed at home" and in spite of the fact that she found the etiquette more "rigid than that which prevailed in Brussels," she had to admit that Vienna had laid on a "splendid spectacle." Her official entry into the capital on the day before her wedding she describes as "magnificent." In a state carriage which had once belonged to the Empress Maria Theresa, she drove through the lavishly decorated streets. "It was in this solemn procession, to the sound of gun salutes, the ringing of church bells, and endless cheering of the populace which testified its loyalty to the Imperial House, that I entered the capital of my future Empire!"

On the morning of her wedding day, in a tasteless dress of heavy silver brocade which she called a "marvel of beauty," she knelt at her father's feet to get his blessing. Resting his long, bony hands on the head which was destined to wear the imperial crown of Austria, the rapacious old charlatan gave her a piece of fatherly advice.

"Remember," he said solemnly, "that the finest crown in the world is the crown of virtue!"

While father and daughter were acting out this pretty scene in one part of the Hofburg palace, the bridegroom, in another, was behaving in a much less sanguine fashion. Countess Festetics, the Empress Elizabeth's lady-in-waiting, emerging from her room dressed for the ceremony, heard the Crown Prince calling her name.

"Countess Marie, don't run away in such a hurry," he begged, "wait a bit."

Turning to face him the Countess was alarmed to see how pale and nervous he was looking. "I am so glad we can still meet as our old selves," he said, standing quite still in the doorway. When she reminded him that the footman had already gone ahead with his bouquet, he replied that he was in no hurry; he had, he said dolefully, all the time in the world. Overcome with sympathy, the Countess murmured, "Oh, your Highness," upon which Rudolf, breaking down, cried out, "In the name of Heaven, say something nice to me." The Countess, through her tears, could only wish him God's blessing and good luck.

"That," she says, "was the prelude to the wedding."

The wedding itself was a glittering affair. By the light of hundreds of wax candles Stephanie dragged her heavy train, trimmed with garlands of silver roses, up the aisle; she moved, says the Archduke Wilhelm, with all the "daintiness of a dragoon." With her big feet and red hands, Stephanie could hardly have been a less fitting bride, he reckoned, "for the sophisticated Rudolf." But the bride herself was conscious of no such shortcomings. As the regimental bands crashed out the national anthems of Austria and Belgium after the exchange of wedding rings, she glanced in happy triumph toward her parents. They were beaming, she said, "with gratification and content."

It was not until after it was all over that Stephanie's aplomb began to desert her. The honeymoon was to be spent at Laxemberg Castle, and it was during the long, cold drive there that she was suddenly "seized with a sense of overpowering dismay." Rudolf seems to have been particularly taciturn, and on their arrival at the castle it was almost as though they had not been expected. The rooms were cold and musty and the furnishings depressingly old-fashioned. "No plants, no flowers, to celebrate my arrival, or to bring a little joy and cheerfulness into the dimly lighted apartments. Nothing seemed to have been made ready! There were no carpets, there was no dressing-table, no bathroom; nothing but a wash-handstand on a three-legged framework."

And there was worse to come. This clumsy, unsophisticated girl had very little idea of what was expected of her. As in the case of Princess Louise, Queen Marie Henriette seems to have done nothing to prepare her second daughter for the occasion.

"What a night!" she says. "What torments, what horror! ... My illusions, my youthful dreams, were shattered. I thought I should die of my disillusionment."

2

The acquisition of the vast Congo domain had merely whetted King Leopold's appetite. Already, between the close of the Berlin Conference and the almost immediate proclamation of the Congo's neutrality, the King had managed a little surreptitious pushing out of the frontiers. Since then, by any means which had come to hand —be they wheedling letters to Queen Victoria, threats to stubborn diplomats or the simple intimidation of local populations—he had extended the southern frontiers to include Kwango and mineral-rich Katanga. It was toward the northeast corner of his new kingdom, however, that King Leopold's gaze was most firmly fixed; he was determined to inch his way forward into the center of the continent until he had gained a foothold on the Nile.

Ever since he had first visited Egypt over thirty years before and there listened to his consul's seductive talk about Belgium's role in Africa, Leopold had dreamed of one day establishing himself on this great river. Both strategically and commercially, it would be a splendid position: he would be in control of the very crossroads of Central Africa and would have access to almost unlimited supplies of ivory. And who could tell, if all went smoothly, the Coburgs—spreading northward through the Sudan toward Egypt—might yet become latter-day pharaohs.

Never, indeed, did the time seem more opportune than at present. With General Gordon having just been killed by the Mahdists at Khartoum, the Sudan was in a state of chaos. Emin Pasha, one of Gordon's subordinates, was still holding out at Lado on the Nile, and as Lado was exactly where King Leopold wanted to be, he hit upon a way of turning Emin's predicament to his own advantage. He would send an expedition under Stanley to relieve Emin and then, as a way of converting the territory around Lado into a province of the Congo, offer Emin the job of governor.

Stanley, obliged to approach Lado from the Congo rather than by the easier route through East Africa, was faced with his most difficult task to date. As usual, by a display of iron discipline and at the cost of hundreds of lives, he accomplished it. He reached Lado, however, to find that not only was Emin not interested in Leopold's offer but that he was not even particularly pleased to be rescued. Stanley, determined to fulfill at least one part of his mission, rescued him willy-nilly and marched him back to Bagamoyo on the East African coast. Here, as a crowning touch of farce to the whole pointless episode, the near-sighted Emin fell off a balcony and fractured his skull.

The Stanley expedition having failed to gain the Nile foothold, Leopold tried other methods. First he set out to convince Bismarck that his presence on the Nile would help stamp out the slave trade, and when this ruse misfired, he about-faced and tried to get Tippo Tib, the famous Arab slaver, to establish a station there. Finally, in desperation, he was obliged to finance an expedition of his own. In 1890, a small army set out from the Congo. By signing treaties with such chiefs as were amenable and by shooting down such as were not, Leopold's expedition slowly gained control of the area. By October 1892, King Leopold was on the Nile. It seemed as though he had made yet another of his dreams come true.

He was not content, however, to let things rest at that; he must now move down the Nile to Khartoum. On a visit to the British Prime Minister, Lord Salisbury, Leopold lost no time in broaching the subject of the Sudan. The King "plunged into the Valley of the Nile," reported Lord Salisbury to Queen Victoria, "and we remained there for more than half an hour. His language was very mysterious." What Leopold was hinting at was that Britain should allow him to lease the Sudan from the Khedive of Egypt and that, in return, Leopold should lend Britain his Sudanese subjects to do with whatsoever they pleased—even to using them in an army with which Britain could then annex China. "His confidences are so extraordinary," wrote Salisbury, "that I hesitate to put them into a despatch."

The Queen agreed. "Lord Salisbury's account of the King of the Belgians' visit is quite preposterous," she wrote, "and really seems as if he [King Leopold] had taken leave of his senses."

Denied British cooperation, Leopold's dream of gaining control of the Sudan faded. Lack of money, moreover, was endangering such dreams as he had already realized. With the Belgians refusing to have anything to do with their Sovereign's grandiose schemes, Leopold had been obliged to finance the whole Congo operation himself. By raising loans, by granting concessions, by issuing premium bonds, by helping himself to his mad sister Carlota's vast inheritance, he managed to stay afloat for a time, but by 1889 he seemed about to go under. In desperation, he turned to the Pope. As the Congo State had been created for the purpose of converting the heathen, argued Leopold, sermons should be preached from every pulpit urging congregations to take up as many Congo bonds as possible. His Holiness remained unconvinced. In a bid for sympathy the King began mortgaging his foreign decorations and his servants' livery; he even cut out a course at luncheon. *"Mais Leopold,"* cried Marie Henriette as her husband, grey with worry, paced the floor, *"tu vas nous ruiner avec ton Congo!"*

That autumn, an Anti-Slavery Conference opened in Brussels and in this Leopold saw his chance to lay his hands on some money. No one was more adept at the conversion of humane sentiments into hard cash. The Berlin Conference had expressly forbidden the levying of an import duty in the Congo; now, to cover what he called his anti-slavery expenses, King Leopold asked to be allowed a ten-percent duty on all goods entering the Congo. Unless he was granted this duty, he protested, the Congo would be unable to play its part in the abolition of the slave trade, and unless the Congo did play its part, the slave trade would not be abolished. It was his old trick of using weakness as strength and, as usual, he got his way. The duty was allowed.

So far, so good, but a ten-percent duty was a mere drop in the ocean of the Congo expenses. He would somehow have to get the money out of the Belgian Treasury. Be it by threats, cajolery or trickery, he was determined to get a loan out of his tight-fisted countrymen. First he threatened to shame them by abdicating. Then he frightened them by declaring that poverty would force him into presenting the Congo to France; "neither Germany nor England would forgive Belgium if we handed over the Congo to France," he sighed. The Belgian Government, moreover, was just beginning to realize the potential of the Congo. It would be a pity to let so rich a prize slip forever from their grasp, and yet they were not prepared to saddle themselves with it until it was proved that it *could* pay its way. If only there were some method of delaying their decision, of remaining free until they could see whether or not it would be to their advantage to gain control of it. Nor, for his part, was the King willing to hand the country over to Belgium. He would consider doing this when he had made his fortune, not before.

As always, His Majesty had the perfect solution. He suggested to his Government that, in exchange for a loan, he should publish a will in which he bequeathed the Congo to Belgium. After ten years the Chamber could decide whether to take advantage of his gift or to demand the repayment of the loan. That way, the King would get his money now and the Government could make up its mind later. Only on receipt of the loan, however, and not before, would he sign the will. To avoid any appearance of sharp practice on his part, he would back-date the will. This, explains one of his more sympathetic biographers, was in order "that the public would not conclude that there was any connection between the solicitation of a loan and the royal bequest."

The transaction was a complete success. Leopold got his loan, the newly drafted but back-dated will was signed, and the complaints of certain politicians at this deepening involvement in Congo affairs went largely unheeded.

If that particular deal had been shady, the next one was diabolical. In 1894 the King informed his Government that, in defiance of the conditions of acceptance of their loan, he had borrowed a further 5,000,000 francs from an Antwerp banker named Browne de Tiège. As security for the loan he had mortgaged a vast area of the Congo to the banker. Now, unable to repay the loan, he would have to grant Browne de Tiège permanent rights over this territory. The Government was appalled. Rather than lose this valuable slice of Belgium's future colony (and as a way of preventing the King from getting into deeper financial straits) the Government reluctantly decided to annex the Congo immediately. The decision produced an outcry from the Belgian public. The Government might be ready for a colonial adventure but the people were not. The protest against annexation, secretly encouraged by Leopold, gathered strength; even the London *Times* (again, it was assumed, on Leopold's instigation) came out against it. In the face of this mounting opposition there was nothing that the Government could do. They were forced to abandon the idea of annexation and to pay Leopold's debt. Striking while the iron was hot, the King suggested that as they were already paying 5,000,000 francs they might just as well add a further 1,500,000. Meekly the Government handed him 6,500,000 francs and Leopold remained master of the Congo. At least, reckoned the Government, he could now pay his debt to Browne de Tiège.

But of course there was no debt. Leopold had never borrowed money from his collaborator Browne de Tiège. He had invented the debt as a way of worming 6,500,000 francs out of his Government. It had all been a cool and gigantic swindle.

Nor were the King's successes merely financial. The Anti-Slavery Conference of 1889 had led to more than that ten-percent duty on all goods entering the Congo. The Conference had, after all, been concerned with the abolishment of the slave trade and although King Leopold had no intention of mounting a great antislavery campaign, there was no reason why he should not turn the prevailing anti-Arab sentiments to his advantage. Rivalry between the Arabs, established in the eastern part of the Congo, and the Europeans, established in the west, had been increasing in the last few years and a clash between them was looked upon as inevitable. It came in 1892. For the following eighteen months the Belgians, fighting bravely, won a series of victories against the Arabs and ended by crushing their power completely. Whatever the reasons for these Arab wars—whether commercial, political or philanthropic—the results, as far as Leopold was concerned, were extremely gratifying. The campaign, presented as an anti-slavery crusade, won him considerable international acclaim and the subsequent "pacification" of the Arab zone added the vast *Province Orientale* to his domains.

Thus far, King Leopold had been merely dishonest; from now on he became inhuman. The Congo, he decided, must begin to pay its own way. A huge slice of a country pledged by the Berlin Conference to free trade and free competition would now secretly be transformed into a monopoly of the King of the Belgians. All so-called "vacant lands" in the Congo were to be exploited by the state; the produce of these lands—ivory and rubber—would become the *fruits domaniaux* of the State. The population of these areas would pay their taxes in the form of labor expended on the collection of these *fruits*. The Africans, who for centuries had lived their lives in their own fashion, were now suddenly forced to work off a tax which they did not even begin to understand. "Inherent in this regime," admits one of Leopold's apologists, "was the temptation to exploit native labor in the interest of a maximum return." It was a temptation to which Leopold was to succumb only too readily and which was soon to bring the whole world about his ears.

3

For year after year, far removed from the turmoil of the court, King Leopold II's brother, the self-effacing Count of Flanders, had been living a life of enviable tranquility. With little love lost between himself and his brother and with deafness making social life difficult, the Count of Flanders was content to play a somewhat negative role during these years of dynastic achievement. He and his Countess would do some obligatory entertaining of visiting royalties, pay a brief state visit to a neighboring sovereign, or make a journey, incognito, to France or Germany or Italy. On Sunday evenings they would dutifully present themselves at the Royal Palace for dinner and, after the meal, would sit through a performance on the harp by Queen Marie Henriette. One hears of them as the guests of honor at a reception in Berlin, with the Count looking, according to Prince Hohenlohe, "most unmilitary in uniform," and the Countess decidedly unsophisticated. Unable to hear what people thought of him, the Count came to care even less; he dressed untidily, he grumbled incessantly, he came and went as he pleased. The Countess, though no more social than her husband, tended to lead a more active life. While he immured himself in his library of over 30,000 books, she busied herself with painting, music and good works. As she was forever involved in some new charitable project, King Leopold would refer to her, sardonically, as "Our Lady of Flanders."

It was within their family circle that the Count and Countess of Flanders were seen to best advantage. Together with their four children—two sons and two daughters—they formed an admirable family group. "They are not perhaps beauties," noted the Infanta Eulalia of the children, "but they are very charming and clever, fair, tall, friendly and altogether very nice." In their palace in the Rue de la Régence the family lived as unpretentious a life as was possible; they were often to be seen on Sunday afternoons strolling, like any good bourgeois, in the park or along the new boulevards. At the Château des Amerois, overlooking the old town of Bouillon in the Ardennes, they spent the summer days exploring the woods and caves of the surrounding countryside. Both parents were deeply interested in the education of their children; nothing was allowed to interrupt the course of their studies and into all four children was instilled a very strong sense of duty. "Do you like working?" someone once asked the youngest child, Prince Albert, when he refused to go out and play. "No," answered the little boy. "I don't like it, but I must."

"A Prince," the Count of Flanders would say on occasion, "is merely a man who has more duties to fulfill than others."

Duty, in fact, seems to have been one of the watchwords of the household. It might have been that the Count of Flanders, with his own distaste for the often meaningless tasks of royalty, was a little sensitive on the question, or it might simply have been a manifestation of the well-known Coburg obsession with the responsibility of princes. Whichever it was, all four children grew up with an unquestioning sense of mission toward their country. "I want them to serve their country," said the Count on one occasion. "Whether from the throne or elsewhere I do not mind, except that, for their own sakes, I had rather they were spared the immense responsibilities of kingship." That was his public opinion; in private he allowed his renowned pessimism free play. "When I am gone," he would say, apropos the dynasty, "everything will be finished."

Not everyone, however, shared his cynicism. Nor could one simply ignore the possibility of those "responsibilities of kingship" eventually devolving on one of his sons. Since the death of King Leopold's only son, the Count of Hainaut, the Count of Flanders had been heir to the throne. But with the King enjoying such robust health, it seemed quite likely that he would outlive his brother and that the throne would pass to Prince Baudouin, eldest son of the Count of Flanders. Baudouin, who had turned twenty-one in the year 1890, seemed as promising an heir as one could wish for; even the irascible King Leopold II was known to approve of him. Tall and good-looking, with a winning ease of manner, Baudouin had very little of his parents' reticence. In the green uniform of the Carabiniers—a smart infantry regiment in which he held the rank of captain—he was an attractive figure. Already he enjoyed immense popularity amongst his future subjects; it seemed as though the dynasty had at last produced a Prince Charming. It was generally assumed that he would marry his cousin, the King's youngest daughter, Clementine.

That was one side of the coin; the other was rather different. Prince Baudouin's private character was distinctly less satisfactory than his public one. Sensitive and highly-strung, he was given to moods alternating between frenetic gaiety and black depression. He suffered, it was said, from "an excess of emotion." He had inherited neither his parents' reserve nor their tranquility and dependability. He was brilliant, but he was erratic.

Very different was the younger son, Baudouin's brother Albert. As a youngster, Albert had been rather unruly, but since his fourteenth birthday (he was six years younger than Baudouin) he had become more studious, more withdrawn. He seemed, in fact, to be developing into a carbon copy of his mild and bookish father. King Leopold was known to refer to him as a "sealed envelope," and when set against his spirited elder brother, he appeared gauche and secretive. His tutors found his shyness disconcerting; it was only after they had spent some time in his company that they came to appreciate his less obvious qualities—his thoroughness, his conscientiousness, his eagerness to learn. Like all the Coburgs, Prince Albert had a passion for geography and an irresistible urge to travel.

At fifteen he was enrolled as a cadet at the *Ecole Militaire* in Brussels. For this lanky, self-doubting, near-sighted youngster, the change from the sheltered atmosphere of the Rue de la Régence to the rough and tumble of a military college was almost too much to bear. Each morning a carriage, complete with liveried footmen, would deposit him at the gates of the school and he would brace himself to face the slang, the skylarking and the uninhibited virility of his fellow cadets. Not until the carriage had fetched him home in the evenings could he shake himself free of the feeling that he was being criticized, patronized or made fun of. "My parents made a great mistake when they sent me there," he said in later life. "I had had no preparation for that kind of life. The studies, the atmosphere, and the talk were entirely strange to me."

Toward the end of the year 1890, Prince Albert caught a bad cold which quickly developed into influenza. From him the illness spread to his sisters Henriette and Josephine, and for a while the princesses were so ill that it became necessary to publish bulletins on their condition. No sooner had the three of them been pronounced out of danger, however, than Prince Baudouin, the eldest, was taken ill. What at first seemed like a mild attack of influenza suddenly developed into pleuropneumonia, and after a week's illness Prince Baudouin died.

The death of this accomplished young prince was a blow, not only to his immediate family, but to the dynasty as well. It was almost as though there were a curse on the first-born sons of the Coburgs of Belgium: Leopold I, Leopold II, and now the Count of Flanders had all lost their first-born sons; was the dynasty never to have enough princes to guarantee the succession? King Leopold II was particularly distressed. This latest tragedy had reopened the old wound caused by the death of his only son twenty years before. To what purpose were all his superhuman efforts to enrich and glorify his realm—his maneuverings to channel the family wealth away from the daughters to the sons that the direct line might grow more powerful; his Congo crown and his dreams of a Coburg pharaoh—when his dynasty was all but dying out? At the funeral the King was said to be "quite overcome by emotion and walked with halting steps, supported on his left by the Count of Flanders, who was himself weeping bitterly." From this time on the embittered old King withdrew ever deeper into himself, keeping even more aloof from both family and countrymen and living his life exactly as he wished, regardless of the feelings of others.

The shy, unsmiling Prince Albert was now the heir apparent; only his most intimate associates could guess how inspiring a king he was one day to be.

4

Blessed with her full share of the Coburg resilience, Princess Stephanie survived the horrors of her wedding night. Marriage to the Crown Prince Rudolf of Austria-Hungary might not be everything she had hoped for, but the situation was not without its compensations. In the flood of festivities which followed the wedding, the disillusionments of the honeymoon were swept aside and Stephanie began basking in the homage due to her in her new position. Her success, according to her self-congratulatory memoirs, was little short of phenomenal. So moving was her first speech to the Hungarian Parliament that "the barriers of etiquette were broken down" and the deputies crowded round her, fighting to kiss her hand. When she visited Transylvania the peasants knelt down in the roadway to kiss the hem of her dress. As she drove through the streets of Prague "a tremor of joy and gratification animated the crowd." On a state visit to Constantinople, "the elegance of my attire and the charms of my person aroused the Sultan's interest"; he could not, she says, take his eyes off her. So popular was she with the officers of her husband's regiment that once, at a regimental banquet, she found herself being lifted shoulder-high by the acclaiming officers and carried into the dining room through a rain of flowers. "My success in these respects made me very proud," she writes. With the navy she seems to have been even more popular. "Words fail to describe the enthusiasm with which I was welcomed by the Navy. This was something more than ordinary rejoicing. It was the expression of the most cordial affection and the highest esteem."

Her father-in-law, the Emperor Franz Josef, "confident that my popularity and my talent for winning people's hearts" would counteract the growing dissatisfaction among the Italian patriots in Austrian-occupied Trieste, sent her on a visit to that rebellious city. It was, she admits readily, no easy assignment but she proved herself equal to it. Before many days had passed she was, as usual, being pelted with flowers and mobbed by the delighted populace. "The antagonistic cries and songs were stilled; as a result of my efforts patriotic lays took their place; and on all hands I heard the name the people had given me: *Stephania benedetta, Stephania carissima....*' "

It cannot have been, then, with quite so much astonishment as she professes, that she listened to the Empress Elizabeth asking her to take over all her official duties. The Empress told her, says Stephanie, "that I had already won all hearts, and that she was happy to have a daughter-in-law who could take so dignified a position." The truth is that no matter how inept Stephanie might have been (and Elizabeth is said to have referred to her as "that tiresome lout of a girl") the Empress would have asked her to take her place. To Elizabeth all official appearances were a nightmare; to Stephanie—for all her professed fear of the responsibility—they were a chance to shine. Henceforth, while the Empress devoted herself to the preservation of her looks and to her search for solitude, Stephanie satisfied her craving for popular acclaim. Her own childhood at Laeken had been so bleak and so loveless; one should not, perhaps, blame her for pretending that she was a nation's darling. "People seem to forget," she once said, "that when a princess marries a crown prince, she naturally wishes to play the part of empress or queen and that her ambition is justified."

When it came to her marriage, she had much less reason to be pleased with herself. Not even she could pretend that it was anything other than a disaster. For the first year or two things were not too bad; Rudolf was kind if somewhat preoccupied and Stephanie imagined that she was doing her best to adapt herself to his way of life. In letters to his old governor, Latour von Thurmberg, Rudolf writes of Stephanie with affection, whereas she, from the very outset, found reason for complaint. She accuses Rudolf at one and the same time of being insanely jealous ("the Crown Prince would lose his temper the instant he saw that any other man admired me in the least") and of neglecting her. He cared for very little, she said, other than "his own pleasure and sport." He was, it is true, excessively fond of shooting, and neither for this nor for his other passion—politics—did Stephanie have any taste. Confessing that she was "never very closely acquainted" with his political ideas, she tended at first to dismiss him (as did many others) as something of a political poseur—what she calls "the prototype of a liberal prince, in accordance with the fashion of the day." Some of his political friends, she feared, were "the sort of people who would never be received at court."

His charm, which seems to have been prodigious, was lost on her. Stephanie's sister Louise, with her husband Prince Philip of Coburg, was living in Vienna at the time and the spirited Louise had nothing but praise for Rudolf. He was, she says, "more than handsome, he was enchanting. Behind his fragile appearance lay reserves of strength and energy. He reminded me of a racehorse; he had its temperament, breeding and caprice. His will power was only equalled by his sensibility.... Like his mother the Empress Elizabeth, he had a way of talking that held everybody, and a faculty for setting all about him agog to solve the riddle of his personality."

It was a riddle which the self-obsessed Stephanie was neither interested in nor capable of solving.

"Thus," says Count Lonyay, who came to know Stephanie very well, "was this hypersensitive neurasthenic and genetically degenerate intellectual joined to a woman whose nerves were as strong as whipcord and whose skin was as thick and hard as armour plate." This lack of sensitivity seems to have been one of Stephanie's most outstanding characteristics. "An obelisk of tactlessness" is how the Emperor once described her. To the Empress Elizabeth, with her family history of mental instability, Stephanie would chatter at length about the incurability of mental diseases. To a hypochondriacal guest suffering from high blood pressure she told an amusing story about a dignitary whom she had expected to drop dead from a stroke. When Rudolf tactfully tried to change the conversation, she imagined that the anguished guest had missed the point and repeated the story. If Rudolf had a headache it never occurred to her to cancel her singing lesson; in a powerful voice which "closely resembled the foghorns of the Danube tugboats," she would sing manfully on. Even her lap dog, intimidated by that voice, would slink away to find cover.

In September 1883, Stephanie gave birth to a daughter. She was named Elizabeth, after the Empress. The parents' initial disappointment at the birth of a girl deepened with the gradual realization that Stephanie was unlikely to have another child. Not only would the dynasty be lacking a direct heir, but there would be less chance of anchoring the restless Rudolf to his home. That he was in need of some sort of anchor was by now obvious to all; and equally obvious was the fact that Stephanie was not the one to provide it. "Speaking generally," she says defensively, "it was the fashion at that time to despise the joys of family life; and I now know that I was not the only wife to suffer as the result of these perverted views and habits."

Nor did their home seem to be a particularly comfortable one. After the birth of little Elizabeth, they had been given an apartment in the imperial palace—the Hofburg—in Vienna. As their apartment boasted neither a bathroom nor a lavatory, Stephanie complains of having to wash in a rubber tub and of the slops having to be carried through the passages "under the eyes and nose of any who might happen to be there." The rooms were permeated with the smell of cooking from the nearby kitchen and in spite of the fact that gas, and even electricity, was widely used in Vienna, they had to make do with paraffin lamps. And Stephanie suffered the additional humiliation of knowing that her husband still retained, and made frequent use of, his bachelor apartments in the same palace.

Exactly how much she knew of his outside activities during the first few years of their life together is uncertain. She would have had to have been deaf, dumb and blind, however, not to have known something of his deepening involvement in liberal movements within the Empire and of his no less intimate association with the racier elements of national life. Even she, self-obsessed as she was, realized that both politically and emotionally he was getting into deep waters. Writing of his subversive political activities, she later claimed that he had never taken her into his confidence; "What I occasionally gleaned of his intentions was wholly repugnant to me," she said. About what she calls his "unwholesome manner of life," she probably knew more. All Vienna was seething with gossip about Rudolf's amorous adventures and Stephanie's sister Louise was never slow in repeating these stories. Of the frustrations of his position, of the tragedy of a talented man condemned to a life of idleness, she understood very little. She saw him merely as a restless, cynical, sport-mad and pleasure-loving young man who should have known better.

By the summer of 1887, however, during the sixth year of their marriage, even she began to realize that there was something seriously wrong with her husband. She returned from an official visit to Pola in present-day Yugoslavia to find him more edgy, more feverish, more sharp-tongued than ever before. Although, as she afterward said, the cause was "still obscure to me," she became thoroughly alarmed by his condition. He was drinking heavily, he was becoming increasingly short-tempered, he never got home until the early hours of the morning. When angry, he would subject her to talk of his "distasteful *amours*"; he even, on occasion, threatened to shoot both her and himself. By October the following year his "decay was so greatly advanced as to have become conspicuous." His skin was flaccid, his eyes restless, his expression almost sinister. "It seemed," noted the bewildered Stephanie, "as if his lineaments had lost the inner substantiality which can only come from strength of will, as if a process of internal dissolution were going on."

Sick with foreboding, she took the unprecedented step of going uninvited to see her father-in-law, the Emperor Franz Josef. He received her kindly and listened patiently to what she had to say. He remained, however, unconvinced.

"You are giving way to fancies, my dear," he said soothingly. "There is nothing the matter with Rudolf. I know he is rather pale, gets about too much, expects too much of himself. He ought to stay at home with you more than he does. Don't be anxious."

Embracing her, he dismissed her. Stephanie, collapsing onto a bench in the anteroom, was suddenly overwhelmed with a sense of dread. "It seemed to me," she said, "that the Crown Prince's fate was sealed."

On the evening of Sunday, January 27, 1889, there was a reception at the German Embassy in honor of the Kaiser's birthday. The Emperor Franz Josef, the Crown Prince Rudolf and the Crown Princess Stephanie were all present. Also attending the reception was an eighteen-year-old girl by the name of Mary Vetsera. She was a small, voluptuous, dark-eyed creature, the daughter of a wealthy and socially aggressive Greek mother, Baroness Helene Vetsera. There could have been very few people at the Embassy that evening who had not heard that the pretty little Mary Vetsera was the Crown Prince Rudolf's latest mistress. Stephanie was certainly aware of it, for although the lovers had known each other for less than three months, all Vienna was talking about the affair. Mary, infatuated by the handsome and melancholy Crown Prince, made very little secret of her feelings. She flaunted herself, very décolleté, in public, she gazed at her lover in open admiration, she was even known to refer to Stephanie as Rudolf's "stuck-up, stupid wife."

That evening at the German Embassy Mary is said to have been looking particularly lovely; she seemed "aglow with some inner excitement." Rudolf was seen to speak to her twice during the reception and there is a story that Mary, on coming face to face with her rival, Crown Princess Stephanie, refused to curtsey to her. "The eyes of the two women met," runs one version, "and I am told they looked for all the world like tigers ready to spring." Only the anguished tuggings of Mary's mother put an end to the embarrassing situation. Mary left the reception early and the Crown Prince Rudolf followed soon after. It was not, however, with the adoring little Mary that he spent the night; he spent it with one of his less emotional flames—a warm-hearted, down-to-earth ex-dancer by the name of Mitzi Kaspar. He left the following day to go shooting with Count Hoyos and Stephanie's brother-in-law, Prince Philip of Coburg, at his hunting lodge at Mayerling.

"Rudolf had expressly informed me," says Stephanie, "that my presence was not wanted on this occasion." She was soon to know why.

At ten o'clock on the morning of January 30, Crown Princess Stephanie started her usual singing lesson. It was a dark winter's day with snowflakes drifting across the windowpanes. She was singing, with customary vigor, "the song of the King's daughter, a woman betrayed, whose heart yearns for the peace of her homeland," when the lesson was interrupted by the appearance of her chief lady-in-waiting. The lady asked to speak to Stephanie privately and together they went into an adjoining room. Hesitantly, the lady-in-waiting warned the Princess that there was bad news from Mayerling.

"He is dead!" cried Stephanie immediately.

It was true. The Crown Prince Rudolf had been found dead in his bedroom at Mayerling. The news had been brought to the Hofburg by Rudolf's companion, Count Hoyos; Philip of Coburg had been too shattered by the discovery to bring the news himself.

Almost immediately Stephanie was summoned to the Emperor and Empress. Franz Josef was seated in a chair in the middle of the room; Elizabeth, dressed in black and as pale as marble, stood beside him. The Empress told Stephanie—for this is what she believed at the time—that Rudolf had been poisoned by Mary Vetsera and that their two dead bodies had been found together in his room at Mayerling. Seating Stephanie between them, the parents assailed her with a "cross-fire of questions," making her feel, she said, like a criminal. When the bemused young woman ventured to defend herself by telling the Empress how she had warned the Emperor,

153

several weeks before, of Rudolf's alarming state of mind, Elizabeth refused to listen. "In her eyes," said Stephanie, "I was the guilty party."

To hush up the scandal, it was decided to announce to the world that Crown Prince Rudolf had died of a heart attack.

Only at dawn the following morning did the Emperor Franz Josef learn the truth of his son's death. It seems that there had been a suicide pact between the Crown Prince and Mary Vetsera. Rudolf had shot Mary through the head on the night of Tuesday the 29th, and early the following morning, having sat beside her dead body all night, he had shot himself.

Now, more than ever, was it imperative that the affair be hushed up. The official announcement that the Crown Prince had died of heart failure was allowed to stand. A secret medical report, suggesting mental derangement, was used to secure from the Pope permission for Rudolf to be given a Christian burial. The Crown Prince's body, with the gaping head wound carefully covered and the burns on the face camouflaged with pink wax, was brought back to lie in state in the Hofburg. It was in the disposal of poor Mary Vetsera's corpse, however, that the workings of the bureaucratic machine were revealed at their most ruthless and efficient.

The imperial commission which had gone to Mayerling to examine Rudolf's body had there found the naked corpse of Mary Vetsera—her long hair streaming over her shoulders, a rose held between her lifeless hands. The body had been bundled into a lumber-room and covered with a pile of old clothes; it was not until Rudolf's corpse had been borne away in solemn state that it was brought out. Two of Mary's uncles were summoned to Mayerling to identify the corpse and to sign a false statement claiming that their niece had shot herself. Then, at dead of night, they were forced to play a part in her macabre funeral. The body, fully dressed in coat, shoes, boa, gay feathered hat and veil, was stood upright between the uncles and, by linking their arms through those of the corpse, the two men guided it carefully, as though walking, down the steps and toward the waiting carriage. Here it was propped up between them in a sitting position. They were then jolted along dark, icy roads to a nearby monastery; each time the carriage lurched, the corpse would bump against the two men and the feathery hat would have to be jammed back on to hide the bullet wound.

At the monastery the body was put into a rough coffin and Mary's uncles joined the police officers already waiting for them in the refectory. The monastery was renowned for its cellars and while Mary's body lay in the mortuary until morning, the atmosphere in the nearby refectory was not unconvivial. "Several of those present became very high-spirited and merry," runs one official report. The hardness of the frozen ground and the force of sleet and rain prevented the funeral from being held, as intended, at an early hour, and it was not until nine o'clock that the body was finally buried. The grisly deed accomplished, the company dispersed, leaving the rain to lash the piled earth on little Mary Vetsera's unmarked grave.

Preparations, in the meantime, were going ahead for Rudolf's grandiose funeral. He was to be buried, with full Catholic rights, in the Hapsburg family vault of the Church of the Capucines.

For his widow, Crown Princess Stephanie, these were bleak days. What she mourned, and she admits it honestly, was the loss of her position. It was true, she says, that Rudolf's death had relieved her of a conjugal life full of anxiety and unhappiness, but only at an enormous cost. "My own future and that of the country, for which I had endured so much with unfailing patience, seemed to have been shattered. Nothing remained but a burning wound in my heart. My hopes, the meaning of life, had been pitilessly destroyed." The Court seemed already to be turning its back on her; even before Rudolf was buried, she was being treated as someone of no account.

The arrival of her parents, King Leopold II and Queen Marie Henriette, alleviated her despair somewhat. Marie Henriette seems to have been particularly sympathetic and even Leopold revealed himself "unusually understanding." What enraged him, claims

Stephanie, was the fact that his daughter had been slighted, that the "prestige of the family had been tarnished."

Of more concern to the mercenary King than the bolstering of his daughter's pride, however, was the bolstering of his own financial position. This was the time when the Congo finances were at their shakiest, and Leopold was resolved to turn the family tragedy to his own advantage. The very first thing he did on setting foot on the station platform in Vienna was to make an appointment with the chairman of an Austrian bank. The next was to reply to a message of sympathy from the Belgian Government. "We thank you for your kind expressions regarding the disaster that has fallen on us," he wrote. "We know the feelings of Ministers and count on their sympathy in the terrible trials which God has laid upon us. Do whatever you can to help M. Van Neuss to place some more shares on the market: this would be most agreeable to me. Once more, I thank you."

Once the funeral was over, Stephanie's only wish was to get away. Taking her little daughter Elizabeth with her, she went to Miramare. Here, in Maximilian's white castle on the Adriatic, she was joined by her mother, Queen Marie Henriette, and her sisters, Louise and Clementine. Gradually, but predictably, she recovered her spirits. "I do not know whether it was thanks to the unceasing wonderful rhythm of the Adriatic which lapped the feet of the palace or whether the aroma of the spring flowers and the songs of the birds soothed my wounded heart—but, in any case, the sense of void gradually departed; once more I found joy in life, became resigned and patient, recovered poise and courage."

The one question, of course, which haunted her throughout the months she spent at Miramare was why Rudolf had committed suicide. It is a question which has not been satisfactorily answered to this day. One theory was that his father, or the Pope, had refused him permission to divorce Stephanie. Another was that he had been in financial difficulties. There was talk of inherited madness; of his will power being weakened by an addiction to morphine; of a political murder made to look like suicide; of a blazing row with the Emperor about Mary Vetsera. Queen Victoria even hinted at details "too shocking to write." The most persistent theory is that he was deeply involved in some Hungarian plot against the Emperor's Government. On the morning of the day that Rudolf had left for Mayerling a footman had handed him a telegram; Rudolf had read it and then muttered, "Yes, it has got to be." What message had the telegram contained? Whatever it was, the telegram was carefully destroyed after Rudolf's death.

Perhaps the Crown Princess Stephanie was not so very wide of the mark after all when, years later, in her matter-of-fact fashion, she declared that: "For me, the root of the matter lies in the instability of his nature."

5

Princess Stephanie's marriage and Carlota's madness had provided the family with two disasters; Princess Louise's extramarital activities were to provide it with still another.

While out driving in the Prater one morning in the spring of 1895, the lively Louise, who shared her mother's passion for horses, noticed a young man battling to control a black stallion. Impressed by his handling of the restive horse, she stopped to watch. As the stallion plunged toward her carriage, her eyes met those of its rider. They did not speak and when the young man had mastered his mount, she drove on. But it had been a significant encounter. "I received," the young man afterward admitted, "a kind of electric shock." In fact, the sight of the thirty-seven-year-old Louise had swept the simple and impressionable young man off his feet. From that moment on, he says, the urge to see her became "necessary to my life."

He trailed her for months, and not until the following year, at Abbazia, on the Adriatic, did he actually speak to her. She learned that his name was Count Geza Mattacic-Keglevic and that he was a lieutenant of the 13th Uhlans. Louise, flattered by the ardor of the handsome and courtly young man, became his mistress and by the time they returned together to Vienna they were in love. As always, Louise made not the slightest effort to hide her feelings and before long there were few who did not know that she and Mattacic were lovers. She paraded him in public, she made light of the disapproval of the imperial court; the two of them spent money like water. The Emperor Franz Josef, annoyed at Louise's indiscretions, forbade her appearance at court and packed Mattacic off to the provinces.

But the affair had gone beyond such conventional remedies. Determined to divorce Philip of Coburg and marry Mattacic, Louise went to Brussels to get her parents' permission. King Leopold would not hear of it. A husband, explained the cynical old King, was a very useful screen; provided one were discreet, what went on behind the screen was nobody's business. Ignoring the advice, Louise left Belgium and joined her lover on the Riviera. With them went Louise's fifteen-year-old daughter, Dora. It was while the three of them were staying at the Villa Paradis in Nice that Prince Philip, egged on by his more pugnacious friends, reluctantly challenged Mattacic to a duel. The challenge was accepted, Mattacic returned to Vienna and on February 18, 1898, the aging and nearsighted Prince Philip faced the young and athletic Lieutenant Mattacic on the sanded floor of the *Reitsaal* of the Spanish Riding School in Vienna. Both men held pistols. Philip's shots went wild; Mattacic fired his into the air. They were then handed swords. "The lieutenant," says Louise, "continued to treat [Prince Philip] with respect," and the whole farcical business was finally brought to a close by Mattacic's nicking the Prince lightly on his right hand. The Count retired, intact, to Nice.

Having failed to get rid of Mattacic by fair means, his enemies now tried to do it by foul. The Count was accused, by Prince Philip, of forgery. Louise's enormous bills, all carrying the guaranteeing signature of her sister Stephanie, were produced as evidence.

Stephanie, it was claimed, had never signed the bills. The signature was a false one and Mattacic was charged with having penned it.

Mattacic, from the safety of France, denied the accusation. But whether the signature was forged or not, the bills remained to be paid and in the ill-founded hope that Queen Victoria would pay them, Louise and Mattacic set out for London. As the Queen had given her "so many evidences of her affection" in the past, Louise felt sure that she would not fail her now. It was as well that she did not put things to the test. The train carrying the lovers to England passed the train carrying the Queen to the south of France, and in London prudent friends dissuaded the couple from approaching Victoria on their return to Nice.

By now they were up to their ears in debt. Louise was borrowing from all and sundry; she was even said to be buying jewels on credit to sell them at half price for cash. When King Leopold visited the Riviera he would neither see her nor give her a penny. An announcement in the local press to the effect that Prince Philip of Coburg was not responsible for his wife's debts brought a small army of tradesmen and moneylenders to her door. They forced their way into the lovers' hotel room and carried off anything of value on which they could lay hands. Even her horses were taken from her. Her daughter Dora's fiancé, Duke Gunther of Schleswig-Holstein, very wisely removed the girl from this degrading atmosphere and deposited her with his parents in Germany.

Unable to remain in Nice, and desperate for money, the lovers decided to return in secret to Austrian territory. They made for Mattacic's stepfather's castle hidden away in the mountains of Croatia and threw themselves on his mercy. Their presence did not remain undetected long. As the authorities were unwilling to arrest them in the home of their influential, but by now uneasy, host, they hit upon a way to get the couple to the nearby city of Zagreb. Mattacic was summoned to present himself at Zagreb—ostensibly for a compulsory military medical examination. Unable to refuse, he took Louise with him and while they were there, their hotel rooms were raided. Mattacic was arrested for forgery and flung into prison. Stripped of his rank and title by a court martial in secret session, he was condemned to six years' imprisonment. Louise, presumably on instructions from the Emperor Franz Josef, was offered the alternative of returning to her husband or being shut up in a lunatic asylum. She chose the asylum.

To legalize her confinement, Louise was certified as insane by a hastily assembled tribunal. She was then committed to the asylum at Purkersdorf.

Without a single voice being raised in her defense, she had been, as she says, "erased from the world and taken to a madhouse." The royal families of Austria and Belgium, considering themselves well rid of an embarrassing member, heaved a sigh of relief. No one, claims Louise, not her daughter Dora, nor her sister Stephanie, nor her mother Queen Marie Henriette, lifted a finger to help her. "As for the King," she says, "he placed appearances above the obligations of his conscience, and took no further interest in the cruel fate of his eldest daughter." But she was wrong. King Leopold did interest himself in the business. He made a point of instructing the superintendent of the asylum to "keep a strict watch upon the madwoman."

6

Almost completely unaware of the march of events about her, the mad Empress Carlota lived on for year after year in the Château de Tervueren. Although her brother, King Leopold, was quite prepared to dip into her vast fortune to help finance the Congo, he is said to have been unable to bear the sight of her. It was left to Queen Marie Henriette and her daughters to pay her occasional calls. Sometimes the Empress recognized them and would behave with a certain decorousness but at other times she seemed completely deranged. She still looked, says one of the princesses, "amazingly beautiful."

In March 1879, in the early hours of the morning, the servants at Tervueren were awakened by the smell of burning. Madame Moreau, the Empress's lady-in-waiting, leapt out of bed and ran to her mistress's rooms. She found the sitting room already thick with smoke, but the Empress, on being urged to get up, refused to budge. *"Cela ne devrait pas être,"* she kept repeating. Only by convincing her that she herself had issued orders for them all to leave could they get her away. Dressing her as quickly as they could, they led her down the staircase and into the park. By now the fire, which had been started by a defective chimney pipe in the linen-room, had swept through the entire building and the Empress stood watching the blaze in some bewilderment. *"Ah, oui, c'est très grave, c'est très grave,"* she said, *"mais c'est très beau!"*

Queen Marie Henriette, as soon as she heard of the fire, came hurrying over from Laeken to fetch the Empress. At first Carlota refused to get into the carriage and when she was finally persuaded to do so, they had to tie her to the framework with a shawl lest she try to jump out. Taking the reins herself, the Queen drove them back to Laeken. For a few weeks Carlota remained with the family at Laeken and was then installed in the castle of Bouchout, a vast battlemented and moated pile, a few miles from Brussels.

Here her condition gradually worsened. Her lucid periods became less and less frequent and although there were intervals of calm, her behavior was often violent in the extreme. She would smash vases, slash paintings and rip books to shreds, always taking care, however, not to destroy any photographs or souvenirs of the long-dead Maximilian. Somewhere in that clouded mind there remained an awareness of her former life. "When I reigned," she once remarked to a tardy attendant, "I simply lifted a finger to summon my lady-in-waiting." Her doctor had only to remind her that her violent behavior was not seemly in an empress for her to lapse into a dignified calm. And she one day sat down at the piano and played—for she could still play accurately and with feeling—the Mexican national anthem.

The widowed Princess Stephanie, in the company of Queen Marie Henriette, once visited the Empress at Bouchout. The year was 1899 and Carlota was then almost sixty years old. Although pale, she still looked very beautiful and was dressed with her usual care. Stephanie ran up to kiss her hand and the Empress, remembering her and obviously delighted to see her again, embraced her warmly. As soon as they sat down, however, the Empress launched into a stream of incoherent chatter; nothing she said made the slightest sense. Then, quite suddenly, she turned her large sad eyes toward her niece and said quite lucidly: "Have you come from Austria, dear child? How is your father-in-law, the Emperor?"

Thereupon she rose to her feet and taking Stephanie by the hand, led her across the room to a life-sized portrait of that other Emperor, Maximilian. Very humbly, the Empress curtsied before it.

"And the other one," Carlota said quietly to her niece, "they killed him."

"It was really heartbreaking," says Stephanie.

Chapter Seven

1

As he grew older, King Leopold II grew more impressive to look at. At the turn of the century, by which time he was not far from seventy, there were few monarchs who looked more kingly than he. Tall and erect, with his piercing eyes, his hawk-like nose and his great white bib of a beard, he was a man of immense presence. There was something patriarchal, almost Biblical, about his appearance; one could never mistake him for anything other than a king. And yet he was not a vain man. He seemed, for the most part, quite unconscious of his looks and paid very little attention to his appearance. His suits were often threadbare, his bald head usually covered with a shapeless old military cap or a battered straw hat, and more often than not there was a button missing from his jacket.

And in the same way that he was unconcerned about his looks, so was he not bothered by what the world thought or said of him. Popularity was something which he had never courted. "My grandfather, Louis Philippe, loved to show himself on the balcony; not I," he one day remarked to Charles Woeste. "I do not seek the applause of the masses." He was never one for winning affection by the friendly wave, the proffered hand or the kindly word. Aloof, cynical and arrogant, he made no attempt to win the hearts of his subjects; if they were not satisfied with him as he was, then there was nothing that he was prepared to do about it. No one could have epitomized less the beer-drinking, home-loving, down-to-earth Belgian than did King Leopold. And no one could have made his distaste for these particular qualities more obvious. "Popularity!" he scoffed. "I had it and it left me; it is like the movements of the title. It is made of light froth; it is not even foam. There remains nothing of it—nothing."

If Leopold found his countrymen dull, he was beginning to find his country even duller. As he grew older he spent long periods away from home. He found the Belgian weather depressing and the atmosphere provincial. "When does the train start back to Paris?" ran the caption to a contemporary cartoon showing Leopold just arriving in Belgium after a sojourn abroad. He was especially fond of France. He liked the French capital for the opportunities it gave him of doing business, of wandering about the streets unrecognized and of satisfying his voracious sexual appetite. He loved the Riviera for the sunshine, for the flowers, and for the chance of a little property speculation. While his yacht lay at anchor off Cap Ferrat, the King would be driving himself along the coast road at breakneck speed; he had a passion for fast cars. Avoiding other holidaying royalties like the plague (they, it must be admitted, were just as anxious to avoid him), he would spend his time in the company of financiers, *bon viviers* and chorus girls. Yet he had no real friends. Even those men who, in earlier days, had shared his dream of a Belgian Empire had long since been frightened off by his unscrupulous methods of winning and maintaining it. He let them go. Rich, powerful and self-sufficient, he had no need of friends.

Only when it served his immediate purpose did he put himself out. His charm, on these occasions, could undermine the most firmly held convictions. Cecil Rhodes, no less of an empire builder himself, once refused an invitation to the palace on the grounds that every dinner accepted cost him another province. And Clemenceau, a hard man to win round, was won round, nevertheless, by the persuasiveness of King Leopold. But it was sarcasm that came more naturally to the King than charm; his wit was almost always malicious. Xavier Paoli, a French *agent de Sûreté* assigned to visiting royalties, complained that "his habit of icy chaff made one feel perpetually ill-at-ease.... One never knew if he was serious or joking. This tall, rough-hewn old man had a trick of stinging repartee under an outward appearance of innocent good-nature." When the anarchist Rubino tried to shoot him and wounded his companion Oultremont instead, the King, feigning an uncomprehending anger, cried out: "What harm has Oultremont done the people that they should try to do away with him like this?" Once, when Leopold was staying with one of his mistresses in his villa at Ostend, a local priest, primed by his scandalized parishioners, reluctantly tackled the King on the subject of his behavior. "The word has gone round that Your Majesty has a mistress," stammered the embarrassed old priest. Leopold, adjusting his monocle, looked at his companion in mock horror. "Could you believe such a thing?" he gasped. "Well, Monsieur le Curé," he continued confidingly, "I was told the same story about you yesterday, but I refused to believe it!"

Scandal about Leopold and his mistresses was not, however, confined to Ostend; by now all the world was talking about the old King's dissolute life. Age seems merely to have increased his sexual virility. After the *Pall Mall Gazette* made its attack on child prostitution in London, King Leopold was named as one of Mrs. Jeffries' clients when she was charged with procuring pre-pubescent virgins; the accusations were never denied. *Le Roi des Belges et des Belles* they called him as a tribute to the stream of young girls who satisfied the almost abnormal royal cravings. "The huge white beard," says one of his biographers, "waved over the opening of the twentieth century as a snowy symbol of vigorous and insatiable elderly desire."

The most famous of the King's liaisons was with Caroline Lacroix, later known as the Baroness de Vaughan. King Leopold first saw this sixteen-year-old prostitute in a hotel corridor in Paris, and within a few days she was brought to him for his inspection. The watery blue eyes approving of what they saw, the King arranged for her to meet him at Bad Gastein and from then on Leopold found himself becoming increasingly fond of Caroline. She was pert, she was coarse, she was quick-tempered, but there was something about her which appealed to the old man. Exactly what it was no one seemed to know. There was talk of her depraved sexual tastes, of strategically placed mirrors and specially equipped couches, of her ability to give him the illusion of youth and vigor. But he might simply have been in love with her. In spite of their incessant public squabbling, in spite of her reputed unfaithfulness, in spite of all her vulgarity, Leopold kept her by his side for year after year, making no secret of his passion. *La Reine du Congo* they called her; and indeed, if Leopold had two kingdoms, why could he not have two queens?

This well-publicized affair between the septuagenarian monarch and the teen-aged prostitute was hardly calculated to enhance an already tarnished reputation. The depraved old King was attacked, not only in the Belgian Press, but in newspapers throughout the world. King Edward VII kept contact between Leopold and himself to a minimum; the Empress Augusta of Germany had the court chaplain exorcise the apartment in which the King had been staying; President Theodore Roosevelt refused to allow him to visit the St. Louis Exposition. "We don't want him," exclaimed the President, banging the table. "He's a dissolute old rake!"

But King Leopold had no intention of changing his ways for anyone. Smiling his sardonic smile and stroking his silky beard, he went limping, like some cold-hearted merchant prince of the Middle Ages, into the twentieth century.

He had by now severed almost all connections with his family. His only interest in his daughters was to ensure that they inherited nothing of the vast fortune he was building up. This wealth was derived mainly from something known as the *Domaine de la Couronne*. This *Domaine* consisted of a slice of the Congo ten times the size of Belgium, a piece of territory belonging to Leopold personally and from which, by ruthless exploitation of the African population, he was earning a great deal of money. This money, he reckoned, would ensure that his ambitious public works were carried out and that the dynasty would remain powerful and independent. As his father, Leopold I, had aggrandized his house by way of advantageous marriages, so was Leopold II doing it by making that house rich beyond compare. And he was determined that this vast inheritance must never be broken up and divided among his daughters; it must remain intact as a guarantee of dynastic glory. As this intention ran counter to Belgian law, King Leopold was ready to employ any subterfuge to make sure that his fortune did not fall into the hands of his daughters.

With the headstrong Louise, now incarcerated in a lunatic asylum, he would have no truck whatsoever. When the Emperor Franz Josef sent an emissary to Brussels to suggest that Leopold pay his daughter's enormous debts, the King's answer was very much to the point. "As far as I am concerned," he said, "my daughter is dead." Why had the emissary not told Leopold, remarked Franz Josef with unaccustomed wit, "that it would become him to pay the debts of even his dead children?"

When the widowed Stephanie, some years after the Mayerling tragedy, decided to marry Count Elmer Lonyay, a Hungarian commoner, Leopold was furious. Although Franz Josef gave his permission for the marriage, King Leopold withheld his. Stephanie married nonetheless, and her father refused to have anything more to do with her.

Clementine, his youngest daughter, was the only one with whom he was on speaking terms. Of the three princesses, Clementine was the best looking. Like her sisters, she was tall and somewhat statuesque but she had been spared both Louise's feverishness of manner and Stephanie's awkwardness of movement. Her profile was fashionably aquiline and she dressed with great panache. But her looks, at this stage of her life, belied her personality. She was a modest, dutiful, long-suffering young woman, very much the stay-at-home daughter of elderly parents. It needed all her tact, however, to cope not only with her father's scathing tongue and her mother's complaints, but with the insolence of the King's mistress. More and more, as the years went by, did Clementine take over the Queen's duties, until the sight of the cantankerous old King, leaning on the arm of his spinster daughter, became a familiar sight throughout Belgium. She began to be known as "the little Queen." It was not so much that the King loved her as that he needed her, and being a selfish man, he was determined to hang onto her for dear life.

But it was probably Queen Marie Henriette who led the saddest life of them all. Ignored, despised and humiliated by her husband, she had been living, ever since the year 1895, at Spa, in the foothills of the Ardennes. She might occasionally go to Brussels to attend some state function or to hear a concert, but for the rest of the time she lived a life of almost complete obscurity. She had bought and converted the old Hotel du Midi at Spa into a little palace and she was usually to be found working in the garden or talking to her various pets. She had two ill-tempered griffons, Caro and Mucho, a Mexican and a Congolese parrot, a horse, Cocotte, whom she had taught to salute with its hoof, and a llama with a tendency to spit in the face of anyone who caressed it. She was still a skilled and fearless driver; she still gave little musical soirées at which she played the harp; she did a great deal of charitable work among the poor of the district. It was a pathetic and pointless existence and it was no wonder that she would sometimes, according to one of her daughters, "give way to her sorrow and allow the cries of her wounded soul to be heard."

Princess Louise tells the story of how once, before she was committed to the asylum, she went to spend a birthday with her mother at Spa. Both Stephanie and Clementine were staying with the Queen, and Marie Henriette decided to give a little dinner party to celebrate Louise's birthday. She booked a room at an hotel and the four women—two of them estranged from their husbands, the third widowed and the fourth unmarried—sat down to a meal. Dinner over, the Queen felt like dancing. She therefore sent for Gerard, her aged *maitre d'hôtel*, and ordered him to partner them. So, while Clementine played waltzes on the piano, the old servant solemnly shuffled each of the husbandless royal ladies around the room in turn. It must have been a strange and poignant sight.

On the afternoon of Friday, September 19, 1902, the sixty-six-year-old Queen, who had been unwell for some time, was playing cards with some members of her suite. The game over, she asked for the results of the afternoon races at the Hippodrome of Sart and then, feeling tired, settled down in a chair for a little rest. At half past seven she asked an attendant to help her rise and as the attendant did so, the Queen heaved a deep sigh and fell back dead.

The King was holidaying in the Pyrenees with Baroness de Vaughan when he heard the news of his wife's death. He set out at once for Belgium. Princess Clementine, who had been on bad terms with her mother for the past year, had hurried to Spa on the very night of the Queen's death and Princess Stephanie arrived from Austria two days later. When King Leopold arrived at Spa at four o'clock on Sunday afternoon, they were already there. On hearing that Princess Stephanie was praying beside her mother's coffin, Leopold refused to go into the room until his daughter had left it. Even in these tragic circumstances, the iron-hearted King would have nothing to do with the daughter who had married against his wishes. He would neither speak to her nor allow her to attend her mother's funeral. Princess Stephanie, her face pale under a long black veil and her shoulders shaken by violent sobs, came hurrying out of the death chamber and took a carriage to her hotel. From here, through a silent, curious crowd, she drove to the station and took a train to Vienna.

Immediately after the funeral, held in the Church of Sainte Gudule in Brussels, King Leopold climbed into his motor-car and was driven, at full speed, toward France. Here, in the company of the Baroness de Vaughan, he resumed his holiday. *Der Wahre Jacob*, a German illustrated paper, promptly published a cartoon of the King, dressed in deep mourning, rushing into the arms of his beloved, with under it the caption: "*Vive le veuvage!*"

2

When the shy Prince Albert, at the age of fifteen, was asked by his uncle, King Leopold, about the sort of girl he hoped to marry, the boy's answer was instantaneous.

"I shall marry a girl with small hands and small feet and fair hair," he said.

"Is that all?" pressed the old King.

"Well, no," added the Prince. "I shall love her."

Love was an emotion which had hitherto played very little part in the marriages of the Coburgs of Belgium. With the possible exception of Carlota, no member of the dynasty had yet married for love. Even Prince Albert's parents, the ideally suited Count and Countess of Flanders, had only come to love one another with the passing of the years. But Albert, for all his shyness, was a resolute—indeed a stubborn—young man, and he meant what he said. No one was going to force him into a political marriage. Once, when the chance of a particularly brilliant match presented itself, old King Leopold was determined that Albert should take advantage of it. But the Prince refused.

"I shall announce the betrothal," threatened the King.

"Then I shall deny it," answered the Prince quietly.

And until the age of twenty-five, in spite of King Leopold's fears that the dynasty would simply die out, Prince Albert remained single. He spent two years at the *Ecole Militaire*, he served as an officer in the Grenadiers, he attended a royal wedding here and a coronation there, he toured the United States, he pedaled his bicycle along the flat roads of Flanders and scaled the cliffs of the Ardennes, but he remained heart-whole. Women might find his simplicity refreshing, his calm reassuring and his modesty touching, but they never succeeded in discovering what lay in his heart.

It was not until the summer of 1900 that Prince Albert fell in love. He had gone mountaineering in the Bavarian Alps and it was here that he met a girl with the obligatory small hands and feet, although her hair was not fair, but auburn. She was the twenty-three-year-old Princess Elisabeth, Duchess in Bavaria, a member of the extraordinary Wittelsbach family.

Her father was Duke Charles Theodore, Duke *in* Bavaria (the Dukes *of* Bavaria belonged to the reigning royal family), a brother of the beautiful Empress Elizabeth of Austria whose aimless wanderings had finally come to an end with her assassination on the shores of Lake Geneva two years before. His cousin was that bizarre King Ludwig II who had been drowned, in strange circumstances, in the lake near the Castle of Berg to which he had been confined as a madman. The strong strain of eccentricity running through the Wittelsbachs had affected Duke Charles Theodore as well; the Ducal ménage at Possenhofen was utterly unlike the usual royal household. Having no taste for the customary pursuits of his position, Charles Theodore had insisted on studying medicine at the University of Munich and in Vienna; having taken his degree, he insisted on practicing. As he was particularly interested in diseases of the eye, he founded three eye hospitals, the chief one being in the Royal Schloss at Tegernsee. Here the "Oculist Duke" would perform his operations. He charged no fees, but such patients as could afford to pay were expected to contribute to the hospital's collecting box. This money was then distributed among the poor.

Very different from the liberal, rebellious and unconventional Wittelsbachs was the family to which Princess Elisabeth's mother, the Duchess Marie-José, belonged. She had been born a princess of Portugal, a member of a branch of the House of Braganza which had been associated with all the most reactionary movements of the nineteenth century. Iron-willed, autocratic, steeped in the theories of absolutism and the divine right of kings, they had not made the slightest effort to adapt themselves to a changing world. At the time of Elisabeth's birth, in fact, one of her mother's sisters was careering about Spain, mounted, armed and uniformed, in a vain effort to place her brother-in-law, the pretender Carlos VII, on the throne of Spain. It was as well that Princess Elisabeth, while inheriting something of the Braganza tenacity, had inherited none of its less attractive characteristics. The Wittelsbach strain—romantic, artistic and unorthodox—was far more evident.

The Duke's five children had been raised with the utmost simplicity. They were an informal, intelligent and compassionate family, with no time for the busy trivialities which made up the lives of so many royalties. They all had a strong sense of duty toward the underprivileged, a concern which was always practical, never patronizing. One of the sons took Holy Orders and worked as a curate in a poor parish. Princess Elisabeth, the second child, was particularly close to her father; she had that same natural, almost bohemian air about her. The Duke had personally supervised her education and had encouraged her in her musical interests and she played both the piano and the violin with considerable skill. She assisted him in his hospital and accompanied him on his rounds of his peasant patients. When he and her brothers went mountain-climbing, she went with them.

That this warm-hearted and unaffected young woman was attracted to the sincere and simply spoken Prince Albert is understandable. At first meeting, almost, they were conscious of a very real affinity. "Not only did they develop swiftly a strong mutual attachment," says one observer, "but that attachment was based on the sure foundation of common tastes, common ideals and common interests." The tall, grave, conscientious young prince and the small vivacious and no less dutiful princess were delighted with each other. "They are together," wrote the visiting Belgian writer, Van Zype, "and it is plain to all beholders that this Prince and Princess are indeed two lovers, for whom, at this moment, nothing exists outside themselves." On the day that Albert, having just risked his neck to pick Elisabeth an edelweiss, summoned up a different brand of courage and asked her to marry him, she consented immediately.

For all the similarity of their tastes, however, Albert and Elisabeth were unalike in many ways. Where he was ponderous, introspective and self-doubting, she was quick-witted, extrovert and assured; where he was cynical and pessimistic, she was confident and enthusiastic. What his character lacked, hers could supply. Unobtrusively and with great tact, she was henceforth to smooth his way and to bring his complex personality to full flower.

King Leopold, appreciating his nephew's independent streak, made no objection to the match. But hating music and having been obliged to sit through so many of Queen Marie Henriette's musical soirées in the early years of the reign, he asked whether Princess Elisabeth played the piano.

"She is a wonderful player," answered Albert proudly.

"Well," growled the old King, "if she insists on playing to you, remember that you insisted on marrying her."

The couple were married in Munich in October. The bride, scarcely reaching her husband's epauleted shoulder, looked a bit small, thought one of the guests, for a future queen. But no such reservations bothered her future subjects. When Albert and Elisabeth arrived in Brussels three days after the wedding, their reception was almost embarrassing in its vociferousness. Whether this was meant as a rebuke to the autocratic old King, who accompanied them on their drive through the city, or whether the crowd really was pleased at the sight of the shyly smiling bride, no one knew. The King's champions, however, always accused the Belgians of ingratitude because of the wave of sentiment in favor of the Prince and Princess which now swept through the country.

Here, at last, were a royal couple after the Belgians' own hearts. They filled the ever widening gap between King and people perfectly. Honest and unassuming, they had a very real interest in social reform, in the problems of disease and poverty and in the intellectual life of the country. In this their attitude was in direct contrast to the imperiousness of the old King. Where Leopold II would not be seen from one month's end to the next, Prince Albert busied himself with philanthropic projects and there were few days on which Princess Elisabeth—"the little Princess"—was not to be seen tramping through the poorest quarters of Brussels, bringing practical aid to the sick and the needy. The naturalness of their home life was likewise appreciated; they both had a marked distaste for excessive formality. "My friend, I am only a man like yourself," said Albert good-naturedly to a gardener who would not stop bowing. To their home in the Place de l'Industrie came artists, writers and musicians, all grateful for the practical encouragement and easy-going unconventionality of their hosts. At the birth of each of the children—Leopold in 1901, Charles in 1903 and Marie-José in 1906—their popularity increased. After the sordid public wranglings of King Leopold's family, the harmony of life in the Place de l'Industrie was a refreshing change. There was something very touching in the unashamed devotion of the parents to their three children. "In Germany," said some visiting Prussian princeling chaffingly to Prince Albert, "men have other matters to engage their attention."

"I have noticed it," answered Albert, "without envy."

For all Prince Albert's growing popularity, his position as heir (his father, the Count of Flanders, died in 1905) was a particularly difficult one. Although King Leopold had grown to appreciate his many good qualities, he was still not prepared to share power with him. The King was extremely jealous of his rights and it needed all Albert's tact not to arouse the old man's animosity. The King might call him in during the discussion of some state business, but he allowed him to play no active part in public affairs. Nor could he resist an occasional malicious slapping-down of his nephew. Once, when Albert opened a window in the King's study, the sudden draught swept all the papers off the monarch's desk. One of the ministers present immediately bent down to collect the scattered documents but the King held him back.

"Pick those papers up," said King Leopold to his nephew.

The minister protested.

"Let him do it," said the King. "A future Constitutional Monarch must learn how to stoop."

The incident has sometimes been quoted as an example of the King's appreciation of democratic principles; it is probably a better example of his sour wit.

What, one wonders, did King Leopold II really think of this unpretentious young couple who were one day to take his place? Was he disappointed to find them so modest, so bourgeois, so seemingly lacking in the stuff of greatness? Although some of the old King's dreams had never materialized—Britain had finally driven him off the Nile in 1906; his recent attempt to gain a foothold in China had failed—he had achieved greatness nevertheless. The world might criticize him (and its most violent criticism was yet to come) but it could not deny the immensity of his achievements. Were this unassuming couple fitting heirs to this spectacular legacy? Were they likely to add yet more luster to the crown of Belgium?

It did not, on the face of it, seem very likely. But unknown to King Leopold, Albert and Elisabeth—in a very different fashion—were to achieve a very different sort of greatness.

3

To ensure that Princess Louise was kept well beyond the reach of an increasingly sympathetic public opinion, she was moved from the lunatic asylum at Purkersdorf to a mental home at Lindenhof, in Saxony. Although she was housed in some comfort ("my cage was certainly gilded") and allowed more freedom, she was still under strict surveillance. Her coachman and footman were policemen and her single lady-in-waiting was obliged to hand in daily reports. The only member of the family to interest herself in Louise's plight was the kindly Countess of Flanders who once talked Louise's married daughter Dora into accompanying her on a visit.

Four years after Louise had been certified as insane, she heard that her lover, Count Mattacic, had been released from prison. His case had been taken up by a Socialist deputy in the Austrian Parliament and, after a sensational, seven-month-long struggle, during which the Coburgs came in for their full share of abuse, Mattacic was allowed to go free. The first thing that this faithful and long-suffering ex-officer did was to make for Saxony in search of Louise. One day, while she was out driving under guard, she noticed a cyclist pedaling toward her carriage; as they passed, she realized that it was the Count. Their eyes met but she had the presence of mind not to cry out. Twice after this, with the cooperation of Louise's lady-in-waiting, they managed short, furtive meetings in the depth of a forest. But the police were becoming suspicious and Mattacic had to leave the district. For months the anguished Louise, longing to be rescued, heard nothing more from her lover. But one afternoon, while she was out in her carriage, a little boy flung a scrap of folded paper onto her lap. As soon as she was alone she opened it. Through her tears Louise read and re-read the one word scribbled on the sheet—"HOPE."

Not until she was allowed to visit the health resort of Bad Elster was there an opportunity of that hope's being fulfilled. Her first few days there took on an almost comic-opera flavor: a tangle of secret letters, whispered messages and meaningful looks, with waiters, night-watchmen and fair-haired strangers playing their parts. What it all signified was that Count Mattacic was in the district, planning her escape. Finally, one evening at dinner, Louise's impassive-faced waiter passed the last message: "It will be tomorrow."

On the appointed night of the escape Louise attended the local theatre. "Of all the plays I have ever seen," she afterward said, "none has left me with so slight a remembrance as that with which the little theatre of Bad Elster regaled its honest audience that evening." The play finally over, she was escorted back to her hotel room. Having said goodnight to her warders, she hurriedly packed a few clothes and waited for some signal. It was one o'clock in the morning before she heard a slight scratching at her door. Hushing her little dog, Kiki, she opened it. In the dark corridor stood the hotel's night-watchman. He whispered to her to be ready to leave at any moment and that he would be returning soon. For two agonizing hours Louise stood by the door, waiting. Just after three o'clock the watchman returned. Once again she silenced Kiki and then she and the watchman tiptoed along the corridor, down the stairs and out of a side door. Here Count Mattacic was waiting for her. Together they crept through the shadowy garden and out into the road. In the bright moonlight two sentries stood chatting. As soon as they parted Louise and Mattacic bounded across the road and into the dark trees on the opposite side. From here they were led by their fellow conspirators to a waiting carriage. It took them to the station and within a few hours they were safely in Berlin. Not until they reached Paris, however (and to get there they had to pass through Belgium), could they breathe freely once more. "I was in a hospitable country," said Louise, "protected by just laws." Her seven-year-long nightmare was over.

But the impetuous Louise was never one for staying out of trouble long. She was still, moreover, in desperate need of money. Queen Marie Henriette's death, two years before, had raised the question of her daughters' inheritance. Louise and Stephanie thus joined forces to claim one-half of King Leopold's vast fortune. The world was now treated to the unedifying spectacle of a lawsuit between a father and his daughters. Paul Janson, the Radical deputy and lawyer, represented the two princesses and day after day the Brussels courtroom was packed with a large and fashionable audience. Although Janson's eloquence on the subject of his clients' unhappy lives and the defendant's callousness brought tears to many an aristocratic eye, he lost the case. The gratified King Leopold kept his money. "He has not even a heart of stone," commented one Viennese paper; "he has a heart of gold, which is harder than stone."

But Belgian opinion against the miserly and licentious old King was beginning to gather strength. While his daughters starved, people said, King Leopold was squandering his Congo millions on his mistresses. Lest this public antagonism affect his carefully nurtured fortune, Leopold hit upon a way of silencing the embarrassing Louise. He sent Sam Wiener, the wealthy lawyer whose hand was to be seen in many of Leopold's schemes, to make her an offer. The King would grant Louise an estate near Cologne and an annual income of £10,000 if she would end her association with Mattacic. It is greatly to Louise's credit that she refused to hear of it. She could not even pay her hotel bill but she never, for a moment, considered leaving Mattacic. She was right when she said that "our mutual fidelity may astonish some people."

In 1907 Louise finally obtained her divorce from Philip of Coburg. The move gave Leopold the excuse to wash his hands of her once and for all. Nor was he the only one. Stephanie, shocked that the family name should be sullied by a divorce, would have nothing more to do with her.

"Louise and I remained devoted friends, connected by the closest ties, until the unhappy hour when our roads parted," she noted prissily. "After her separation from Prince Philip in the year 1907, she was no longer regarded as a member of the Saxe-Coburg-Gotha family."

4

By the turn of the century the world was beginning to wake up to the fact that something extremely sinister was going on in King Leopold's Congo. Missionaries, defying possible expulsion, began reporting atrocities by state officials against the African population. It was believed, at first, that such horrifying reports must be exaggerated and it was not until Sir Charles Dilke raised the matter in the British Parliament that the evidence began to be taken more seriously. The diary of a Congolese officer named Tilkens, falling into strange hands, made shocking reading, and still more damning evidence was presented by Edmund D. Morel, the journalist. His exposures, first in the press and then in his two impassioned books, *King Leopold's Rule in Africa* and *Red Rubber*, did much toward rousing public opinion.

In 1903 Herbert Samuel, by bringing certain grisly details to the attention of the House, stirred the British Government into action. A Note was sent to the signatories of the Berlin Act and—what proved to be of more practical value—Roger Casement, the British Consul at Boma, was commissioned to make a report on the matter. The Casement Report, published in 1904, more than confirmed the allegations. His findings were subsequently backed up by the evidence of many others—Consuls, Vice-Consuls, American, British and

Danish missionaries and unbiased travelers. The Congo Reform Association, founded by Morel, held protest meetings in Britain and America. Morel himself petitioned President Theodore Roosevelt to demand reforms in the Congo. King Edward VII referred to the matter in a speech from the throne, and from pulpits throughout Britain the clergy spoke in terms of "a terrible blot upon the name of Christianity." The phrase "Congo Horrors" became a rallying cry, and the demand for some sort of action became more and more insistent.

What, exactly, were these horrors? They were the almost inevitable result of King Leopold's monopoly system. The King's only interest in the Congo was to make as much money out of it as quickly as he possibly could. In 1901, when he had been due either to repay the Government loan of ten years before or to hand the Congo to Belgium, he had managed, in his usual adroit fashion, to do neither. The Government obligingly passed a bill postponing repayment of the loan indefinitely, and King Leopold remained in control of the Congo. Not even he, however, imagined that he would live forever and his milking of the Congolese cow was now accelerated to provide the funds for his many unfinished projects.

Rubber provided the main wealth of the Congo and it was in the collecting of rubber that the African population was forcibly engaged. Leopold, interested in quick profits only, made no effort to conserve the rubber vines or to plant new ones; as the supplies of wild rubber dwindled, so did the search become more frantic. If the Africans were slow in delivering their quota, they must be made to work faster. The easiest way to do this was to terrorize them. And the best way to terrorize them was to kill those guilty of not working fast enough. To prove to King Leopold's impatient agents that a punitive raid against a dilatory village had indeed been carried out, severed human hands were brought in as testimony. The more hands that were brought in, the more efficiently had the punishment been carried out and the more efficiently, presumably, would the rubber be gathered by others in future. Reliable witnesses saw baskets of human hands being hauled along by Africans to a local European official for his inspection. When the soldiers (often cannibals from different tribes, chosen by officials for their brutality) were accused of wasting too many bullets, they would simply hack the hands off living men to make up the pile. Nor did the atrocities stop at shootings and hand-hackings. Villages were burned, men flogged, women mutilated, children chained in sheds as hostages or flung into crocodile-infested rivers, whole clans wiped out. Tribes fled in terror across the borders. Those who survived lived a nightmare existence. Senator Picard saw "a continual succession of blacks, carrying loads upon their heads; worn-out beasts of burden, with projecting joints, wasted features, and staring eyes, perpetually trying to keep afoot despite their exhaustion.... They totter along the road, with bent knees and protruding bellies, crawling with vermin, a dreadful procession across hill and dale, dying from exhaustion by the wayside...." It has been estimated that in fifteen years, through massacres, through flight and through disease, the population of the Congo fell by some three million.

It was horrifying, but it was profitable. King Leopold, in the ten years between 1896 and 1906, made almost £3,000,000—then $15,000,000—in clear profit for his *Domaine de la Couronne*. For almost every life lost, in fact, he gained a pound sterling.

When faced with these accusations, King Leopold pooh-poohed them. He dismissed his critics as impractical idealists, as meddling do-gooders, as rapacious businessmen jealous of his success, as land-hungry rivals trying to steal his territory. As usual, he played one critic off against the other. By insinuating that Britain had designs on the Congo, he aroused the suspicions of France and Germany; by implying that the Protestant missionaries wanted to get rid of a Catholic sovereign, he alarmed the Catholics. He set up a secret Press Bureau to disseminate favorable propaganda. He expended vast sums of money on buying the support of leading public figures. He paid state visits to Paris, Berlin and Vienna. He sent the President of the United States a silver-framed photograph of himself.

But he was blowing against a hurricane. No one believed him. A less notorious personality might have got away with it, but with the sort of reputation he enjoyed, the charges stuck all too easily. The world already knew that he was depraved, mercenary and hard-hearted; that he had betrayed his wife and ill-treated his daughters; that he was moving heaven and earth to rob these daughters of their inheritance. If he was capable of such behavior toward his own flesh and blood, could there be any doubt that he was guilty of atrocities toward unknown savages?

To the chorus of vilification were now added the voices of such eminent writers as Anatole France, Conan Doyle, and Mark Twain. "In fourteen years," thundered Mark Twain, "Leopold has deliberately destroyed more lives than have suffered death in all the battlefields of this planet for the past thousand years ... this mouldy and piety-mouthing hypocrite, this bloody monster whose mate is not findable in human history anywhere, and whose personality will surely shame hell itself when he arrives there—which will be soon, let us hope and trust."

With no chance of riding out this particular storm, Leopold agreed to organize a Commission of Enquiry. Its findings, although couched in the most tactful language, confirmed previous allegations. The King, after a considerable delay, announced various innocuous reforms. They did almost nothing toward alleviating international hostility. By now it was beginning to be realized that the only answer was for Belgium to annex the Congo. Even King Leopold could appreciate this. He was not, however, going to let it go cheaply. With the vigor of a man half his age, he now prepared a series of intricately worked-out and arrogantly worded documents in which he set out the conditions upon which he was prepared to hand over the Congo to Belgium. From out of the pages of verbiage emerged one significant fact: Leopold was planning to keep his personal Congolese estate, now known as the *Fondation de la Couronne*, intact. If he was successful in preserving this, then what Belgium would inherit would be little more than an empty shell.

But the stubborn old man was fighting a losing battle; the Belgian Government was no longer prepared to dance to their Sovereign's tune. Annexation without provisos was becoming inevitable. Finally realizing this, Leopold decided to salvage what he could. Money was hurriedly shifted from the *Fondation de la Couronne* to secret depots in Europe. In a typically complicated financial maneuver, he set up an illegal body known as the "Foundation of Niederfullbach." To circumvent Belgian law, the Foundation was headquartered in a castle near Coburg—cradle of the dynasty—and into this new secret body Leopold deposited the wealth of his doomed Congo *Fondation*. It was not, of course, that he wanted the money for himself; he wanted it for the power that it gave him. He must be rich enough to do as he pleased. He must be able to build palaces and enlarge harbors and erect triumphal arches without having to beg his Government for the money. He must be able to continue aggrandizing Belgium whether she wanted it or not. He must force greatness on her willy-nilly.

Only when Leopold had drained off as much money as he possibly could did he signify that he was ready to hand over the Congo But even now, at this eleventh hour, he could not resist cornering Belgium into further obligations. She reluctantly agreed to take over and complete the great public works hitherto financed by his *Fondation*. And finally, he forced them into granting him a further £2,000,000 as "a mark of national gratitude."

Seldom has a pill been more generously sugared.

On November 15, 1908, the sky-blue flag with its golden star, once assumed to be a philanthropic symbol and in reality the symbol of so much suffering, was hauled down. The Congo Free State became the Belgian Congo. Leopold II had defied the world for over thirty years but the world, in the end, had got the better of him.

5

While this storm was raging about her father's head, the modest Princess Clementine announced that she wanted to get married. Her choice was Prince Victor Napoleon, heir to the imperial throne of France. His father had been the irascible Plon-Plon, cousin of the Emperor Napoleon III; his mother had been the pious Princess Clotilde, daughter of King Victor Emmanuel of Italy. Already in his forties, Prince Victor had been living in exile in Belgium for some years; his home was a sumptuous mansion on the Avenue Louise. Apart from his looks, Prince Victor had inherited very few of the Bonaparte characteristics. He had neither the family licentiousness nor its ambition and, except for some violent quarrels with his late and unlamented father, he had led an extremely uneventful life. His political activities as Bonaparte pretender were minimal. A manifesto here, a round of royal visits there, an article somewhere else marked the extent of his dynastic campaigning. "Prince Napoleon is a Pretender who seems to have no pretentions," they quipped in Brussels. Not even in Republican France was he considered anything of a threat. He seemed, on the face of it, an excellent choice for Princess Clementine.

But Leopold was having none of it. It was not so much that he feared the insult to France by allowing his daughter to marry the Bonapartist Pretender, as that he was loath to let her go. Not only did he find Clementine extremely useful, but she provided him with his last shred of domestic respectability. He flatly refused to give his consent.

For once in her life Clementine rebelled. She continued to see Prince Victor, she immersed herself in Bonapartist literature (the French writer, Frédéric Masson, was releasing a flood of it at this time), she pressed her father time and again for his permission. Unable to talk her out of her obsession, Leopold fell back on typically oblique methods. He offered her a bigger allowance, he got various statesmen to speak to her, he asked the Prime Minister to send him a letter of protest against the marriage, he even had the newspaper *l'Indépendence Beige* run a leader on the subject. The hand of the King was only too obvious in the sonorous phrases about the Princess's "duty" toward her father, the dynasty and the Belgian people. And

Clementine, not strong enough to withstand this barrage, surrendered. While youth slipped by, she remained at her father's side—dutiful, diffident, uncomplaining.

Toward the equally unobtrusive Prince Victor, Leopold had now developed a strong antipathy. One morning, while the King was waiting on the station platform at Bâle for the train to Brussels, Prince Victor suddenly emerged from the refreshment room. On realizing this, Leopold turned at once to his companion.

"Let's go and look at the engines," he said sourly and, turning his back on the advancing Prince Victor, went limping away.

While King Leopold was denying his daughter the right to marry, he himself was thinking of taking a second wife. His young mistress, the Baroness de Vaughan, had by now been established in the Villa van der Borght near Laeken, and the old King seems to have been as besotted with her as ever. She had already borne him two sons—Lucien in 1902 and Philippe in 1904. Leopold, delighted at being the father of these two sturdy little boys (although there was a rumor that he was not the father of the second) was all for legitimizing them. In this he came up against the implacable opposition of his family, his Government and his subjects. The Baroness was attacked in the streets of Brussels by a scandalized populace and Leopold's daughters, bitterly resentful of the amounts of money being squandered on a prostitute, appealed to the Pope. His Holiness suggested that Leopold either break with his mistress or marry her. It was a risky pronouncement. Given the choice, Leopold plumped for marriage. He would marry the Baroness, he said, as soon as the storm of public disapproval had died down. In the meantime he would persist in his efforts to legitimize the children.

But the Belgian Government remained as obstinate as ever and Leopold had to be content with recognizing his sons as German Princes of Saxe-Coburg-Gotha.

Not until later, and then in bizarre circumstances, did he marry the Baroness.

6

How far had King Leopold succeeded in realizing his ambition to make Belgium "greater, stronger and more beautiful"? If the half-hearted annexation of a huge slice of Africa constituted greatness, then he had made her greater. If the transformation of Brussels from a medieval town into an imperial capital, of Ostend from a fishing village into an international resort, of modest royal residences into flamboyant palaces meant beauty, then he had indeed made her more beautiful. But he had not yet made her stronger. This was not for any want of trying. Year after year, decade after decade, in season and out, King Leopold II had urged successive governments to look to Belgium's defenses. But nothing seemed to shake them out of their complacency. The majority of Belgians dismissed their monarch as a warmonger and turned their minds to what seemed to them like more pressing problems.

But in this, as in everything, the King persisted. In 1887, after years of threats, pleas and cajolery, the King got a disgruntled Chamber to agree to the fortification of Liège and Namur on the River Meuse. Germany, fearing a French attack through Belgium, had also requested the erection of these forts; by an irony of fate these same forts were one day to hold up the German attack, through Belgium, on France. At Antwerp the King had less success. King Leopold I's plan to convert Antwerp into a great national redoubt had never fully materialized. The predominantly Catholic, Flemish-speaking population remained firmly, even violently, opposed to fortification. Yet Leopold II, to the very end of his reign, kept hammering away at the subject.

Of even more importance to the King was the business of *remplacement*. This was the system whereby youths purchased exemption from military service, a system which had the unqualified support of the majority of Belgians. King Leopold was determined to ditch *remplacement* for what was called "personal military service," and so build up a bigger, more efficient army, but each move to do so brought an hysterical outburst from his subjects. *Remplacement* was seen by progressives as a symbol of personal liberty and by Catholics as a means of keeping their youth away from the depravities of barracks life. They would not hear of compulsory military service. King Leopold, once more, seemed to be hitting his head against a brick wall.

In 1904 King Leopold paid a state visit to Berlin. Here the Kaiser, thrashing about for allies in face of the rapidly developing Anglo-French *Entente Cordiale*, tried to tempt King Leopold with an extraordinary bargain. While the old King listened "open-mouthed," the Kaiser spoke about the possibility of recreating the old Duchy of Burgundy; by the annexation of Artois, French Flanders and the French Ardennes, Leopold could revive the glories of that old Burgundian Empire. When the King, laughing nervously, reminded his host that things had changed since the fifteenth century and that his Government would never countenance such a project, the Kaiser lost his temper. He stormed at his fellow monarch for allowing himself to be guided by parliaments rather than by "the Lord who reigns in Heaven" and assured him that he, the Kaiser, was not one to be lightly crossed. Whoever was not with him in the event of a future European war would be against him, he threatened; if Belgium refused to join him, then Germany's actions would be motivated by "strategic considerations only." Belgium's long-guaranteed neutrality, in other words, would count for nothing. The Kaiser could not have made himself more clear. It was no wonder that when King Leopold, just before leaving, reviewed the troops at the station, he put on his ceremonial helmet back to front.

Now, more than ever, was it essential to build up Belgium's strength. The fortifications must be carried out and *remplacement* must go. To these ends King Leopold devoted his still unflagging energies. He made speeches, he harangued deputies, he bombarded ministers with instructions. At last, toward the end of 1909, after a year of parliamentary battling, a bill abolishing *remplacement* was passed by the Chamber. It was the Kind's final triumph.

For by now the seventy-four-year-old King was dying. He had arrived back from a stay at Balincourt, country home of the Baroness de Vaughan, on December 1, 1909, and had complained of feeling unwell. In an effort to resist old age, the King had been following an exceptionally rigorous course prescribed by an American therapeutist and it had proved too much for him. On arriving at Laeken, he decided to put up in the Pavilion des Palmiers rather than in the palace itself. In this octagonal, glass-walled pavilion, part of that great maze of greenhouses which he loved so well, King Leopold played out the last bizarre act of his life. All about the old King's sumptuously furnished ivory-colored bedroom stretched the silent greenhouses; the atmosphere was heavy with the scent of flowers, the leaves of palms and ferns dripped ceaselessly. Not a breath of air stirred the great masses of waxy, riotously colored blooms. When he felt up to it, the King would take the arm of an attendant and hobble along the glassed-in galleries, "tasting the joy," says Count Louis de Lichtervelde, "of being for the moment only an old gardener passionately fond of flowers."

King Leopold II was not the man, however, to neglect more serious business. He worked at state papers, he received his ministers, he followed—with avid interest—the progress of the Military Bill through Parliament. On the morning of December 13, Leopold was told that he would have to undergo a serious abdominal operation and that he had a ten-percent chance of surviving it. He received the news calmly. He made only one stipulation: the doctors must keep him alive until the following Tuesday, for that was the day of the final vote on the Military Bill and he wanted to be able to sign it before he died. He then sent for the Baroness de Vaughan, who had arrived from France some days before, and told her that he was going to marry her.

The ceremony was performed by the palace chaplain. The King wore a white dressing gown and his bride a black silk dress. "Let me introduce you to my widow," said Leopold to one of the witnesses when it was over.

He next tackled the question of his remaining personal possessions. Lest his daughters get their hands on anything of value, he instructed his lawyer to transfer practically every bit of movable property—state carriages, furniture, silverware, jewelry—to his secret Foundation of Niederfullbach. With his daughters thus safely disinherited, he consented to see the only one of them with whom he was still on speaking terms—Clementine. Taking care to avoid meeting the Baroness—by now her stepmother—Clementine spent some time by her father's side.

In the afternoon the King received the Last Sacrament. He spurned the offer of Cardinal Mercier, who had come hurrying to Laeken to perform the last rites, and entrusted the ministering to the local parish priest. He then received his heir, Prince Albert, and his Prime Minister, Frans Schollaert. Unable to rise from his bed, he still found the strength to lecture Schollaert on the importance of not giving up an inch of Congo territory. "If you yield," he threatened, "your old King will rise up from the tomb to reproach you." The Prime Minister left the room, they say, with tears in his eyes.

The operation was performed on the morning of December 14. "I am ready," Leopold had said to the surgeon, "but on my awakening I want to find myself on this couch, for I have work to finish." And that is where he did find himself. The work which he had yet to finish was brought to him that evening: it was the Military Bill, passed by Parliament and now waiting for his signature. He signed it with a wavering hand. For two days longer he held on and early on the morning of December 17, on the forty-fourth anniversary of his accession, he died. With him, at the very end, was the Baroness de Vaughan.

She did not remain there long. The first thing that the royal family did after the King's death was to throw her out. She ran shrieking across the ornamental bridge connecting the Pavillon des Palmiers to the Villa van der Borght. But Princess Louise's lawyers had got there before her. The Baroness found the doors locked and seals placed on the boxes of Congo stock which Leopold had given her. She fled, at once, to France.

But it was going to take more than mere expulsion to erase her memory. King Leopold, appreciating his unpopularity only too well, had asked to be buried early in the morning at a simple, private ceremony with Prince Albert as the only member of the royal family attending. But in the same way that King Leopold I's wish to be buried at Windsor had been overruled, so was his son's request ignored. King Leopold II was buried on December 22, 1909, with all possible pomp. It was not, however, for the galaxy of foreign princes who followed the coffin, or for the solemnity of the scene at Sainte Gudule, that King Leopold's funeral was chiefly remarkable; it was for the scurrility of the pamphlets, dealing with the King's private life, that were being sold like hot cakes all along the funeral route.

Albert I
King Against Conqueror
1909-1934

Chapter Eight

1

King Albert faced a formidable task. Leopold II, in his obsession with strengthening the dynasty, had neglected the one sure way of doing so: he had never put himself out to win the loyalty of his subjects. If the monarchy was to survive both the internal and external pressures threatening the country, then Albert would have to make sure that the crown remained the symbol of a united Belgium. Both his predecessors—Leopold I and Leopold II—had been as much concerned with their prestige as monarchs as with the affairs of their country. Albert, in letting it be known that he preferred the title Albert, King of the Belgians to that of Albert I, immediately set the tone of the new reign.

The first step was to ensure his personal popularity. For this, Albert was hardly better equipped than his uncle had been. It was true that the simplicity of his manner and the decorousness of his home life had gained him a certain amount of respect, but he had neither the taste nor the talent for winning popular acclaim. For one thing he was extremely self-conscious about his appearance. He was abnormally tall, his body was heavy, his walk shambling, his eyesight poor and his hair unruly. He looked uncomfortable in uniform and far too comfortable in civilian clothes. He seemed more like an absent-minded professor than a king. With his far-away, abstracted air, he always looked, it was said, "as if he wished to build something."

Nor did he have any aptitude for projecting his personality. He was embarrassed in crowds and tongue-tied with strangers. He could make neither interesting small-talk nor rousing speeches. He seldom smiled. Awkward himself, he was incapable of putting others at their ease. His severe expression, magnified by his glasses, tended to make his guests even more inarticulate than he was. He never knew how to bring an interview to a close. On one occasion a guest, in strained conversation with the King, glanced up at a looking-glass behind the King's head; in it he saw reflected the image of Queen Elisabeth peeping through a doorway and making frantic signs to her husband to dismiss his visitor. "You must go," said the King abruptly, and then added, as a means of softening the brusqueness of his order, "but don't forget your handkerchief." As the guest, in complete bewilderment, looked down at a scrap of lace-trimmed fabric on a nearby table, a voice suddenly sounded from the doorway. "It's *my* handkerchief," said the Queen.

Not only did King Albert have very little taste for courting popularity but he tended to regard it with some cynicism. A delighted aide-de-camp once remarked on the size of the crowds that had flocked to see the King. "They will be just as big," said Albert dryly, "when I am led to the scaffold."

It was with much more enthusiasm that the King applied himself to his less public challenges. Away from the glare of public scrutiny his particular qualities showed to much better advantage. His compassion, his intelligence, his devotion to duty, his quiet strength, his capacity for leadership were more apparent in the study or the council chamber than on the platform. "It is impossible," says one of his ministers, "to come near the King without feeling the prestige of his personality, and without being filled with admiration for his scrupulous conscience and his wide knowledge."

Albert was determined, by appeasing political and linguistic enmities, to develop a spirit of unity throughout the country. Whereas King Leopold II had often chaffed against the restrictions imposed on the sovereign by the Constitution, Albert's behavior was always impeccable. In the struggle between the ruling Catholic party and its Liberal and Socialist opponents, he remained strictly neutral. Those who, because of the King's apparent diffidence, assumed that he would be a tool in the hands of the conservatives were to be proved as wrong as those who, because of his sympathy with the poor, imagined that he would become a "Socialist King." Tolerant, adaptable and progressive, he steered a careful course between capital and labor. "In the ministerial council," says a minister, "he exerted the influence of a chief. This influence did not impose itself through the expression of some decisive and dictatorial opinion; it insinuated itself through his words, uttered somewhat slowly, as if he were in search of a more precise form, and accentuated by a few constructive gestures."

It needed all this tact and firmness to deal with the country's internal upheavals. These early years of the reign were marked by the steadily mounting campaign for universal suffrage. An extension of the franchise in 1893, during King Leopold II's reign, had greatly benefited the Socialists; now, by way of strikes and demonstrations, they pressed for a further extension. At the opening of Parliament in 1910, the new King, seemingly unperturbed, was forced to ride through a rain of petitions in favor of universal suffrage. And hand in hand with this spread of Socialism went the spread of Republicanism. "Between Socialism and Monarchy," declared a Socialist Manifesto published on the eve of the King's accession, "there is no possible reconciliation, and when official Belgium prepares itself to acclaim Albert I ... a loud clamour of hope and defiance will rise from all the workers' breasts; *Vive la République Sociale!*" It depended on King Albert, almost entirely, to divorce this creed of Republicanism from that of Socialism.

Another of his problems was the growing antagonism between Flemings and Walloons. The struggle between these two language groups—the Flemish-speaking, largely peasant population of the northwest and the French-speaking, more industrial population of the southeast—had hitherto been confined to a small intellectual circle. Resenting the nineteenth-century tendency to belittle the Flemish language, a group of Flemish writers had set out to resurrect and champion it. Toward the end of the century their purely scholarly cause had been transformed into a political one; Flemish Socialists attacked French as the language of the rich ruling classes and Flemish priests accused it of being the language of atheism. That French should be used, almost exclusively, not only by the Government, but in the courts, the army, the universities and the secondary schools was a state of affairs bitterly resented by the Flemings. There had even been a case of two innocent Flemings condemned to death and guillotined, after a trial conducted in French—a language which neither of the men had understood.

With increasing vigor and in the face of considerable opposition, the Flemings—or the *flamingants* as they called themselves—pressed for reform. Little by little their demands were complied with and by the time of Albert's accession Flemish, in Flanders, had regained considerable prestige and was being widely used in local government, in courts and in schools. But the struggle, hitherto confined to Flanders, now spread across the entire country; the *flamingants* were determined on nothing less than equal language rights. Flemish must be introduced into the central administration and become as much the language of the country as French.

King Albert, sympathetic to the Flemish struggle, gave his full support to linguistic reform. He encouraged the growth of Flemish culture, he used Flemish (which he spoke fluently) when addressing Flemish audiences, he was the first Belgian sovereign to take the oath of office in both languages. He wished the Belgian people, he said, "to cultivate the feelings which united them, and not those which divided them." But this was easier said than done. An important section of the Flemish population remained discontented. It was a discontent which was to manifest itself, in significant fashion, during the First World War. It was a discontent which plagues Belgium to this day.

Another of Albert's tasks was to counteract the increasing isolation into which King Leopold's blithe disregard of world opinion had driven the country. He and the Queen went on a round of visits to the various capitals of Europe and in the summer of 1910 the *Exposition Universelle* in Brussels gave him the opportunity of playing host to his brother sovereigns. Opening the exhibition on April 23, the King spoke of it (more in hope, one imagines, than by conviction) as "a work of peace and prosperity in which free competition has replaced the armed conflicts of former days." It was toward the saber-rattling Kaiser Wilhelm II that this innuendo was chiefly directed; King Albert was becoming increasingly apprehensive of the aggressive attitude of his powerful neighbor. Skeptical of Germany's intentions of respecting Belgium's neutrality in some future war, King Albert had begun, from the very outset of his reign, to urge the further strengthening of Belgium's army. At the end of that exhibition summer he was able to mention his hopes for peace to the Kaiser personally. Wilhelm visited Brussels in October and Albert, in his speech of welcome, assured his royal guest that he had every confidence "that your noble efforts will continue to preserve the peace of the world and thus benefit all nations." To this plain hint the Kaiser made a fulsome but noncommittal reply.

The royal visit, as far as Wilhelm was concerned, was an immense success. The streets were gratifyingly aflutter with German flags, the crowds were flatteringly enthusiastic, the speeches were suitably congratulatory. The Kaiser rhapsodized over the glories of Belgian art and architecture and had a great deal to say about the "success which the Belgian people has won in all the domains of commerce and industry." He, who so loved brilliant uniforms, was somewhat disappointed by those of the Belgian officers; at one reception, however, he caught sight of a particularly gorgeously dressed officer and made some surreptitious enquiries in the hope that he himself might be granted an honorary rank which would allow him to wear so striking a uniform.

In his anxiety to win Belgian support, the Kaiser laid frequent stress on the ties which united the royal houses of Belgium and Germany. The Saxe-Coburg family was German, Queen Elisabeth was a Bavarian, and King Albert's mother, the Countess of Flanders, was a Hohenzollern princess. It was thus almost incomprehensible to the German Emperor that King Albert, half Hohenzollern himself, should pay so much attention to the opinions and aspirations of his subjects.

"Why grant so many audiences, and to men of no account?" he one day asked Albert. "You have your policy—it is for them to follow it."

"My country and I, we make our policy together," explained the King.

"But we Hohenzollerns," replied the Kaiser grandiloquently, "are the bailiffs of God."

It was no wonder that King Albert felt apprehensive.

Before leaving Belgium the Kaiser, flushed with the success of his visit, assured Baron van der Elst, the Secretary-General at the Belgian Ministry of Foreign Affairs, that Belgium had nothing to fear from Germany. "You will have no grounds of complaint against us," he said expansively. "I have a great affection for your King who, through his mother, belongs to our House. I will allow no one to do him harm. I understand perfectly your country's situation."

Just how imperfectly he understood it was to become apparent very soon.

2

King Leopold II was hardly cold before his three daughters set about flouting his final wishes. The two eldest, Louise and Stephanie, immediately embarked on a lawsuit against the late King's estate, claiming—with some justification—that the wealth of the Foundation of Niederfullbach was part of the royal fortune and therefore belonged to them. As their lawyers dug deeper, so did they uncover layer upon layer of the old King's complicated trusts and foundations; he had been richer, it seemed, than anyone had ever imagined and his bland assurance, in his will, that he possessed nothing other than the sum bequeathed to him by his parents was patently nonsense. The lawsuit dragged on for years. Stephanie backed out after a while leaving the more resolute and more impecunious Louise to carry on alone. She never won her case but in 1913 the Belgian Government agreed to settle £230,000 on the two Princesses. The outbreak of war prevented Louise, then living in Germany, from receiving her share and it was not until five years later that the sum was finally handed over. Throughout the war she had been obliged to beg and borrow as best she could and when, at the end of hostilities, she was searched by Communist officials in Budapest, one of them exclaimed: "Here is a King's daughter who is poorer than I am!"

In her vitriolic and scarcely coherent memoirs, published just after the war, Louise attempted to clear her name of the many calumnies still clinging to it. The book was dedicated, curiously enough, to "the Great Man, to the Great King, who was my Father." Louise did not long survive the publication of her book; she died, at the age of sixty-six, at Wiesbaden in 1924. Her sister Stephanie, having written and published her own self-applauding memoirs, outlived Louise by over twenty years, dying, at the age of eighty-one, in 1945.

King Leopold's youngest daughter, Clementine, had played no part in her sisters' financial hagglings. "She accepted from the Belgian Government that which the State was pleased to offer her," scoffed Louise. But Clementine was no less actively engaged in repudiating her late father's wishes. No sooner had he been buried than she began making plans to marry the faithful Prince Victor Napoleon. The wedding took place less than a year after Leopold's death and in spite of all the late King's professed apprehensions, it caused not a ripple of disapproval in Republican France.

It was at the castle of Moncalieri, Italian home of Prince Victor's mother, the devout Princess Clotilde, that the ceremony was performed. The bride, according to one enraptured witness, looked "radiant in beauty and charm ... majestic and amiable." By this marriage the Coburgs, already linked to almost every royal house in Europe, were united to the most colorful dynasty of them all and Princess Clementine, according to her friends, became "*plus Bonapartiste que le Prince.*" The couple had two children: a daughter,

Clotilde, born in 1912, and a son, Napoleon, born in 1914. Twelve years later, on the death of Prince Victor in 1926 (Clementine lived on until 1955), this boy—the grandson of King Leopold II—became the Pretender to the imperial throne of France. He remains so to this day. The breach between King Leopold I and the Emperor Napoleon III had at last been well and truly healed.

3

In Queen Elisabeth, Belgium gained its first queen of any real stature. King Leopold I's queen, Louise, had been too self-effacing for the position; King Leopold II's queen, Marie Henriette, too disillusioned. Elisabeth, on the other hand, had not only the aptitude for the task, but a streak of unconventionality that was to lift her high above the ordinary run of royalties and make her one of the most controversial figures of her time.

She was no beauty. She had the advantages of neither height nor bulk nor natural dignity. The calm, the hauteur, the commanding air of so many royalties she lacked almost completely. She did not, in these early years, even dress particularly well. But when set against her remarkable force of character, these shortcomings were as nothing.

She had an alert, mobile face; her nose was sharp, her eyes bright, her smile dazzling. She was small and slender, with a quick, bird-like quality and boundless energy. Unlike her husband, she enjoyed her public duties. She delighted in her popularity and responded warmly to admiration and applause. Her manner, both in public and in private, was relaxed and confident; only in the company of the pretentious, the arrogant or the ostentatious was she ever less than charming. With empty ceremonial, with excessive protocol, with the activities of so-called society she had very little patience. Rows of pompous dignitaries would often be held up while she chatted, with unfeigned vivacity, to some poet or musician or social worker. Her interests were wide-ranging and she brought to them an unflagging enthusiasm and a very real intelligence. There was a professionalism, a complete absence of royal dilettantism, about everything she touched.

Music was her first love. The eminent violinist Eugène Ysaye had been giving her lessons for some years; now she consulted him on the whole question of advancing the musical life of Belgium. Musicians must be encouraged, trained and supported; they must be assured of a respected place in the life of the community. Her interest in the other arts—in poetry, in writing, in painting, in sculpture—was hardly less intense. Leopold II, with is taste for the immense and the flamboyant, had had very little sympathy with the cultural movements of his country. Now, with the encouragement of both Albert and Elisabeth, Belgium looked forward to an artistic renaissance. That some of the country's cultural leaders, like the Flemish poet Emil Verhaeren, were dedicated republicans bothered Elisabeth not one scrap; her interest in their work was always genuine and wholehearted. She was never one for using her patronage to wean them from their beliefs. "Who would have dreamt," Verhaeren once exclaimed, "that I should ever be a Court poet. But you know, it is not a Court like the others, it can scarcely be called a Court!"

Already, during her years as Crown Princess, Elisabeth had shown an interest in the health and well-being of her future subjects. Oblivious to hostile stares, she had tramped through squalid, working-class, staunchly republican districts, visiting the sick, questioning the poor, acquainting herself with such matters as wages, amenities and living conditions. The knowledge gained was now put to practical use. With the help of some of the country's most eminent doctors, such as Doctor Depage, she founded various societies and associations to deal with the sick and the needy. She started, among other things, a holiday fund for children, a home for the blind, a campaign against tuberculosis, an association for the improvement of workers' houses. The Queen spent so much time visiting hospitals, said the King dryly, that he would never be able to claim her full attention until he had broken a limb or contracted a fatal disease.

Her recreations were pursued with equal zest. She painted, she practiced the violin, she visited exhibitions, she arranged private concerts. To the consternation of her suite, she went up in an airplane and down in a submarine. Gardening was one of her chief delights and her rose garden, on which she lavished so much care, was to become world renowned. She enjoyed supervising the vast flower arrangements for state receptions rather more than she enjoyed the receptions themselves; it was in small, intimate parties, where the guests were musicians or writers or scholars, that she took the greatest pleasure. She was unappreciative of good cooking. Both she and Albert, to the despair of the royal chef, insisted on simple, wholesome meals, and both drank mineral water in preference to wine. Albert, in time, became a vegetarian. It was a decision that would have shocked his hearty, meat-eating subjects.

Bohemian, said Charles d'Ydewalle, rather than bourgeois, would be the word to describe both the King and the Queen. "They were Bohemian in their unprejudiced outlook, their absolute lack of snobbishness, their unique position, their love of adventure, their indifference to danger, etiquette and criticism. They were in nowise confined within the conventional limits of the bourgeois conception of life."

Yet they could be regal when occasion demanded it. The state visits, the balls, the receptions, the banquets were magnificently staged affairs; the Queen could always be relied upon to bring a touch of royal theatricality to these occasions. Each May she held a garden party at Laeken. As there are few days in Belgium on which it does not rain, the reception would be held in the great conservatories. Dressed in white or pale blue, the Queen would move through these exotic, sweet-scented galleries, impressing all with her ease and vivacity. The annual state ball was another never-to-be-forgotten affair. Brand Whitlock, the United States Minister in Belgium, always remembered "the dancers under the brilliant chandeliers, the jewels and the gleam of white shoulders, and the gold lace of the officers of the Guides—their trousers cherry red; and old generals whose breasts were heavy with orders; and suddenly the King, in black evening dress...."

Elisabeth was a devoted mother. All three children—Leopold, Charles and Marie-José—had inherited something of her effervescence of temperament and had to be firmly controlled. Their education was thorough and strictly supervised but both parents had a capacity for joining in their games and hobbies. Elisabeth helped them with their gardening and when they were holidaying in the country the King, who always retained a certain boyishness, was often to be seen leap-frogging with them over haystacks. Family life was as simple and as natural as it was possible to make it and there seems to have been a genuine affection between parents and children. "Through their well-ordered, simple and busy life," wrote Prince Leopold's tutor, General Maton, "the parents spread among the family an atmosphere of sincerity and devotion to duty." They made, as one Belgian writer has put it, a "*bon ménage*."

Brand Whitlock, watching the royal family at the annual *Te Deum* in Sainte Gudule in honor of the founding of the dynasty, has left a picture of the scene. "The King, tall, broad-shouldered, tanned somewhat from his outing by the sea—he had just come from Ostend—was in the lieutenant-general's uniform he always wears; behind the thick lenses of his pince-nez his intelligent eyes were taking in the scene, noting who was there. The Queen, frail, delicate, with the unconscious appeal of sweet, girlish eyes and the delicate, sensitive mouth, had the three royal children beside her: the two princes, Leopold the Duke of Brabant, and Charles the Count of Flanders, grave, fair, slender boys in broad batiste collars and grey satin suits, and Princess Marie-José, with her pretty, mischievous little face and elfish tangle of crisply curling golden hair....

"I stood there and watched this most interesting family—a very model, in its affection and in the sober good sense of the young parents, of all the domestic virtues."

In the year 1911 the Queen contracted typhus. She was so ill that it was thought she would die. Her recovery was slow and during the long weeks of her convalescence she was not even allowed to see her children. When, for the first time after her illness, she made a public appearance, her reception was overwhelming. The cheering crowds flung flowers into the roadway and pressed so closely about her carriage that it was frequently brought to a halt. Eager arms stretched out to touch her and to clasp her little hands. Flushed and exultantly smiling, the Queen was driven slowly through the acclaiming crowd to the safety of the palace. Her tolerance, her sincerity, her warmth of heart had already won her the love of her subjects; in the terrible days that lay ahead, they were to come to regard her as little less than a saint.

4

In November 1913 King Albert paid a visit to the Kaiser Wilhelm II at Potsdam. Growing yearly more suspicious of Germany's intentions, Albert had come to determine them for himself. He was not left in ignorance long. Moving awkwardly amongst the superbly uniformed, tightly corseted, heroically mustachioed German officers, Albert was able to find out, only too clearly, what his hosts were up to. On the occasion of a Court ball the Kaiser pointed out General von Kluck as the man who was "to lead the march on Paris." On another evening, before a state dinner, Wilhelm launched into an impassioned harangue against France; because of continual French provocation, ranted the Kaiser, war had become inevitable. When Albert, with habitual calm, protested that the French wanted nothing but peace, Wilhelm refused to listen to him. After dinner, at which the table had been strewn with violets and during which Albert had looked extremely grave, the argument was continued by General von Moltke, the German Chief of Staff. The General had a great deal to say about the invincibility of the German army and the aggressive spirit of the German people. "This time we must make an end of it," he declared. "Your Majesty cannot imagine the irresistible enthusiasm which will permeate the entire German nation on 'The Day.'"

That both the Kaiser and his Chief of Staff were trying to frighten King Albert into coming to terms with Germany there was no doubt. The so-called Schlieffen plan, whereby Germany hoped to bring France to her knees within a matter of weeks, depended on the swing of a massive German right wing through Belgium. The fact that Germany had been one of the guarantors of Belgium's neutrality in perpetuity was looked upon as nothing more than an unimportant technicality; what was important for Germany was that Belgium should allow German troops to pass through her territory unhindered. At worst, Germany expected Belgium to make some sort of token resistance and then to fall back, leaving the German armies to roll across Belgium, into northwestern France and on to Paris. That way the Germans would have trapped the French armies, drawn up along the Franco-German frontier, in a vise. The success of the Schlieffen plan thus depended almost entirely on the attitude of Belgium. It was an attitude which King Albert, on his return to Brussels after his disturbing Potsdam visit, made crystal clear.

"We are resolved," he stated in a memorandum, "to declare war at once upon any power that deliberately violates our territory; to wage war with the utmost energy and with the whole of our military resources, wherever required, even beyond our frontiers, and to continue to wage war even after the invader retires, until the conclusion of a general peace."

This resolve, so firmly and unequivocally stated, was not treated very seriously in diplomatic circles. No one seemed ready to believe that Belgium intended defending her neutrality. With the countries of Europe becoming ever more firmly locked in alliances or sympathies—Russia with France and France with Britain, Germany with Austria—it seemed unlikely that strategically placed Belgium would remain unattached much longer. She was merely biding her time, it was generally assumed, until she saw which group of powers was likely to be victorious. France suspected her of being in secret alliance with Germany and Germany suspected her of being in secret alliance with France. That she was determined to defend her frontiers, be that attacker France or Germany, or Britain, for that matter, was a simple truth which no one was prepared to believe. When the Belgian Minister for War assured the British Military Attaché in Brussels that a British army landing on Belgian soil for the purpose of attacking Germany would be met with a Belgian "*coups de canon*," he was no less sincere than the Belgian Military Attaché in Berlin who told General von Moltke that a German invasion of Belgium would be resisted to the utmost. To King Albert, Belgian neutrality was something positive, something to be cherished, protected and defended, not something to be bartered. Any Belgian approach to one of the rival powers, no matter how tentative, would give the other side all the excuse it needed to violate this neutrality. There is no doubt that an agreement with the *Entente* powers—to whom Albert naturally inclined—would have benefited Belgium enormously, but the King remained stubbornly and meticulously impartial. If Germany attacked Belgium the Belgian defense might be weak but her conscience would be clear.

"Belgium," explained the French President, Raymond Poincaré, in some astonishment, "was so scrupulous in the matter that she preferred to sacrifice herself rather than to seem for one moment to ignore her neutrality by entering into … conversations with us."

In default of an alliance with France and Great Britain, King Albert had to build up Belgium's own defenses as best he could. In spite of the famous Military Bill, signed by King Leopold II on his deathbed, Belgium's army was still in a sorry state. Not until 1913 could King Albert push through a new Military Bill introducing compulsory military service. As yet, this bill had had very little effect. With his General Staff the King was having even less success. According to the Belgian Constitution, the King assumed supreme command of the army on the outbreak of war—but not before then. Until the very last moment he was obliged to defer to the opinions of the General Staff. Hamstrung, among other things, by the uncertainty of who the first violaters of Belgian territory were likely to be, its members could decide on no definite plan of campaign. They bickered for months and in the end adopted, but never really finalized, a compromise plan. For Albert, so acutely conscious of the dangers, this shilly-shallying was almost more than he could bear. "During his whole reign," wrote his personal military adviser, Emile Galet, "his thoughts had been dominated by one central idea—that of preserving his country from being caught unprepared by the outbreak of an unexpected war.... And now disaster was in sight. Nothing that he had intended was ready. The storm found Belgium without a plan and with a command divided against itself."

It was on August 2, 1914, that the storm broke. At seven o'clock that evening the German Minister in Brussels delivered an ultimatum to the Belgian Foreign Minister. Out of all its velvety phraseology one steely fact emerged: the German army, with or without Belgian permission, was going to cross Belgium into France. The country was given twelve hours in which to comply with, or to reject, the German proposal. The ultimatum having been translated, it was taken by the Prime Minister, Baron de Broqueville, to the King.

Albert had been expecting it. Ever since the murder of the Archduke Franz Ferdinand a month before, things had been speeding toward a climax. There had still been a slight chance, however, that Belgium might not be involved in the coming struggle. The request from the British Government for a formal assurance from France and Germany that they were prepared to respect Belgian neutrality had received an immediate affirmative answer from France. Germany, however, had remained silent. In the face of this continuing silence, King Albert had decided, on the evening of August 1, to write a personal letter of appeal to the Kaiser. He had an idea that the Kaiser might be able to give him some sort of private reassurance on the matter—a reassurance which the Kaiser could not, for political reasons, make public. With the help of the Queen, Albert drafted the letter.

"All her remarks," says Baron van der Elst, who was with them on the occasion, "were sound and betrayed a sure judgment and that particular tact which often makes women better psychologists than men." She spoke softly, he says, almost timidly, putting her views in the form of questions. Every word, every phrase of the important letter was carefully considered. When it was finished, the Queen suggested that she translate it from French into German. To ensure that it was done with the utmost accuracy, she fetched a dictionary from an adjoining room and, placing it on an armchair beside her, knelt in front of a low table and began to write. Behind her, bent anxiously over her shoulder, stood Albert. She sometimes paused to explain why she was using one word rather than another, and again and again she moved the King aside so that she could consult the dictionary.

It was while waiting for an answer to this carefully composed appeal that King Albert received, from the hands of his Prime Minister, the German ultimatum. Once he had read it, all his uncertainties dissolved.

"It is war," he said simply.

At nine that evening he presided at the Council of State assembled to discuss the German ultimatum. "Our answer must be 'No,' whatever the consequences," were his opening words. That these consequences were likely to be disastrous, that Belgium might be laid waste and incorporated into the German Empire, was fully understood by everyone present. There was no question, however, of giving in to the German demands. A reply was drafted and at seven o'clock on August 3, exactly twelve hours after the delivery of the ultimatum, the Belgian answer was handed over to the German Minister. Even now there was a faint hope that the firmness of the Belgian rejection might cause Germany to think again before putting herself so obviously in the wrong. Lest this hope be wrecked, King Albert insisted that no approach be made to either England or France; Germany must not be provided with the slightest pretext for justifying her aggression.

That evening the King received the Kaiser's eagerly awaited answer to his letter. It was in the form of a telegram and was merely another attempt to get the King to accept the terms of the ultimatum.

"As the conditions laid down made clear," telegraphed the Kaiser blandly, "the possibility of maintaining our former and present relations still lies in the hands of Your Majesty."

For the first time during the crisis King Albert lost his temper. "What does he take me for?" he exclaimed and immediately gave orders for the blowing up of the Meuse bridges at Liège and of the railway bridges and tunnels leading to Luxembourg.

At eight o'clock the following morning, the first German troops crossed the Belgian frontier.

Two hours later the King, in simple field uniform, rode to the Palais de la Nation to address Parliament. Behind him, in an open carriage, drove Queen Elisabeth and their three children. Through streets packed with wildly cheering crowds and past buildings bright with flags and flowers, the little procession made its way toward Parliament. "I shall always remember him," wrote an eyewitness of the King, "as he rode forward slowly and steadily among the acclamations and the flags. I thought of the occasion of his accession to the throne which seemed still so recent, when he passed through Brussels in an atmosphere of universal illusion, and of the salute he gave in answer to these joyful demonstrations, his grave smile scarcely perceptible behind his gold-rimmed glasses. Today it was the vivid and unadorned reality, a reality which took you by the throat. To all appearances, Albert I had remained the same. His composure restored confidence. Without hurry and without hesitation, this young and just man went straight where duty called him."

His speech within the hall was simple and without rhetoric. He looked calm, almost impassive. He neither depressed his listeners with talk of possible defeat nor misled them with promise of glories to be won on the field of battle. "In these grave circumstances," he said, "two virtues are indispensable: cool and steady courage and union among all Belgians." When, reminding them of the Congress of 1830 which had created an independent Belgium, he asked, "Are you inflexibly resolved to maintain intact the sacred heritage of our fathers?" the excited deputies rose to their feet and cried out *"Oui! Oui! Oui!"*

Listening intently to his father's every word was his twelve-year-old heir, Prince Leopold. Seated with his mother, the Queen, and his brother and sister, he kept his eyes fixed on the tall, uniformed figure at the lectern. "What are the thoughts in that boy's mind?" wondered Brand Whitlock, as he watched the absorbed expression on the face of the slight, satin-suited Prince. "Will this scene come back to him in after years? And how? When? Under what circumstances?"

The situation was to repeat itself to the watching Prince only too clearly and in circumstances hardly different from the present ones. Twenty-five years hence the boy, as King Leopold III, would face a second German violation of Belgium's neutrality. His subsequent course of action, however, was to be very different from that of his father.

The King's speech over, he took up his *képi* and, with sword clanking, strode out of the hall. He was followed by the Queen, the great white plumes on her hat trembling as she curtsied to the deputies. "Then that stillness again in the chamber," says Whitlock, "intense, vibrant with emotion, the thrill of patriotism, the sense of tragedy, the consciousness of assisting at an historic scene." His eyes, he suddenly discovered, were wet with tears.

King Albert, now Commander-in-Chief of the Belgian Army, set out for Headquarters, established in the Town Hall of the picturesque and ancient city of Louvain, lying between Liège and the capital. "Soldiers," said the King in his rousing Order of the Day, "I am leaving Brussels to place myself at your head." It was eighty-three years since King Leopold I, with similar defiance, had led his army against the sudden invasion by superior Dutch forces. Did King Albert's mind, one wonders, revert to that Ten Days War? Were the disasters and humiliations of that campaign to be repeated? Although the people were as enthusiastic now as they had been then, the army was in hardly better shape. There was no agreed plan of campaign, the General Staff was divided, the troops were under strength, ill-disciplined and badly trained, there was a shortage of machine guns and an almost total lack of heavy field artillery. Six Belgian divisions, ragged and poorly equipped, faced thirty-four divisions of the strongest and most efficient military machine in the world.

It was no wonder that Europe stood amazed at the brave and resolute fashion in which Belgium prepared to defend her independence. It was to be even more amazed at the doggedness with which she was to continue to defend it. But contrary to more cynical European opinion, Belgium had no choice. Her neutrality had been violated and she had to defend it. Years later, when the war was over and King Albert's bravery had become legendary, a French statesman praised him for his heroism.

"Yes," answered Albert in that wry, self-depreciating fashion, "we were cornered into heroism."

Chapter Nine

1

The months of August, September and October 1914 were to be the most tragic, and the most glorious, of King Albert's life. Considered hitherto, by those who did not know him, as a colorless if well-intentioned sovereign, he was to emerge as a bold and resolute leader of men, the living symbol of little Belgium's stand against a powerful and ruthless invader. While his allies floundered about in a swamp of indecision, his country was to bear the brunt of the German attack and he to earn for himself the well-merited title of "Albert the Brave."

At noon on August 4, by which time it was quite certain that the Germans had crossed the border, King Albert appealed to France and Great Britain for help. Suspecting that the main German attack, in accordance with the Schlieffen plan, was to be made through Belgium, and confident that the Allies, realizing this, would hurry to his aid, the King prepared to hold up the enemy advance until the arrival of reinforcements. As his General Staff had refused to adopt his scheme for defending the line of the Meuse, he had to content himself with the less satisfactory plan of concentrating the army before Louvain, leaving the Meuse forts of Liège and Namur to look after themselves. With luck, the two fortresses, built, ironically enough, on the insistence of the Germans some thirty years before and considered all but impregnable, would pin down the enemy until the arrival of the French and British forces. Unknown to King Albert, however, the Allies had no intention of rushing troops to Belgium's aid. France, obsessed with regaining the provinces of Alsace and Lorraine, lost to the Germans in 1870, was determined to make its thrust directly across the Franco-German frontier, and Britain, after a period of exasperating indecision, finally bestirred itself into sending four divisions to strengthen, not the Belgian resistance, but the French left wing, over fifty miles from the Belgian front line. Thus, for more than two weeks, Belgium faced the tremendous onslaught alone.

For King Albert it was an agonizing fortnight. Young and inexperienced, beset by doubts and misgivings, he was obliged to make a series of momentous decisions. That they had to be made in the face of hostile criticism from his allies, his General Staff, his troops and the civilian population rendered them all the more significant. Two factors influenced his actions: he had to conserve his little army, and he had to keep it on Belgian soil as long as possible. His strategy, though frequently unpopular, was invariably proved right. "They always managed to escape our grasp so that their army has not been decisively beaten nor forced away," growled the exasperated General von Kluck.

The first test came at the very opening of the campaign. The Belgians, fighting magnificently, repulsed the Germans before Liège. With Brussels going wild with excitement and newsboys shouting "*Grande Victorie Beige!*" the more impulsive members of the General Staff were all for ordering an immediate offensive against the enemy. Only King Albert's level-headedness kept them in check. An offensive at that stage would have been suicidal. A few days later he had occasion to display an equally admirable firmness. When Germany, still convinced that Belgium would not be so foolish as to offer any serious opposition, proposed that as Belgium had now "upheld its honour by heroic resistance to a very superior force" she allow them to pass, Albert rejected the proposal out of hand. Rebuffed, the Germans bombarded Liège into submission. As the enemy came pouring over the Meuse, Albert made the much-criticized but sensible decision to fall back, thus keeping his army intact. He realized by now that he could expect no immediate help from his allies. "We are alone," he said dispassionately to his Prime Minister. It was quite possible, he added, that the Germans would overrun central Belgium and occupy Brussels. "The greatest victory during this period will be to have gained time; the final issue of events is still uncertain." The King refused, however, to retreat southward to join the French left wing; for patriotic reasons he retired to the great national fortress of Antwerp. "It is not a question of shutting ourselves up in an entrenched camp," he explained to the disappointed French, "but of taking breath before an eventual counterblow."

Here, in this great seaport on the Scheldt, fortified by King Leopold I and King Leopold II against just such a day as this, King Albert and his army came to seek refuge. The Queen, the royal children and the Government had already been established there for some days. On August 20, the Germans occupied Brussels. For three days and three nights the seemingly endless German army marched through the silent capital. From here they swung southward, in a massive curve, toward France, leaving Antwerp, still intact, on their right flank. And for the following six weeks, while King Albert waited anxiously for relief and harried the enemy's flank as best he could, the Germans carried out a ruthless and systematic terrorization of the country.

The Belgian resistance had infuriated the Germans. The Schlieffen plan had made no allowance for a prolonged campaign in Belgium; the German army was meant to sweep swiftly through the country in order to reach Paris within a matter of weeks. The Belgian stand at Liège, at Namur, and the sorties from Antwerp had already delayed the German advance and given the tardy Allies time to prepare their defense. If the Schlieffen plan was to be adhered to, then the Belgian resistance would have to be stamped out once and for all. And the only way to do this, reckoned the Germans, was by intimidation of the civilian population.

While King Albert looked on in impotent horror, his country was subjected to a series of atrocities the like of which had never before been experienced in European warfare. Using the activities —real or imagined—of civilian snipers as an excuse for retaliation, the

Germans inaugurated their reign of terror. They looted, they smashed, they destroyed; they set fire to farms, to hamlets, to villages, to towns. The countryside was scarred with blackened, roofless ruins; the deserted villages were as quiet as the grave. Toward the end of August they sacked and burned Louvain. This ancient city, renowned for its Town Hall, its churches, its University and its superb library, was viciously destroyed. For days the Germans rampaged through the town, killing, pillaging, battering and burning until not a single house remained undamaged and corpses lay rotting in the streets. Worse still were the mass executions. As soon as the Germans entered a town or village a number of civilians—often as many as five or six hundred—would be rounded up, marched off to a nearby field and shot. Sometimes the entire population, including priests, women and children, would be herded into the square where they would be fired upon until not a person was left standing. Each time the Belgian army harried the invader, reprisals would be taken against the civilian population. By the end of August the roads toward the sea were choked with panic-stricken refugees. If there had hitherto been any doubts as to why the war was being fought, the German rape of Belgium removed them. Not only had Belgian neutrality been violated but her stubborn stand against a powerful and merciless invader had won her the sympathy and admiration of the world. The magazine *Punch* published a cartoon at this time, showing King Albert and the Kaiser standing face to face on the ruins of a devastated Belgium.

"You see," the Kaiser is saying, "you've lost everything."

"Not my soul!" replies Albert.

It was during these weeks in Antwerp that the Belgian soldiers came to know their King. Until now he had been something of an unknown quantity to them. To help distract the Germans from their main objective—the southward thrust into France—King Albert organized two important sorties against their rear, and during these attacks he was always to be seen in the thick of the fighting. He moved openly among the men, encouraging them and sharing their dangers. Although never sparing himself, he was extremely sparing of his men; he considered no military success worth the loss of too many lives. His calm, his common sense and, above all, his unostentatious courage earned him at first the trust and then the wholehearted devotion of his troops. "The attitude of the King and Queen through these tense and tragic days was magnificent," wrote Winston Churchill, who visited beleaguered Antwerp at this time. "The impression of the grave, calm Soldier-King presiding at Council, sustaining his troops and commanders, preserving an unconquerable majesty amidst the ruin of his Kingdom, will never pass from my mind."

The Allied victory on the Marne, which finally halted the German advance into France and put paid to the Schlieffen plan, caused King Albert to hope afresh for the long overdue reinforcements from France and Britain. With the Germans now falling back, he assumed that the Allied armies, moving up through Flanders to protect the Belgian coastline, would link up with his own army and thus save Antwerp from falling to the enemy. He hoped in vain. From September 15, by which time there was still no sign of relief, the Germans began to concentrate their attack on Antwerp; their advance halted, they could not risk leaving the entrenched Belgian army on their right flank. For three weeks, and in the face of merciless bombardment, the citadel held out, but by October 5 King Albert realized that if he did not soon evacuate his army, his line of retreat would be cut off and all hope of joining up with the Allied forces would be gone. He could not, he said, recalling the capitulation and subsequent downfall of the Emperor Napoleon III in 1870, afford another Sedan. He left Antwerp on October 7 and three days later the Germans entered the town. With the fall of this great national stronghold, so long looked upon as the impregnable heart of the country, it was assumed that the two-month-long resistance had come to an end. Belgium, it seemed, was lost. Except that it had gained a little time for the Allies, the sacrifice had been in vain.

These were terrible days for King Albert. Confused and demoralized, his army was fleeing helter-skelter toward the coast. The weather, until now, had been perfect. "August," wrote one observer, "that terrible August, passed away in the flood of its beautiful sunshine, and its days of blue and gold gradually merged into the silvery light of September." But now the "miracle of persistent sunlight" came to an end; the rain swept down like a curtain on the scene of retreat. Under lowering skies, along roads deep in mud, the ragged troops merged with the great mass of refugees heading for France. It was *sauve-qui-peut*. Through this panicky, disorderly mass drove the King and Queen, no more certain than their subjects as to what was likely to happen to them. The Government had already fled to Havre in France; only the Prime Minister remained with the King. "If ever a doubt of final victory penetrated his soul, it must have been at that moment," wrote Emile Cammaerts. At Selzaete, on the road to Ostend, the Queen, usually so brave, was seen wandering in a rose garden, sobbing her heart out. Belgium would have to be abandoned and the little Belgian army, stripped of its independence, would become an anonymous, expendable part of that great host massed on the Western Front.

The King's apprehensions were confirmed when he met the French and British representatives at Ostend on October 10. As tactfully as possible the two Allied generals persuaded the King to withdraw his army to France, "leaving us," as General Rawlinson put it, "to deal with the military situation as best we might for the Allied cause." Broken-hearted, Albert acquiesced.

But within forty-eight hours he had changed his mind. He was resolved to retreat no further. Courage in adversity was a trait which he had always admired; he told his officers how the Mexican leader Juárez, when fighting his uncle-by-marriage the Emperor Maximilian, had held out in a natural mountain stronghold against the imperial forces until such time as he was able to reconquer his country. He, King Albert, was about to make a similar stand. A few miles south of Ostend the river Yser flowed into the sea; some miles inland it was joined by the Ypres Canal. Together, these two waterways formed a natural barrier while between them and the French frontier lay a few square miles of Belgian territory. On this last enclave of his country's soil, wedged in the far western corner of Belgium, King Albert was determined to dig himself in. Come what might, the Belgian army was going to remain in Belgium.

On October 13 the King issued a resounding proclamation to his troops. They were to fall back no further. "It is for you to maintain the reputation of our arms by the tenacity and bravery of which you have already given such ample proofs," he urged. "Our national honor is at stake." To his divisional commanders he delivered a more practical set of instructions. Under no circumstances whatsoever was there to be a retirement. To the officers of the General Staff, who seem to have remained persistently uncooperative, he had a special message. They were to remain in the front line during the fighting, he said, "encouraging others instead of grumbling...."

From this moment on, King Albert seemed like a different man. Having made his decision, he threw every ounce of his energy into abiding by it. The position had simplified itself; death had become the only alternative to defeat. "This leader," wrote one of the King's biographers, "who had always been ready to take advice, who professed to persuade rather than to command, was transformed into a dominating personality, following his own counsel, acting with the utmost determination and speaking in such a stern voice that even those who were intimate with him wondered at the change."

When the representative of French Headquarters, Colonel Brécard, who in the early days of the war had found cause to complain of King Albert's stubbornness in retiring on Antwerp rather than toward France, now visited the King on the Yser, he was deeply impressed by his defiant attitude. "His country is now almost completely invaded," wrote Brécard, "he is entirely cut off from Brussels, his government is at Havre, his Minister of War at Dunkirk, his country recruits at Cherbourg; and his Army, which has already suffered such severe losses, and has been separated from the Allies, still defends with the utmost energy the last corner of land which remains Belgium. In the face of this tragedy—the end of which no-one can foresee—the King is alone, absolutely alone with the Queen, facing his responsibilities. Both are sustained by their deep patriotism and the sense of duty toward their people. What an example and what a lesson."

Albert's new-found determination was soon put to the test. On October 18, and for the following twelve days, the Germans launched a massive attack on the Belgian position along the Yser. For day after day the Belgian army, depleted, exhausted, short of guns and ammunition, beat back the enemy. It performed, said King Albert, "prodigies of gallantry." When the French, who had consistently underestimated the strength of the forces ranged against the Belgians, demurred about sending reinforcements, Albert came close to losing his habitual control. He bitterly resented, he wrote tartly to General Foch, "the belittling of his soldiers' immediate opponents which had gone on ever since the beginning of the campaign."

That King Albert had every reason to be proud of the Belgian defense there is no doubt. The Battle of the Yser, by which the Belgian army halted the German advance along the Channel coast, thus saving the French ports, was a magnificent achievement. It marked the turning point in the Belgian defense, restoring the prestige lost after the fall of Antwerp and securing a foothold for the army on Belgian soil. It allowed the Belgians to link up with, and to form the extreme left wing of, the Allied front stretching all the way from Switzerland to the Channel. And it established King Albert's reputation as one of the wisest and most tenacious military leaders of the Great War. What came to be referred to as the "immortal glory of the Yser" remains, indeed, one of the proudest moments in Belgian history.

After a week of almost superhuman effort, the Belgians were forced off the left bank of the Yser and were obliged to take up their position behind the embankment of a nearby railway line. Even the belated arrival of French reinforcements could not regain the lost ground. The troops were exhausted. It was now that the King decided to open the sluice gates at Nieuport, on the Channel, and flood the valley of the Yser. Once the culverts piercing the railway embankment had been blocked up to prevent the flooding of the Belgian trenches, his army would be separated from the enemy by a vast sheet of water. Before reaching a firm decision, however, the King, in a final effort to get more reinforcements, paid a visit to British Headquarters. The result, as usual, was negative, but the King seems to have been particularly struck by the "phlegmatic imperturbability" of his British allies.

On the night of October 29, a party of Belgian soldiers crept into no man's land and, within a few steps of the German outposts, surreptitiously opened the lock gates. Swiftly, silently, the water rose and spread itself over the banks of the Yser. Canals, ditches, roads and shell holes were quickly filled and leveled. The water crept around islands of high ground, sending groups of soldiers splashing to the safety of the sand-bagged defenses. Relentlessly and noiselessly it spread, until nothing but an immense sheet of water, glistening darkly under the night sky, stretched from the embankment to where the Germans were scurrying back toward the rising ground in the east.

The Battle of the Yser had been won. The Belgian army and the Belgian King were to remain, henceforth, on twenty square miles of Belgian soil.

2

As a German, Queen Elisabeth was in a difficult position. Not only had she been born in Bavaria but her brother-in-law Crown Prince Rupprecht of Bavaria, husband of her favorite sister Marie-Gabrielle, was in command of the German Sixth and Seventh Armies, now fighting the French. The Germans, hoping to undermine Belgian faith in their Queen, lost no time in spreading rumors to the effect that her sympathies were entirely with the enemy; she was in constant touch, they said, with German agents in Switzerland. Needless to say, there was not a grain of truth in these assertions. When, before the war, the Kaiser had tried to break down King Albert's meticulous impartiality by appealing to Elisabeth's native loyalties, her answer had been discouragingly succinct." "My husband and I are one," she said. "I abide by his decisions." It had proved to be the one occasion on which Kaiser Wilhelm II had not given wholehearted approval to wifely subservience. Now that Belgium and Germany were at war, Elisabeth identified herself unequivocally with her husband's country. "It is finished between me and them," she once said of her German connections; "henceforth an iron curtain has descended between us which will never be raised."

From the very first she flung herself into war work. As soon as the Germans crossed the Belgian border, she converted a wing of the palace into a hospital. For this, and for the years of nursing which lay ahead, her youthful experience in her father's hospitals in Bavaria proved invaluable. The American Minister, visiting the Brussels Palace soon after the German invasion, was amazed at the transformation. The Queen, dressed in a simple pale blue gown and wearing no jewelry other than her wedding ring, led him through the state apartments, all vastly different from when he had last seen them "thronged with men in brilliant uniforms at a Court ball." Beneath the tinkling chandeliers there were now rows of hospital beds, the white coverlets already turned down in readiness for the wounded. At the foot of each iron cot was fastened a little Belgian flag.

"The children put them there," explained the Queen with "that faint, exquisite smile."

When Brussels had to be abandoned and the army retired to Antwerp, the Queen continued her work there. Each day she visited the wounded, helped the doctors and gave practical relief to the thousands of panic-stricken refugees who had crowded into the besieged camp. With the town being subjected to Zeppelin raids—a novel and terrifying experience—she decided to take advantage of Lord Curzon's offer to look after her children for her. It would be as well to remove the heir from the danger zone. At the end of August she took all three children to England and spent a few days at Hackwood, Lord Curzon's country home. She was seen here by Margot Asquith who noticed how profound an effect the war was having on the normally vivacious Queen. "She appeared numbed, sensible, whispering and refined," she said. When Margot Asquith announced that she thought the war would last as long as two years, Elisabeth professed herself "amazed."

The two young princes, Leopold and Charles, and their sister, Marie-José, quickly settled into life at Hackwood. If the boys' clothes were considered somewhat bizarre ("very décolleté at the neck … naked legs encased in high leather boots") their behavior seems to have been perfectly normal. They remained at Hackwood for several months and Queen Elisabeth crossed the Channel as often as she could to visit them.

After the great battle of Ypres, of which the Belgian defense on the Yser had been a sterling episode, the war bogged down, quite literally, in the trenches. Except for the gain of a few hundred yards here and the loss of a few hundred yards somewhere else—always at the cost of thousands, and often tens of thousands of lives—the Western Front remained static for four long years. The combatants dug themselves in and life immediately behind the lines took on a semblance of normality.

It was in the little seaside resort of La Panne, some eight miles from the front and a stone's throw from the French border, that King Albert and Queen Elisabeth established themselves. Here, on a sparkling summer's day over eighty years before, King Leopold I had entered Belgium. Leaving behind his French escort, he had driven from La Panne into his new kingdom. "This is where my grandfather arrived in Belgium," King Albert would say to his companions. "This is where they would like to drive me out." La Panne, in Leopold's day, had been a small fishing village set in a windy desert of sand dunes; it was now a sizable little resort, bustling in summer and desolate in winter. In a stolid, red brick villa, situated at the far end of the sea-front, Queen Elisabeth now set up home. The house was sparsely and tastelessly furnished. The bedrooms were without heating and there was no hot water. From the windows, when the swirling winter mists allowed one to see out of them, was a view of the flat grey sea. More often than not it was raining. The dunes spread to the very steps of the villa. In the little garden nothing but salt grasses swayed in the wet sea wind. Such, for many years, was the home of the King and Queen of the Belgians. Yet Elisabeth refused to change anything. When the visiting Princess Alice, Countess of Athlone, once asked her how she could bear to live in such surroundings, Elisabeth explained that to make the house more attractive would be to accept it as a home; she could not allow herself to believe that she would go on living there much longer.

Once the front line had been stabilized, the royal children were able to rejoin their parents. In the spring of 1915, the thirteen-year-old Prince Leopold joined the 12th Regiment of the Line as a private. A fair and exceptionally good-looking boy, he spent the following six months in the army. At the end of that time he was sent to Eton. During the holidays, when his friends returned excitedly to their homes, he came back to the dangers, and the dreariness, of life at La Panne. The Baroness de T'Serclaes, then nursing with the British troops near Ypres, always remembered "poor little Prince Leopold, so pale and delicate-looking, as a private in the trenches…. I often saw him and thought what an absurd arrangement it was. Imagine … being expected to be a nice little schoolboy for part of the time and for the rest to mix with men whose whole outlook and attitude had often—and inevitably—been coarsened and made callous by surfeit of death and frustration and destruction." It was this familiarity with the horrors of war during his most impressionable years, thought the Baroness, which was largely responsible for the future King Leopold's much-criticized behavior during the next war.

The eleven-year-old Prince Charles followed his brother to Eton but the little Princess Marie-José remained with her parents; not until 1916 did she leave La Panne for school in Florence. She was "a lovely little girl with fuzzy hair and fussy skirts, extremely short," says one observer. So unruly, in fact, was her great mop of hair that the British officers at La Panne called her "Fuzzy-Wuzzy." Several times each year the King would mark the height of his growing children on the frame of the sitting-room door. The marks, with their dates and comments ("*21 janvier 1917—Leopold sans souliers*") were carefully preserved for many years after the war was over.

The sameness, the never-ending despair of the Queen's days were sometimes relieved by the visits of British royalties, foreign statesmen or personal friends. "I enter a drawing room very simply furnished," wrote Raymond Poincaré, the President of France. "The Queen, dressed all in white, receives me most graciously. Delicate and frail, it seems as if she should have been broken by the storm; but she has an indomitable soul; she has given herself wholly to her husband, her children and Belgium. She lives only for her family and for her adopted country."

From among that host of friends who had once flocked to Elisabeth's bohemian Court came Ysaye the violinist, Claus the painter, Saint-Saëns the composer and Verhaeren the poet. Of all Elisabeth's admirers, Verhaeren, the republican, was to become the most enthusiastic.

When the French writer Pierre Loti was granted an interview, he discovered that Elisabeth had not, in fact, quite lost her bohemian aura. Something of that theatricality, that eccentricity almost, remained. Leaving a crowd of cake-eating, orphaned children for whom she was giving a party, the Queen led Loti to her bungalow on the grounds of the villa. It was a temporary structure, made of wooden sections, and could be moved, noted Loti, "from one place to another in an hour or two, like a nomad's tent." The simile was apt, for the interior was "entirely hung with delicate blue Persian silk, relieved by a touch of rose color, scrolled with a large design representing the porticos of a mosque. It contained nothing in the way of furniture but a writing desk and divans, on which were piled brightly hued cushions printed with simple but extremely original patterns." The conversation was confined almost entirely to the religions of the East. Loti described the Queen, as well he might, as being "different from anyone else."

"Although she is fragile and highly-strung," greed Poincaré, "she has a spirit like a tempered sword-blade."

And there were less illustrious guests than these. One day, while Elisabeth was wandering alone by the seashore, she was approached by three young French officers. Assuming her to be a local resident and not having enjoyed the company of a charming young woman for weeks, they boldly suggested that she take them home for a cup of tea. She agreed and led them to the red brick villa nearby. "Now," she said as they seated themselves, "I want you to meet my husband." Swallowing their disappointment, the officers assured her that they would be delighted. Behind her, when she returned with the tea tray, came a grave, gangling man wearing spectacles. "My husband," introduced Elisabeth as she sat down to pour the tea, "King Albert."

But such diversions were rare. It was to the wounded that Queen Elisabeth devoted most of her time. As soon as she arrived at La Panne, she assisted Doctor Depage and Doctor Nolf in the setting up of field hospitals. It was she who inaugurated a three-stage system of first-aid posts, intermediary centers and base hospitals, with the first-aid posts being situated much closer to the front line than had hitherto been the custom. During her years at La Panne, over 200,000 wounded were treated in the field hospitals; of these only 10,000 died. With Belgium having been so speedily overrun by the enemy, almost all hospital equipment and medical supplies had had to be abandoned. The main field hospital, l'Hôpital de l'Ocean at La Panne, lacked even the most elementary facilities. To overcome this seemingly hopeless situation, the Queen resorted to the bold and simple remedy of telephoning Harrods' stores in London and ordering whatever was needed. Nothing daunted, Harrods fulfilled the order and delivered it safely to La Panne within a matter of days.

The Queen visited the hospitals every day. Sometimes she assisted the doctors; at other times she comforted the wounded. Once, while she was visiting a hospital near the front line, an emergency case—a soldier with a perforated lung—was brought in. With the wounded arriving in a continuous stream there was a shortage of nurses; the Queen immediately offered to assist the surgeon in what would obviously be a difficult operation. Calmly and efficiently she rolled up her sleeves, put on an overall and a mask and took her place beside the operating table. "She knew exactly what to do," said the doctor afterward. "I did not have to tell her anything."

Her calm in the face of danger always astonished the men. Whether in the wards or in the trenches, she would continue her rounds, seemingly impervious to bursting shells. Once, when a hospital was struck and set ablaze, she refused to be hustled away to safety. She worked tirelessly, helping the nurses get the patients out of the burning building. When the raid was over and the wounded had been accommodated elsewhere, the doctor in charge complimented her on her courage.

"*My* courage!" she answered with a wry smile. "In what way did it differ from that of your nurses?"

She always claimed that she never felt fear. "The people I admire," she once said, "are those who are afraid and don't show it. I have never experienced any sensations of fear. I do not know what it means to feel afraid."

Dressed in white, the Queen would spend hour upon hour with the wounded. She would move from one bed to the next, smiling, questioning, comforting. Dying soldiers would call for her as to a mother; many died in her arms. The face of their little Queen was the last thing to be seen by many a Belgian soldier. "Your Majesty has been able in a wonderful way to replace for us our absent mothers," ran a message from a gruff squad of soldiers. "We cannot express the fullness of our affection for you in consequence. From the bottom of our hearts we are grateful, and remain attached to you till death."

Such simple tributes touched Elisabeth profoundly. As the men drew strength from her humanitarianism, so did she draw strength from their gratitude.

As the years went by, so more and more did Queen Elisabeth become an object of veneration. She was the sun, it has been said, of that grey winter. So small, so frail, she seemed to epitomize the spirit of the Belgian resistance. The poet Verhaeren saw symbolized in her white-clad figure all the purity, the grace, the refinement of Belgian civilization as opposed to the black barbarism of the enemy. She became "The Heroine of the Yser," the "Mother of the Army," the "Soul of Belgium." To the men, bogged down for year after year in the hell of the trenches, it seemed in no way excessive when it was predicted that their Queen would one day be known as Saint Elisabeth of Belgium.

3

Rising like an island of calm in the turbulent sea of occupied Belgium was the castle of Bouchout, home of the mad Empress Carlota. To the gates of the castle had been affixed, by the German officer commanding the troops in the district, a notice to the effect that all German soldiers were to pass by without singing and were in no way to despoil the property. The reason for this unusual courtesy was the fact that the castle was occupied by the sister-in-law of "our revered ally the Emperor of Austria." The ghost of the long-dead Maximilian could still provide his Belgian widow with some measure of protection.

Brand Whitlock, the American Minister, who was concerned with the organization for the feeding of the Belgian population, once had a request from the castle of Bouchout. Would it be possible to supply the Empress with white bread, as she was unable to eat the grey? "It was the one problem of *revitaillement* easily settled," he commented. But Whitlock never saw her; "we could see the facade of the chateau, the windows staring baldly and sometimes flashing back the sun, when there was sun," he said, and wondered "what news of the present dark tragedy of the world had found its way behind those bleak walls."

Indeed, to what extent the seventy-four-year-old Carlota realized that there was a war on, or that Belgium had been overrun, was difficult to say. The thunder of guns could be heard quite clearly from Bouchout and one day in August 1914, the Empress was heard muttering to herself about the fighting. "Monsieur, one sees red," she said. "One thinks something is happening for one is not gay ... the frontier is dark, very dark ... the prisoners should not be surrendered!"

What the Empress Carlota would certainly not have known about were the extraordinary wartime activities of Sedano, the late Emperor Maximilian's natural son by Concepción Sedano y Leguizano, the pretty young wife of the gardener at Cuernavaca in Mexico. It is unlikely, in fact, that Carlota even knew of his existence. Concepción had not long survived Maximilian's execution in 1867 and their son, for whom the Emperor seems to have made some provision, was sent to France. Here Sedano grew up fully aware of, indeed inordinately proud of, his illustrious parentage. His beard was styled as his father's had been styled, he affected what he assumed to be a regal air, he delighted in being pointed out as "the imperial bastard." But of his father's idealism, chivalry and charm he had almost nothing. Sedano was an irresponsible wastrel, always in debt and incapable of settling down to any regular employment. He was a poseur, pure and simple.

In 1914, at the outbreak of war, Sedano was in Spain. Desperate for money, he offered his services to a German espionage organization in Barcelona. Having duly instructed him, they sent him back to Paris and from there, for some two years, Sedano posted off military secrets, written in invisible ink, to an address in Switzerland. Had he written his invisible messages between the lines of a seemingly ordinary, previously prepared letter, he might have got away with it, but with characteristic recklessness Sedano wrote out his information on what looked like blank sheets. Eventually one of the letters was intercepted, a reagent to develop the ink discovered, and one evening, as Sedano was about to post yet another message, he was arrested. Twenty-nine of his letters—all of them containing valuable military information—were produced at his trial and, in spite of a smooth-tongued defense, Sedano was convicted and sentenced to death.

On the morning of October 10, 1917, Sedano faced a firing squad at Vincennes. The sentence, read out by the officer in charge, had a bizarre ring. "Sedano y Leguizano, son of the Emperor Maximilian of Mexico, you will be shot as a traitor." Refusing to be blindfolded, Sedano remained haughtily composed until the moment that the volley rang out and he slumped dead against the wooden post to which he had been tied.

It was almost half a century since his father had been similarly executed on a hilltop outside Querétaro, in Mexico.

That Sedano was the Emperor Maximilian's son there was no doubt, but whether someone with an infinitely more illustrious war record was the son of both Maximilian and Carlota has never been proved. But there has persisted for many years a rumor—and it is nothing more—that shortly before leaving Mexico for Europe in 1866, the Empress Carlota became pregnant by her husband. During the first months of her insanity, when she was still shut up in the garden villa at Miramare, she is said to have given birth to a son. The Emperor Franz Josef, anxious to avoid the dynastic complications raised by the birth of the child, is said to have made a deal with Carlota's brother, King Leopold II, whereby all details of the birth and parentage would be suppressed and the child taken to Belgium.

The birth of a male child, of unknown parents, was subsequently registered with the civil authorities in Brussels. The boy, who had been given the Christian name of Maximilian, grew up in Belgium and then joined the French Army. His career was brilliant and whatever the name of his parents might have been, he won world renown as General Maxime Weygand.

4

For four long years King Albert and his army remained on the Yser. Although not a day passed without some action along the Belgian front—often slight, occasionally massive—the war had become very largely one of attrition. Boredom, frustration and despair were as prevalent as danger. Ahead of the front line stretched the murky waters of the flooded Yser, with here and there a blasted tree stump or a ruined farmhouse breaking the surface or crowning an islet of high ground. The front line itself was a confusion of muddy trenches, sodden sandbags (*"Vaderlandjes"* the Flemings called them, in reference to the sour joke that if the war lasted much longer the entire country would be put into sacks), barbed-wire entanglements, gaping shell holes, crumbling roads and blackened ruins. Behind, beyond the reach of the German bombardment, lay the monotonous Flemish landscape, its lines of poplar trees reflected in the canals, its long grasses flattened by the wet sea wind. An occasional clock tower rose starkly against the grey sky. In summer the scene was warmed by a watery sun, in autumn it was shrouded in a damp mist, in winter it was swept by torrential rains, and for a few weeks in the spring it was transformed, as though by magic, into a sea of gaily nodding, flame-red poppies. If the King was due to visit the trenches, the men, with blithe disregard of snipers' bullets, would gather armfuls of these poppies with which to decorate his path.

Stories of the King's unheralded appearances among his soldiers are legion. "Close the bloody door," shouted a private as his Sovereign, with characteristic awkwardness, came shuffling into a wooden hut. "Careful with the sandbags," commanded another when the King looked in to see what he was doing. On asking this same and by now highly embarrassed soldier the time, and finding out that he had no watch, the King saw to it that a wrist watch was delivered to him the following morning. "It has been admired by every soldier in my regiment as the gift of His Majesty the Soldier-King," announced the man proudly. One day, on walking past the villa in which one of his officers had been billeted, the King noticed the young officer sitting in the garden. Beside him, contrary to regulations, sat his wife. It was too late for the young woman to escape into the house, and the young officer hurried forward to make his excuses. "Your Majesty has caught me out," he stammered. "I am here with my wife."

"And I also am here with mine," answered the King quietly.

It was this fairness, this broadmindedness, this lack of any tyrannical streak, so often prevalent in army life, that made King Albert so popular with his men. "*Il est juste, mais bon,*" they said of him. Once, when two soldiers were wandering about the dunes in search of rabbits, they saw a superior officer trudging toward them.

"A general!" exclaimed one, preparing to bolt.

"No," answered the other, visibly relieved, "only the King."

Albert returned their salutes gravely and strode on across the sands.

To read through the war diary kept by King Albert during these dismal years on the Yser is to come to some appreciation of the strength of his character. He emerges from the scrawled pages as simple as modest, as prudent, as realistic and as brave as legend has always claimed him to be. There are no histrionics, no delusions, no vindictiveness; the tone throughout is practical, highlighted by that vein of cynicism which ran so strongly through his nature. In spite of all temptation he remained serene, refusing to indulge in what he called the "exaggerated patriotism" of some of his colleagues or in the defeatist attitudes of others. He never lost his sense of proportion. So honest himself, he found the meaningless rhetoric of some of the Allied politicians highly distasteful. "They take refuge, as does public opinion," he wrote, "in formulas whose apparent logic is far removed from any reality. What does a struggle for right mean? Or a fight for civilization? Or to go on to the end?"

Nor would he allow himself to indulge in the general and near-hysterical condemnation of all things German. When someone once accused the German troops of being cowardly, King Albert's reply was deflating. "Barbarians, yes," he said, "but in the mass not cowards. They have been misled, shamefully misled, but they die as bravely for their country as my men die for theirs, and I myself have seen some magnificent examples of heroism—heroism that has made me wish with all my heart it were in a better cause."

It was all so different from the rantings of Kaiser Wilhelm II.

King Albert's aims, from first to last, remained constant. He was dedicated to defending Belgian independence and Belgian neutrality. He was seeking neither glory nor revenge nor gain; he was simply fighting for the right of his country to live in peace, free of any international entanglements. With those—some of his ministers at Le Havre amongst them—who cried out in terms of vengeance, of eventual territorial aggrandizement at the expense of the enemy, he would have no truck. "These politicians," he noted sardonically, "think they are enhancing their own glory by affecting a die-hard and aggressive patriotism which accords perfectly with the care they take to keep as far away from danger as possible."

And in the same way that he refused to listen to talk of territorial compensation at the expense of Germany, so did he resist the temptation to form long-term alliances with his allies. "Belgium must be no one's vassal," he said, "neither England's nor France's." She had been neutral before the war, and neutral she must henceforth remain. When the Allies compiled a joint answer to President Wilson's Note on their "war aims," the King resisted his Government's pressure to include Belgium in the answer. "Our war aim is not the same as Great Britain's," he explained to his uncertain ministers; "we are not under arms to destroy Germany." As a result of his stand, Belgium sent a separate answer to Washington.

The sparing of Belgian lives and Belgian property was always one of his chief concerns. His allies might consider him stubborn and uncooperative and over-cautious, but he refused either to hand over control of his army to one of the Allied commanders or to allow it to take part in any operation which he considered ill-advised. "The King holds the command of the army from the Constitution, that is to say, by the will of the Belgian people, whose first servant he considers himself," he claimed. To relinquish this command would be to allow his men to be used in the costly and pointless offensives which were such a feature of the Western Front. Too often had he seen thousands upon thousands of lives flung away in attacks of which the only result was a temporary gain of a few hundred yards. And he fought tooth and nail against all proposals to launch a major attack across West Flanders. An inch-by-inch campaign across this rich, densely populated countryside would leave some of Belgium's finest towns and cities in ruins; a thrust through the undulating and relatively deserted area farther east would be much more practical.

Already, without the possibility of this threat being carried out, the sufferings of the Belgian people were causing him acute concern. That occupied Belgium was being cruelly exploited there was no doubt. The country was being drained of its resources, a crippling war contribution had been levied, tens of thousands of workmen were being forcibly deported to labor camps in Germany. "It was the atmosphere, the moral odour of invasion, that was the hardest to bear," wrote someone who lived through these bleak years. "To those who had been used all their lives carelessly to breathe its air, liberty, now that it was lost, became a very real and beautiful thing." A rash of posters, telling the Belgians what they might or might not do, broke out across the walls of the towns and cities; the streets were full of German soldiers and the public buildings guarded by German sentries; the population was hamstrung by a mass of humiliating regulations. But what caused the King the greatest anxiety of all was the German attempt to break up the unity of the Belgian State by encouraging the differences between Flemings and Walloons. So stuffed with racialistic theories themselves, the conquerors saw in this linguistic feud an excellent opportunity of undermining Belgium's carefully nurtured cohesion. With the aid of a section of Flemish extremists known as "Activists" (as opposed to the majority of Flemings who were dubbed "Passivists") the Germans set about granting a great number of long-fought-for Flemish demands. The University of Ghent was turned into an exclusively Flemish institution. A so-called Flemish National Congress was allowed to elect a *Raad van Vlanderen*—a Council of Flanders. Belgium was divided into two administrative units: the Flemish provinces, with part of Brabant including Brussels, formed Flanders, while the remaining provinces, with Namur as their capital, formed Wallonia. Flemish was declared to be the official language of the new Flemish territory. The *Raad van Vlanderen* was permitted to go so far as to draft its own constitution and to prepare a declaration of independence. "The oppression under which the Flemish people has lived since 1830 has ceased," ran the heroic phrases. "The state of Flanders is born. Flanders follows the current of world politics—the independence of nationalities. The Flemish people have finally been saved." There was even some talk of realizing the dream with which the Kaiser had once tried to cajole old King Leopold II—that of annexing French Flanders to the new state.

But not all the news from occupied Belgium was somber. For the most part, the nation remained loyal, defiant and confident of eventual victory. When the display of the Belgian flag was prohibited, women surreptitiously introduced the national colors into their dresses. When shops and restaurants were prevented from decorating their windows on the day of the anniversary of Belgian independence, they remained stubbornly closed. When a decree was issued forbidding the display of pictures of the King and Queen, mothers sewed little medallions bearing the royal likenesses into the clothing of their children; "*Beige toujours!*" ran the message on these medallions. A secretly printed news sheet, called *La Libre Belgique* and described as a "bulletin of patriotic propaganda," continued to be published in spite of all enemy efforts to suppress it. Try as they might, the Germans could never discover its editors or its publishers. A copy of the sheet would appear, mysteriously and with infuriating regularity, on the desk of the German governor each time it was published. On July 21, the Belgian national day, the crowds in the churches would break into *La Brabançonne*—the forbidden national anthem—ending with great shouts of "*Vive le Roi! Vive la Belgique!*" Adolphe Max, Burgomaster of Brussels, won international renown for his refusal to be cowed by the German authorities; even after his arrest and deportation to a German prison, his example acted as an encouragement to other Belgian burgomasters. And as Burgomaster Max epitomized civil defiance, so did Cardinal Mercier come to symbolize spiritual resistance. In his famous pastoral letter entitled "Patriotism and Endurance," read in every church in the land and circulated secretly among the populace, he exhorted the Belgians to remain faithful to their King and their laws and assured them that the power exercised by the invader deserved "neither esteem, nor loyalty, nor respect."

"Always oppressed but never conquered" was what Baudelaire once said of the Belgians, and it was due, very largely, to a particularly Belgian sense of humor, a national *esprit frondeur*, that the nation was able to endure the miseries of the occupation. In the capital, this savory wit, *la zwanze bruxelloise*, was everywhere in evidence. Even the children of the Quartier des Marolles, the slum district of Brussels lying under the shadow of King Leopold II's vast Palais de Justice, afforded examples of it. Playing at soldiers, the urchins would march and countermarch to the commands of a ragged little leader.

"*Achtung!*" the boy-captain would shout, brandishing a homemade wooden sword in imitation of a German officer. "*Nach Paris!*"

And then the little troop, doing an exaggerated goose-step, would begin to march—but backwards.

A piece of news from out of occupied Belgium which afforded the King particular pleasure concerned the daring raid on Zeebrugge by Vice Admiral Roger Keyes. By blocking the mouth of the Zeebrugge Canal, thereby bottling up some forty German destroyers and submarines at Bruges, young Admiral Keyes struck a severe blow at the enemy's naval strength and provided the despondent Allies with a rare and almost deliriously applauded victory. King Albert was among the first to send Keyes his congratulations and a few days later he invited the Admiral to luncheon at La Panne, informing him that he "wanted to see him about something." After the meal the two men walked onto the sand dunes and there, "very shyly," the King presented Keyes with the Star of a Grand Officer of the Order of Leopold. The little ceremony marked the beginning of Lord Keyes's long association with, and championship of, the Belgian royal family.

During luncheon the conversation had been about wild birds and, more particularly, the flight of wild geese. From this the talk had turned to the now famous raid and the Queen had been anxious to know when the Admiral was planning to attack the coast again. She begged to be allowed to watch the bombardment from one of his ships. "Suppose anything happened to you," protested Keyes, "it would be awful for me, and *I* might not be killed."

"But I could stand quite close to you," joked the Queen, "and then, if anything happened, we should both be killed, and it would be all right."

Chaffingly, they decided that the Admiral was to send Elisabeth a cryptic message when next he was about to set out on a raid. "As for instance," suggested Keyes, "'The wild geese fly tonight.'" That, said the Queen, would be splendid.

As they strolled along the seashore after the informal investiture, Keyes noticed a gentle wind blowing in from the sea. This was exactly what he needed for a raid and, having given secret orders for his ships to stand by, he took hurried leave of his royal guests. As he shook the Queen's hand he suddenly whispered, "The wild geese will fly tonight, Ma'am," and Elisabeth, delighted, wished him the best of luck.

Only rarely, during these war years, did King Albert leave his patch of Belgian soil. He paid short visits to the French and Italian fronts and in 1918 he and the Queen went to England to attend the silver wedding of King George V and Queen Mary. His decision to remain put was a wise one. He became ever more closely identified with and admired by his troops, and his very remoteness enhanced his prestige amongst his allies. When he visited London in 1918 he was amazed at the warmth of his reception. He and the Queen were given a tumultuous welcome. "In the King and Queen of the Belgians," enthused the *Times*, "Great Britain salutes the very soul of loyalty to a word pledged, high minds not cast down by long misfortune, hope and confidence indomitable." When, in the company of King George and Queen Mary, the royal couple attended a Symphony Concert in the Albert Hall, they were accorded an almost overwhelming ovation. "So very small she looked," wrote the watching Lady Diana Cooper of Queen Elisabeth, "and dressed in gleaming white from head to toe." Beside her King Albert, his face ruddy and his hair bleached from long exposure to sun and wind, stood in bemused and embarrassed silence while the great hall echoed and re-echoed with applause. They cheered, claimed Lady Diana, "as I have not heard cheering before."

From the triumphs of London, the royal couple returned to the dreariness of life in the red brick villa in La Panne. "It is impossible," noted the Belgian writer Louis Dumont-Wilden when he visited the villa, "to imagine a sadder place of exile." Its windows, he said, "opened on a grey seascape veiled with thick mist; the sky seemed melting into water. The rain, which had lasted already several days, was still falling." For King Albert, who was so passionately fond of mountains and mountaineering, the flat, featureless landscape must have been especially depressing. There was not even the excitement of battle to relieve the monotony of the days; nothing seemed able to break the murderous deadlock of trench warfare. It must have seemed to the King, at times, as though the war would go on forever.

But he never complained. His concern was for his army and his country, not for himself. Whatever his innermost feelings might have been, the King appeared as confident and as steadfast as ever.

Perhaps the most telling tribute to King Albert's fortitude comes from his biographer, Emile Cammaerts. "Those who saw La Panne during the years of waiting," he afterward wrote, "will never forget the tall and austere figure on that last strip of Belgian shore confronted with stormy clouds and foaming sea, watching with calm courage during that long vigil, with all the regal splendour stripped from his Court, and almost all his land torn from his friendly grasp, alone against the blind elements and the blinder injustice of man, with no comfort but his Queen, brought as low as any Sovereign could be brought by the forces of destiny, and as high as any man can be raised by the conviction of his right and the faith in his cause...."

One afternoon, when the King was visiting the trenches to ask the men if there was anything they needed, one soldier, bolder than the others, asked in return, "And you, Sire, don't you want anything?"

For a moment the King was silent. Then, very haltingly, he gave his answer. "I should like to go back to Brussels," he said.

As one, the men moved forward and crowded round him.

"Let us take you there!" they cried.

5

Not until the autumn of 1918 were King Albert's soldiers able to fulfill their promise to take him back to Brussels. In September that year Marshal Foch, now Supreme Commander of the Allied armies, offered the King command of the *Groupe d'armées des Flandres*. This force, made up of the Belgian divisions, the Second British Army and three French divisions, would form the left wing of Foch's gigantic offensive against the enemy. The King accepted the command and the date for the joint offensive was set for September 27.

At dawn that day, following a formidable bombardment, the Belgians advanced through squelching mud and streaming rain toward the enemy's positions. After three days of desperate fighting and at the cost of over 10,000 killed and wounded, they achieved the first phase of the offensive. The Battle of the Crest of Flanders had been won. With the Germans now drawn up behind a strong defensive line known as *Flandern I*, the King's forces had to wait for the artillery to be brought up from the Yser, and it was not until two weeks later that the second attack was launched. It proved as successful as the first. *Flandern I* was overwhelmed and the enemy forced back. On October 16 the Germans finally abandoned Nieuport on the Channel, thus opening the road to Ostend, and two days later the Belgian cavalry went clattering over the cobblestones into Bruges. When an American division, recently added to King Albert's command, broke through the German lines farther east, it was welcomed by a group of Flemish civilians who had been forced to work for the enemy. "The King!" asked the excited civilians of their deliverers. "How is the King?"

The King, in fact, had already paid a short visit to his recently occupied country. Admiral Keyes, realizing how much the royal couple longed to set foot in their kingdom again, hit upon a way in which they would be the first Belgians to re-enter Ostend. As soon as he heard that the Germans were leaving Ostend, Keyes sailed to Dunkirk to pick up the royal couple and on the night of October 17, the destroyer *Termagant*, with the Belgian flag at the main, steamed silently into Ostend harbor. Having ascertained that the enemy had, in fact, vacated the town, the royal party transferred to a whaler and pulled in to an iron ladder leading to the top of the quay. That the climb up the ladder was long and slippery bothered the King and Queen not at all; although their aide-de-camp tumbled backwards into the black water, they both reached the quay safely.

Ostend was pitch dark but in no time the news spread through the town that the King and Queen had arrived. As the little party of five walked toward the Grand' Place, doors and windows were flung open and a crowd of enthusiastically cheering townsfolk began to fill the streets. Entering the council room of the Hotel de Ville, the Sovereigns surprised a group of councillors drinking champagne to celebrate the German withdrawal. The Burgomaster's deputy, mastering his astonishment, launched into a speech of welcome, but Admiral Keyes, anxious for the safety of his charges, cut short the ceremonial and hurried the party back to the quay. The populace were now treated to the singular sight of their Sovereigns disappearing, one after the other, down the iron ladder and into the blackness below.

The royal entry into Bruges, eight days later, was a much more formal occasion. Accompanied by the Queen, Prince Leopold, Prince Charles and Princess Marie-José, the King rode through the acclaiming streets toward the Grand' Place. "Bruges is full of belfries and carillons," wrote one witness, "and on this glorious autumn day the bells pealed out with all their might." That night King Albert took up residence in the Château de Lophem, four miles south of the town. This vast, red brick, mock-Gothic pile, looking more like a basilica than a castle, was to be his home for the following month. "The country people of the district," remembered a resident, "often observed a Belgian horseman of gigantic stature, alone, and surveying the scene through a pair of field-glasses, with a worn and melancholy look on his face ... it was King Albert." The Queen, on the other hand, never looked sad. With victory in sight, she was exultant. She left, at Lophem, the memory of a lively and smiling young woman with a tendency to gallop her horse across the autumn countryside at breakneck speed.

It was while he was at Lophem that the King, besides planning the last of his military operations, received various Belgian political leaders. With one burden about to be lightened, the King was preparing to shoulder the next. It was while he was at Lophem, too, that he heard, on November 11th, that the Armistice had been signed. Spa, where Queen Marie Henriette had dragged out her last sad years, was the scene of the Kaiser Wilhelm's inglorious abdication. From here the once mighty German Emperor was driven to the Dutch border and into exile.

A week later the royal family left Lophem, bound for Brussels. Charles d'Ydewalle, writing of this departure thirty years afterward, remembered seeing little Princess Marie-José holding up a rabbit, a present from some local children, and urging it to wave good-by with its paws.

On November 22 the King entered his capital. At the Porte de Flandre, where he was met by Prince Albert (the future King George VI of Great Britain), he left his car and, mounting a horse, began his triumphant ride into the city. Dressed in khaki, with a steel helmet topping his lined and weather-beaten face, he rode slowly through the gaily decorated streets. Beside him, mounted on a huge white charger and wearing a faded grey riding habit, rode the Queen. Behind, the one in khaki and the other in the blue of a midshipman, came Prince Leopold and Prince Charles. They say that no one who was in Brussels that day could ever forget this homecoming. Every rooftop, every window, every inch of pavement was packed with people. Flags fluttered, handkerchiefs waved, cheer upon tumultuous cheer crashed out as the procession passed by. Throats were hoarse, arms were limp, faces were wet with tears. Even the King, usually so serious, smiled with happiness at this heartfelt welcome. It was the Queen, however, who was the most moving sight of all. "Plainly overwhelmed by their reception," remembered one eyewitness, "she sat erect and motionless on her white horse, her face piteously grave in the midst of so much rejoicing, and her eyes stonily fixed on the road ahead, as though she dare not glance to right or left for fear of breaking down."

Chapter Ten

1

"The real peak of Albert I's achievement," claimed the historian R. C. K. Ensor, "was that he was the best constitutional monarch who has ever reigned on the Continent of Europe."

It would have been for this, rather than for his exploits during the war of 1914-1918, that King Albert would have liked to have been remembered. Because the Belgian Constitution had obliged him to assume the leadership of the army he had done so, but in spite of his praiseworthy achievements, it was with very little regret that he relinquished his wartime powers and returned to the path of constitutionalism. In him the general would always be subordinate to the statesman; the commander would always take second place to the counsellor. "*Je suis un Roi con-sti-tu-tion-nel*," he would say in his slow, emphatic fashion and it was a fact which he never for a moment allowed himself, or anyone else, to forget.

During the last weeks of the war a certain section of the Belgian population, influenced by the right-wing doctrines of the *Action Francaise*, longed for the King to take advantage of his enormous prestige to assume dictatorial powers. For four years he had governed by decree; why should he not continue to do so? Even if he did not go so far as to stage a *coup d'état*, he should at least take advantage of this opportunity to strengthen the Executive. The monumental task of reconstruction, they argued, would be simplified were the King able to work unhampered by party political squabbling.

To these urgings King Albert did not even deign to reply. He was bound to the Constitution by this oath. That, as much as his distaste for autocratic rule, ensured his rejection of any such scheme. When he talked, sometimes, of the "elasticity" of the Belgian Constitution, he was thinking in terms of the further sharing, and not the limiting, of political power. In fact, while still at Lophem in 1918 the King, in consultation with his ministers, agreed to the immediate introduction of universal suffrage and to the gradual granting of various reforms to the Flemings. These moves were to be followed by sweeping social legislation. By this broadening of the base of political life, King Albert placed himself, once and for all, above party politics. No longer could the Socialists, growing yearly more powerful, identify him with the privileged classes. The introduction of universal suffrage increased his prestige enormously; he became less of a political figure and more of a national symbol, the respected and impartial arbitrator between the Catholic, Liberal and Socialist parties. Flexible, and with enough sense of history to realize that the day of the power-wielding monarch was over, King Albert kept well within the limits imposed upon him by the Constitution. He could occasionally have taken a firmer stand but he was wise enough not to try.

A rumor spread, soon after the King's return to Brussels, that while at Lophem he had been terrorized into granting these reforms. A riot, instigated by dissatisfied German soldiers and supported by some Belgian revolutionaries, had erupted in the streets of Brussels on the day before the Armistice. Tricolor cockades, red flags and the strains of the *Marseillaise* had frightened a section of the population into believing that a revolution was imminent. The disturbance had soon been quelled but news of the revolutionary threat was said to have been purposely exaggerated in order to frighten an unwilling King Albert into conceding reform; this supposed coercion of the King by certain men of the Left came to be known as "The conspiracy of Lophem." The rumor was without a grain of truth. Nothing was calculated to make the King more angry than the insinuation that he had granted these concessions under pressure. "You remember Lophem," he said to someone thirteen years after the event. "I have been treated as a coward or a fool, or both, for the decisions that I made there in full awareness of all the facts and of my own free will. I want you to know that what I did at Lophem, I did of my own accord, actuated by no one but myself."

After the King's death, Emile Vandervelde, that great Socialist leader, explained how it was due, almost entirely, to the scrupulous constitutional behavior of the King that Socialism had finally been divorced from Republicanism. "Those who … have reproached us with the betrayal of our republican principles in becoming, in agreement with our party, 'the King's ministers,'" said Vandervelde, "simply proved that they knew nothing of the personality of the first citizen of Belgium and of the country's institutions. King Albert was the ideal incarnation of this 'Republican Monarchy' which the authors of our Constitution wished deliberately to create in 1831."

Things had come a long way since the Socialist Manifesto marking King Albert's accession had pronounced that "between Socialism and Monarchy there is no possible reconciliation."

But it was by no means roses all the way for King Albert. Once the first delirious flush of the royal homecoming had faded, the King faced a daunting and disillusioning task. Belgium, whose prestige had stood so high during the first few months of the war, had lost the world's attention in the sterile years that followed, and she was treated in a distinctly off-hand manner at the Peace Conference at Versailles. Only after the King's personal intervention was she accorded the privileges due to her special position among the Allies. The Peace Treaty itself disappointed the King. He sensed that it would lead to future strife. But to a journalist who asked for his opinion of the treaty King Albert gave a characteristic reply. "What would you have?" he said. "They did what they could."

That national unity, that working together of all Belgians at the task of reconstruction for which King Albert had appealed so ardently at the end of the war, never materialized. Before long the country was being torn by the usual party political rivalries. To these was added the old struggle, but in an even more violent form, between Flemings and Walloons. Exasperated at the delay in the introduction of linguistic reform, certain discontented Flemings organized themselves into the Front Party. Made up of wartime Activists, disgruntled ex-soldiers and minor clergy ("*alles voor Vlaanderen, Vlaanderen voor Christus*" was the rallying cry) they espoused a doctrine of regionalism, of separation from Wallonia. In the general election of 1929, eleven "Frontists" were returned to the Chamber.

King Albert made every effort to placate Flemish susceptibilities. Their regionalism—that Belgian love of his own clock tower—which had always infuriated King Leopold II was something which King Albert understood very well. He was never patronizing about Flemish aspirations. Unlike the great majority of upper-class, French-speaking Belgians, the King had no prejudice against Flemish art and literature. Both he and Queen Elisabeth identified themselves wholeheartedly with Flemish cultural movements. The King took every opportunity to address Flemish audiences in their own language and to praise the achievements of Flemings past and present. But he never ceased to remind them of the economic interdependence of Flanders and Wallonia and he never ceased to preach unity among all Belgians. "The very name of Belgium," he once pointed out, "is much older than that of all our present provinces and most of our cities."

Gradually, through the years, the majority of Flemish demands were complied with, until by the middle of the 1930's the Flemings had realized all their major linguistic demands. But this by no means marked the end of the struggle. From now on extremists were to concentrate on greater autonomy for Flanders and the movement to become increasingly impregnated with the doctrines of fascism.

The purely physical aspect of national regeneration was somewhat more successful. To an Allied general who had once congratulated King Albert on the success of his final attack through West Flanders, the King had replied, "Yes, but what ruins! Europe will take ten, perhaps twenty years to recover." Belgium, in fact, took less time than this to clear away the ravages of war; within five years the work of reconstruction had been all but completed. Railways had been rebuilt, factories reopened, devastated areas recultivated, the population re-housed and public buildings lovingly restored. A financial collapse was narrowly averted in 1926 and for the remainder of the decade the mood throughout the country was fairly optimistic. If King Albert was somewhat disenchanted by the fact that his hopes for a *Union Sacrée*, for a great working together of the Belgian people, had come to nothing, he at least had the satisfaction of seeing his country relatively prosperous.

To escape, sometimes, from the pressures and set-backs of these postwar years, King Albert made several long journeys. Like all the Coburgs, he was an indefatigable traveler. Ill-suited to a sedentary life and intensely curious, he delighted in new landscapes, strange cities and different customs. "Man is the same everywhere," he once said, "but he expresses himself differently. That is why traveling is so interesting."

In December 1918 he visited Paris and in the following year, accompanied by the Queen, he made an extensive tour of the United States. If the King was sometimes embarrassed by the exuberance of his American reception, he was extremely touched by its sincerity. In 1920 the royal couple visited Brazil, returning by way of Portugal, and in 1921 the King visited Madrid. Here, because of his great love of animals, Albert made a point of asking that no bullfights be staged in his honor. The King and Queen visited Rome the following year and India three years later. In 1928 they visited the Congo where the King was able to appreciate the enormous changes that had been effected since his last visit, almost thirty years before. At Leopoldville he unveiled a statue to King Leopold II and made an obligatory reference to the genius of his uncle's "powerful personality." In a speech made at Elisabethville he emphasized to his listeners that "nothing great and lasting can be achieved without reconciling the interests of the two races who are engaged in fruitful collaboration." Unlike his predecessor, King Albert was always very conscious of Belgium's obligations toward its African population.

While the King was in Katanga, one of the colonists complained to him of the loneliness of life out there. "You should have seen the Katanga," countered the King, "as I saw it in 1909."

"Ah, Sire," answered the man knowingly, "a King has traveling facilities which are beyond the reach of common mortals."

"Indeed," said the King, "I traveled through Katanga on foot."

It was when touring incognito that King Albert was at his happiest. Dressed more shabbily than ever ("Pick the worst-dressed fellow of the bunch," he once advised a worried official who asked him how he could recognize the King), he would go shambling down the streets of some foreign city, headed for the museum or, with as much pleasurable anticipation, for the cinema. He one day dragged his companion, Comte de Grunne, to no less than five films. "I love Paris," he said to Dumont-Wilden, "first of all because it is a beautiful city, but also because I can pass unnoticed there. My wife and I like to go to the cinema, but in Brussels we can seldom do so because we are too well known. In Paris we visit all the cinemas of the Boulevards and sometimes forget to dine."

But his incognito was not always successful. "You look remarkably like the King of the Belgians," said a stranger who once met Albert in the Tyrol.

"You are not the first to tell me that," answered the King unblinkingly; "this likeness has already caused me serious inconvenience."

It was mountaineering, however, that remained the King's first love. He was never more content than when climbing. This was the one time when he was able to lose himself completely. More and more, as the years went by, did climbing answer some physical and spiritual need. To pursue this sport, he kept himself in excellent physical condition. He adhered to a strict vegetarian diet, he drank no wine and he gave up smoking. He walked, he cycled, he skated. He had by now completely shed the surplus weight of his early days and looked ten years younger than his age. He had a horror of growing old and of losing his vigor. "So-and-so is sixty," he would say when he himself was not far off it. "He is an old man. I am twenty years younger than he is." Not a year passed without a visit to the mountains of Switzerland, Italy or Austria. The little Italian town of Cortina d'Ampezzo was one of his favorite spots. To mingle, incognito, with the other climbers, to chat of inconsequential matters with the guides, to sleep in some simple mountain hut, afforded him enormous enjoyment. "After a seven hours' climb," remembered one of his fellow climbers, "we reached the shelter at the summit of the Jungfrau. The weather was wonderful. Albert did not talk much; he was no doubt tired, as we were, but he looked particularly happy."

Such climbs, of course, were dangerous, but the King would always dismiss the perils as *"un risque du métier."* When urged to be more careful, he would give the assurance that he took more precautions than most. "Do you think," he would add smilingly, "that so much trouble should be taken in order to be sure to die in one's bed? Think of the tragedy of the deathbed."

He was to be spared that particular tragedy.

2

As King Albert became yearly more shabby, so did Queen Elisabeth become yearly more chic. She made the fashions of the late 1920's—the cloche hats, the velvet coats, the luxurious fur trimmings—peculiarly her own until, with the exception of Queen Victoria Eugenie of Spain, she became the best-dressed queen in Europe. In her 1930 portrait by Herman Richir, showing her in a wealth of draped lamé and gleaming satin, Elisabeth looked as much like a fashion model as a queen. Seldom has a royal couple appeared more ill-matched than did Albert and Elisabeth. In his Stetsons, his floppy collars, his creased jackets, and his baggy trousers, the King would go loping beside his short-skirted, beautifully groomed wife, endeavoring to match his long strides to her tiny footsteps. Queen Elisabeth was in her early forties during these first years of peace, and maturity had ironed out the last vestiges of shyness or hesitancy in her manner.

Her grace and her assurance were by now exceptional; her curiosity, her vitality and her enthusiasm unimpaired.

Once the war was over Queen Elisabeth never harked back to it. The work which she was to do during the years of peace was to be of far more lasting value to her country than her more publicized efforts on the Yser. She could now put into effect the many plans for the physical and spiritual well-being of Belgium which had been interrupted by the war.

She applied herself to the problems of those disabled or orphaned by the war; she founded the National Defense League against Tuberculosis; she concerned herself in research work against cancer; she formed, after her visit to the Congo, the *Fondation Reine Elisabeth pour l'assistance médicale aux indigènes*. She allowed nothing to discourage her. When she was congratulated on her bravery in founding her League for the Prevention of Venereal Diseases, she claimed that it was the "hypocritical silence" on the subject that had decided her. "My duty was to lead the way when other women hesitated because of convention and prejudices," she said. "Since I could, I must." She was tireless in raising funds for her various projects and, once the work was under way, in encouraging those concerned with the running of them. Belgium is still rich in the homes, the crèches, the orphanages, the preventoria, the laboratories and the research centers which were inaugurated through her efforts. The *Fondation Médicale Reine Elisabeth*—a vast institute for medical research—was one of her finest achievements. In time her various Leagues and Foundations came to be known, collectively, as the *Front Blanc de la Santé*.

The Queen busied herself no less enthusiastically with cultural matters. Writers, poets, painters, composers, musicians, photographers, ornithologists and gardeners all benefited from her patronage. Laeken, during these years, became a center of intellectual and artistic life. A passionate Egyptologist, she traveled to the Valley of the Kings at Luxor for the opening of the Tomb of Tutankhamen. This resulted in yet another *oeuvre*—the *Fondation Egyptologique Reine Elisabeth*. But her most valuable contribution to the cultural life of the country was undoubtedly the building of the Palais des Beaux Arts. Due to her practical interest and encouragement there rose, in the Belgian capital, a vast, complex structure housing concert halls, exhibition rooms, lecture halls, rehearsal rooms, a theatre, a cinema, a library and a *salle des fêtes*. Its opening, in 1928, secured for Belgium a leading place in the artistic life of Europe. It was a building which the Queen, with her deep love of music, frequently visited and one in which she felt eminently at home.

Her multiple activities did not, of course, go uncriticized. There was some resentment among a certain section of the Belgian *haut monde* at her continuing concern for the lower classes. A little charitable work was all very well but this excessive humanitarianism, this deep involvement in social problems, showed a want, it was thought, of royal dignity. Nor did her open championship of Flemish culture, at a time when the linguistic feud was at its height, endear her to the Walloons. She seemed too impulsive, too ill-disciplined, too lacking in majesty for a queen. In common with all the Wittelsbachs, she was more than unconventional—she was eccentric.

Elisabeth, like Albert, was always grateful for a break in the royal routine. She, too, delighted in travel, and on her long journeys to the United States, to Brazil, to India and to the Congo she was as excited as a child. She loved sea voyages and she loved the sun. She once had herself lashed to the mast of a boat so that she could enjoy a storm, and long before sunbathing became fashionable, she would stretch out in the sunshine of the park at Laeken. On her journeys she was tireless. She was equal to any occasion—be it a ticker-tape welcome in New York, a donkey ride in the Egyptian desert, a visit to a leper colony in the Congo, a long air flight to the Middle East, or a tramp along the banks of the Seine. If a conversation interested her, nothing could get her away; Albert was often obliged to drag her out of the room in order to get her to bed. "You see ..." she once said over her shoulder to a companion as Albert marched her out of the door, "the cow is being taken to its stable."

She was interested in so many things. She studied music, sculpture, painting and photography. She cultivated her famous rose garden. She swam, she played golf, she drove, she flew. She was an enthusiastic ornithologist. She took courses in physiology, psychiatry and yoga. She studied Lamaistic Buddhism and Hinduism. She spent hour upon hour with Dom Columba, the well-known Abbot of Maredsous, discussing religion. The Pope presented her with the Golden Rose as a tribute to the "most courageous, virtuous and wisest of Sovereigns."

Even her handwriting, it was said, was "like a call to arms—bold, exultant, and imperious."

Providing a sure foundation for the somewhat baroque structure of her life was the love between her husband and herself. Albert and Elisabeth were a devoted couple. "The King has two main preoccupations," said one of Albert's secretaries, "to watch over the country's well-being, and to make the Queen happy." Though their two natures were quite different, said another observer, "their hearts beat in unison." There were times, of course, when the King found her rather trying. Her infuriating unpunctuality, the exhausting zest with which she threw herself into projects in which she was interested and the blithe indifference with which she treated those in which she was not, frequently rubbed up against his own steady, dutiful nature. But he relied greatly on her instinct and her judgment, and even politicians became accustomed to the King's habit of deferring certain decisions until "after lunch." Elisabeth was her husband's collaborator in every sense of the word.

Whenever Albert returned from a climbing expedition in the Alps he would bring her a little bunch of those flowers which he had first picked for her on the day that he had asked her to marry him— edelweiss. "Take them," he would say in his hesitant, embarrassed fashion, "I have gathered them for you."

And yet, for all her intelligence, Elisabeth remained, in many ways, charmingly naive. There was a touchingly unspoiled quality about her. Once, when she and King Albert were visiting Palestine, they were taken to see the treasures in the Armenian Church near Jerusalem. Deeply interested, the Queen, accompanied by a priest, moved slowly from one exquisite object to the next. Coming to a jeweled bird, she cried out, "What a charming little owl!" "Owl?" answered the scandalized priest. "That is the Holy Ghost."

"Oh yes, of course!" exclaimed the Queen, moving closer. "I see now it is a pigeon."

"Dove, Elisabeth," muttered the anguished Albert, *"dove!"*

3

Prince Leopold, heir to the Belgian throne, was an extremely handsome young man. Erect and slender, with fair hair and blue eyes, he was like a prince from some fairy tale. "I realised," wrote the irrepressible Rosita Forbes when she first met him in 1926, "how good-looking the young man was with his splendidly thick air and clear skin, and above all, his look of strong, stalwart good health. In his full-dress uniform with lots of gold on it, he was a fine figure." For all these golden good looks, however, Prince Leopold was a grave young man; his manner was serious and he rarely smiled. Perhaps those years in the trenches had indeed left their mark or he may simply have inherited his father's shyness. Even in his early twenties his sense of royal duty was remarkable. "I am touched by the favorable appreciation which you express concerning my eldest son," wrote King Albert ponderously to his Prime Minister on one occasion. "You may be convinced that all our efforts, the Queen's and my own, aim unceasingly at preparing our sons to fulfill the most important duties which the country has the right to impose upon members of the dynasty." It was small wonder that Prince Leopold so seldom smiled.

His demeanor might be grave but he was by no means dull. He was an extroverted young man, active and impatient and a sportsman, fond of swimming, skiing, golf and fast cars. Like his father, he loved climbing. He was widely traveled, having visited the United States,

Brazil and the Congo and having several times accompanied his vivacious mother on her journeys to Egypt. "You know," he once said to an acquaintance, "if I hadn't got to be a king, I'd have liked to be a captain and master of my own tramp steamer. I'd have a grand time going all over the world." The ambition might have been trite but that did not make it any the less sincere.

It was while on one of his journeys—to Scandinavia this time—that Prince Leopold met his future wife. Princess Astrid was the third daughter of Prince Charles, brother of the King of Sweden. The young couple seem to have been attracted to each other immediately and, having met again at the baptism of a son of Prince René de Bourbon, they decided to become engaged. The decision, said the approving King Albert, was reached "*en toute spontanéité.*"

In the twenty-year-old Princess Astrid the dynasty gained a princess of exceptional qualities. If there was something of a fairy-tale prince about Leopold, there was everything of a fairy-tale princess about Astrid. She was beautiful, she was graceful, she was charming, she was gay. "*Un cadeau de del*" was how the King of Sweden always referred to her. Raised at the informal Swedish Court, she had a refreshing naturalness of manner and a very real warmth of heart. "I might not, even had I tried, have succeeded in finding for my son an ideal bride," said Queen Elisabeth, "but Leopold has done more, he has found for me an ideal daughter-in-law."

They were married at a civil ceremony in Stockholm in November 1926. From the Riks-Sal in the Royal Palace, in which the ceremony was held, they drove in a torchlight procession through the crowded streets to the bride's home. King Albert, in the Swedish capital for the wedding, was amused at being refused entrance to the Royal Palace after one of his early morning rambles through the city; even in democratic Sweden he obviously looked too little like royalty. From Stockholm Princess Astrid sailed on an all-white cruiser, the *Flygia*, for Belgium where the religious ceremony was to be held in Brussels. (As yet Astrid was a Protestant and would not enter the Catholic Church for another four years.) Smiling radiantly and dressed entirely in white, the bride stepped ashore at Antwerp to the cheers of a delighted populace; they nicknamed her, inevitably, "the snow princess." During the following emotion-packed days, culminating in the brilliant wedding ceremony at Sainte Gudule, her manner remained remarkably unself-conscious. Unlike her less confident husband, Astrid was always at ease in public.

The couple made their home in the little Belle Vue palace in Brussels and at Stuyvenberg, near Laeken. After the birth of their first child, Josephine-Charlotte, in 1927, Princess Astrid would often wheel her pram through the public park, pausing every now and then to chat with the other mothers. "Whenever that exquisite lady talked to you she made you feel assured, interesting and terrifically liked!" remembered one acquaintance. "She does like people enormously," Prince Leopold explained proudly. "That's her secret. She likes everybody so much, and is so pleased to see them that she takes it for granted they're glad to see her, too."

Prince Charles, King Albert's second son, was very different from his extrovert brother. He had spent the greater part of his youth in England. During the war he had followed Leopold to Eton (King Albert had the Coburg regard for an English education) and from there he had gone to the naval college at Dartmouth. By the time he had finished his tour of duty on board the *Renown*, he had spent over eleven years abroad. Less good-looking than his brother, Charles was more scholarly, having inherited his mother's interest in the arts. He, too, played the violin. From his father came his simple, democratic manner and his distaste for formality. He stood patiently in cinema queues, he carried home his own parcels, he always traveled incognito. Rumors about his romantic attachments (the most persistent of which concerned Lady Anne Cavendish-Bentinck) always proved groundless. Like his bookish grandfather, Philip Count of Flanders, Prince Charles seemed destined to play a minor role in the affairs of the dynasty. Time, however, was to prove otherwise.

In 1930, the King's only daughter, Princess Marie-José, married Crown Prince Umberto of Italy. The days when the British soldiers at

La Panne had nicknamed her "Fuzzy-Wuzzy" had long since passed and Princess Marie-José was now a tall, svelte, highly accomplished young woman whose hair, if still springy, was worn fashionably short and tucked into the head-hugging hats of the period. King Albert was particularly fond of Marie-José and thought rather more highly of her than he did of his sons. "She ought to have been the heir to the throne," he said on one occasion. Cultured and serious-minded, Marie-José was the worst possible choice for the handsome, charming and pleasure-loving Umberto. As a tribute to his irresistibility to women, the Italians dubbed him a *donnaiolo*. It was as well, perhaps, that Marie-José was as much in love with Italy as she was with him.

Things seemed to go wrong from the very start. As Prince Umberto, in Brussels for the engagement, was laying a wreath on the tomb of the unknown Belgian soldier, an Italian by the name of Da Rosa fired two shots at him. They missed, but at the trial of the would-be assassin, his lawyer was able to draw public attention to the fascist affiliations of the family into which Marie-José was marrying. Then the wedding in Rome, which should have been magnificent, was plagued by mishaps. Guests, arriving at the Quirinale soon after eight in the morning in order to be in time for the ceremony at ten, had a four-hour wait before the arrival of the bride. The long trains of both Queen Elisabeth and the Princess Marie-José came off and had to be stitched back on; the bride, in fact, lost her train three times before she finally reached the altar. The ticklish business of precedence was hopelessly mismanaged, with the future King George VI of Great Britain trailing well behind ex-King Amanullah of Afghanistan. The latter monarch, emerging from the Quirinale, was so carried away by the warmth of the acclamations, which he assumed to be directed exclusively toward himself, that he grabbed the nearest silk hat and waved it frantically to the delighted crowds. Only when he put on the hat and, with a jaunty tap, knocked it right over his face did his gratification fade.

King Albert's comments on the day's festivities were typically ironic. "It was really a very fine ceremony," he reported. "Just imagine, I saw there the ex-King Manoel of Portugal, the ex-King George of Greece, and even the ex-King Amanullah of Afghanistan, for as you know, there are many unemployed in our trade."

Early in 1927, while the younger members of the dynasty were looking toward the future, a dynastic link with the past snapped. On January 19 that year, the Empress Carlota died of pneumonia in her castle of Bouchout. She was eighty-six years old. Until the very end she had still been able to startle her listeners with occasional shafts of lucidity. Once, when the visiting Queen Elisabeth, in conversation with Carlota's lady-in-waiting, was trying to remember the name of some long-dead Austrian politician, Carlota suddenly lifted her head and supplied the name, loudly and clearly. On another occasion, when one of her ladies happened to mention the age of a certain prince to her dinner companion, the Empress corrected her. "No," she said firmly, "he is thirty-nine." After dinner the ladies checked the date of the prince's birth and discovered the Empress to have been right. But at other times her memory failed her completely. When Albert and Elisabeth, in the fourteenth year of their reign, came one day to see her, she afterward informed her companions that, "One has had a visit from the Flanders."

A little while before the end she spoke to Baron Goffinet who came sometimes to lunch with her. "I want to go to Laeken," she said. "One goes up and up and then finally disappears behind the towers." She was referring to the crypt in the Church of Notre Dame at Laeken in which all the members of the dynasty were buried. She had her wish, and on a snowy day in January 1927 her coffin was followed into the crypt by a handful of shuffling old soldiers who, over sixty years before, had landed with the Emperor Maximilian in Mexico at the start of what had been meant to be such a glorious and God-inspired enterprise.

4

In the year 1930 independent Belgium celebrated its centenary. On July 21 that year, a century after King Leopold I had assumed the crown, King Albert and Queen Elisabeth attended a *Te Deum* at Sainte Gudule and then drove to the Parque du Cinquantenaire for the opening of the Centenary celebrations. Here, within the shadow of the immense triumphal archway erected by Leopold II to mark the fiftieth anniversary of independence, the King inaugurated the festival.

Although the country was still plagued by racial strife and financial uncertainty, the dynasty itself had every reason for self-congratulation. It had proved remarkably durable. As the King had said, there were by now so many unemployed in his trade. Of those royal houses who, a century before, had spurned the new King Leopold I, not one remained: the Hapsburgs, the Hohenzollerns, the Romanovs had all fallen. So too had those other once-powerful dynasties—the Bourbons, the Bonapartes and the Braganzas. The King of Spain was to lose his throne the following year and the King of Italy was little more than a puppet in the hands of Mussolini. King Albert, by his pliability, his conscientiousness and his sound common sense had weathered the storm; his popularity, in this centenary year, stood almost as high as it had in those delirious days of his return from Yser.

As a crowning point to the Centenary celebrations, a son was born to Prince Leopold and Princess Astrid that September. The birth of this heir apparent was announced from the balcony of the Maison du Roi in the Grand' Place in Brussels and the crowd roared with delight. He was given the evocative name of those ancient Belgian kings of Jerusalem—and of King Albert's long-dead brother—Baudouin.

Gratifying as all this adulation might be, King Albert was not the man to enjoy it. The summer-long celebrations called for endless public appearances and inspiring public pronouncements, and the King had never accustomed himself to this aspect of his duties. He remained self-conscious and self-doubting. "He appeared deeply serious and anxious," noted one journalist. "He never smiled, he never relaxed. He left the impression of being a man weighed down with the anxiety of high office." The speeches which he wrote were excellent and he would conscientiously learn them by heart; at the last moment, however, his courage always failed him and he would take them from his pocket and read them out. His delivery was poor and he had very little ability to rouse an audience. Returning from some official function he would sigh and say, "One did not put up much of a show." Acutely conscious of this lack of fluency he would say, "Let us be short, for the sake of those who are going to listen to us."

Nothing could convince him of his popularity. "In a crowd," wrote the Comte de Lichtervelde, "he saw at once the ten fellows who did not take off their hats." He might be myopic, but he could always spot the one man who was not applauding. "I have received many ovations," he once said, "but I have read enough history to realize that they are ephemeral."

And in the same way that he avoided histrionics himself, so did he distrust it in others. "I suppose I shall once more be greeted with acclamations as the warrior-king!" he once muttered before a reception. "I am getting so *bored* with it."

More and more, as the years went by, did this cynicism manifest itself. The King by now was a disillusioned man. Not only was he aware of his own shortcomings but he despaired of his own country, and of Europe, ever settling its problems. Belgium had been badly hit by the depression of 1929 and unemployment was rising. The feud between Flemings and Walloons simmered dangerously, with the Flemish nationalists winning more seats in the Chamber each election. France was being racked by financial scandals and in

Germany National Socialism was becoming daily more aggressive. The dreams of 1918 seemed to be turning into nightmares.

"What a profession!" the King once exclaimed. "I shall soon abdicate. Leopold is old enough to succeed me. My wife and I will go to Haslykorn, and in that corner of Switzerland, I shall live happily amidst my books and the mountains." But he did not mean it; he had become too much a part of Belgium to desert her now. His ministers always claimed that he was the only man who really understood the country. When, after the King's death, someone once declared that Albert would have been happier as an engineer or a colonial administrator or a teacher, one of the King's close associates denied it. "You are wrong," he said. "He was purely a King, just as a monk is a monk, and a soldier a soldier. His position as King had absorbed all his faculties to such an extent that kingship became second nature to him. The King and his kingship were one and indivisible."

In 1933 King Albert again visited the Congo where he had the satisfaction of studying the progress of one of his most cherished projects—the Parc National Albert. A great lover of nature, the King had been responsible for the creation of this vast nature reserve between Lake Kivu and Lake Albert. From the Congo he flew to Palestine to join the Queen. Here, where the Belgian Baudouins had reigned for almost a century, the King disported himself with all the enthusiasm of an informed traveler and all the fervor of a pilgrim. Albert was said to be a devout Christian. On one occasion, when he had been missing for a considerable time, he was discovered by his agitated companions on the shores of Lake Genezareth—a tall, untidily dressed figure, lost in meditation.

The King and Queen spent several weeks in the Middle East and at the end of the tour they flew home. For some reason or other they decided to take a later plane than that on which they had originally been scheduled to travel. As they flew over southern Italy the following morning, they saw, scattered far below them in the snow, the wreckage of the plane on which they should have made their flight.

One day in February 1934, the King decided to do a little rock climbing. Often, to make a break from the sedentary life at Laeken, he would drive to the Ardennes and spend a day or two scaling various cliffs; the exercise kept him in trim for his more serious mountaineering in the Alps. On this particular day, however, he had to be back in Brussels at six in the evening to witness a bicycle race at the Palais des Sports. He would have to content himself, therefore, with a climb among the rocks of the Meuse, less than an hour's run from the palace.

He left Laeken at noon and, in the company of his valet, Van Dyck, made for the area known as Marche-les-Dames on the Meuse near Namur, where a line of rocky pinnacles rise up among the trees and tower above the swiftly flowing river. They left the car at nearby Boninne and after the King had done about an hour's climbing and the two of them were returning to the car, Albert suddenly decided that as it was still early, he would return to the foot of the rocks to make one more ascent. He instructed Van Dyck to continue on toward the car and assured him that he would rejoin him in an hour's time—at four o'clock. The King strode down toward the base of the towering *Roche du Bon Dieu* and Van Dyck continued on in the direction of Boninne.

When the King, usually so punctual, did not return at the appointed time, Van Dyck began to worry. He waited a further hour and then, in the gathering dusk, stumbled through the thicket toward the rocks, calling his Sovereign's name. His voice echoed, unanswered, among the cliffs. In rising panic, he hurried back to the car in the hope that the King might have returned there by another path. The car was empty. By now thoroughly alarmed, Van Dyck enlisted the help of a passing lorry driver and two local woodcutters and, by the light of lanterns, the four men searched the area below the rocks. There was nothing to be seen. At seven Van Dyck telephoned the palace. Captain Jacques Dixmude, the King's *officier d'ordonnance*, set out at once, followed some time later by Comte de Grunne and the King's doctor, Professor Nolf. To spare the Queen what might yet prove to be unnecessary anxiety, it was decided to tell her nothing; the King, as far as she knew, was presenting prizes at the Palais des Sports.

For four hours, in bitter cold and by the feeble light of torches, they searched for the King. Comte de Grunne, an enthusiastic alpinist, explored all the intricate crags of the *Roche du Bon Dieu*, exhausting himself in the process, while the others scoured the leafy, sharply sloping floor of the forest behind. Soon after midnight they decided to send for five of Belgium's leading climbers to help in the search. While waiting for their arrival, Captain Jacques, descending the leaf-carpeted slope behind the *Roche du Bon Dieu*, tripped over a rope. It was attached to a body. He shouted to the others and, by the light of a half-dozen torches, the group saw the corpse of their King. He was lying on his back with his arms outstretched. On the right side of his skull was a gaping wound and all about him were scattered his belongings—his cap, his rucksack, his straps and his gold-rimmed glasses.

It appears that the rock on which the King had been resting at the end of his climb had given way and that in his fall he had knocked his head against the side of the pinnacle. Death had been instantaneous. There appears to have been no truth whatsoever in the inevitable rumors that the King had been killed for political reasons or that he had committed suicide.

They put his body in a car and drove it back to Laeken. Here it was washed, bandaged and neatly laid out. Only then was the news broken to the Queen. She had known, by now, that the King was missing but not that his dead body had been found and brought home. She was sitting alone on a sofa, in the grey light of dawn, when they came to tell her. For twenty minutes she said nothing. She simply sat motionless, her eyes tightly closed. Eventually she rose, and asked to be shown the King's body. Only when she discovered that hands other than her own had washed his face and dressed his wound and cleaned his clothes did she lose control. She was furious. It was to be her last flash of temperament for many months to come.

Amongst the hundreds of glowing tributes—from kings, presidents, statesmen, politicians, friends and strangers—paid to King Albert after his death, there was one which he would have appreciated more than any of the others. Some years before, the French, in his honor, had given a mountain peak in Savoy the name of Pic Albert I. On the day after the King's death, four local guides who had often accompanied him on his climbs braved a blinding snowstorm to reach the top of Pic Albert I. On its windswept summit they planted the flag of Belgium.

Leopold III
King Against Countrymen
1934-1950

Chapter Eleven

1

King Leopold III was a very different man from his father. It was true that he had that same strong sense of vocation but his conception of his royal responsibilities differed considerably. The Belgian Constitution, originally considered so gagging for the monarch, seemed, by the standards of the 1930's, to allow him far too much say. Appreciating this, King Albert had never exercised his powers to the full. His son, on the other hand, saw no reason why—provided he remained within constitutional limits—he should not do so. The policy of the new King, complained one of his ministers, was to make use of his royal prerogatives to the utmost; "When the Constitution could be interpreted in two alternative ways," he said, "the King always chose the interpretation that gave him the most power." Acutely conscious of the fact that his reign followed that of three kings who had been, each in his own way, outstanding men, Leopold III was determined to make his mark. And the way to make it, he had decided, was by a show of strength. "Authoritarian democracy," a term much bandied about at this period, was one which very nearly summed up what the King had in mind.

And not only in this notion of a strong, positive monarchy did Leopold III differ from his father but in his handling of his ministers he was not nearly so tactful. Where Albert had guided, Leopold tried to lead; where Albert had been long-suffering, Leopold was impatient; where Albert had always suggested, Leopold invariably lectured. Proud, headstrong and stubborn, with a taste for power and an urge for action, the King had little of his late father's political flexibility. If Albert had been the beau ideal of a twentieth-century constitutional monarch, then there was more than a whiff of the eighteenth century about his son's ideas of kingship.

But for all this, King Leopold III was no tyrant. Like his parents, he had a strong social conscience and a very real concern for the welfare of his fellow countrymen. He could, when relaxed, be utterly charming. "What's this I hear about your being cross with me?" he once cajoled a minister to whom he had recently given a severe reprimand. "Come, come, now...." And because they realized that whatever he did was in the sincere conviction that he was doing his best for Belgium, his ministers usually swallowed their resentment and allowed themselves to be coaxed into forgiving him. After all, it was merely an excess of the customary Coburg conscientiousness that made him seem so didactic.

That Belgium was in need of some strong guidance during the mid-1930's there is no doubt. The problems which King Albert had found so distressing during the last years of his life worsened considerably during the first years of his son's reign. Not only was Nazi Germany—in the face of French and British apathy—growing daily more menacing, but Belgium itself was floundering about in an economic and political morass. The world depression threatened the country with financial ruin, the major political parties were divided, fascist movements in both Flanders and Wallonia were undermining national stability. Normal parliamentary processes seemed incapable of handling the situation. Cabinets followed one another in rapid succession and there were no less than eighteen different governments in the twenty years between the two World Wars. In 1935 the exasperated King Leopold III was obliged to make the most of his powers by calling upon the economist Paul Van Zeeland from outside Parliament to assume the Premiership and save the country from economic collapse. Van Zeeland, an ex-cabinet minister and man of the Center, accepted the invitation and headed a national government made up of Catholics, Liberals and Socialists. By this bold move—the first of many—the King gave weight to the growing belief that he was a man to act swiftly and independently when it came to the greater good of his country.

Premier Van Zeeland was just beginning to get things under control when he was faced with the sudden emergence of the so-called Rexist party. This was a militantly fascist organization founded by a young journalist named Léon Degrelle. Professing to be more Catholic than the Pope, more royalist than the King, the enemy of "international high finance" (he was, in fact, being financed by various big businessmen), the most ardent of patriots and the "tribune of the people," Degrelle won immediate and widespread support. His appeal was to certain members of the aristocracy who still dreamed of a royal dictatorship, to reactionary army officers and ultramontane Catholics, and to those members of the petite bourgeoisie who had been hardest hit by the depression. In Degrelle's often-voiced boast that he enjoyed the support of the King there seems to have been not a grain of truth. Certain members of the King's entourage might have given him some encouragement, and the fact that Leopold was known to favor a strong executive might have led Degrelle to believe that his politics would find favor at Laeken, but there was no more to it than that.

In the elections of May 1936, the Rexist party, barely six months old, won twenty-three seats. Degrelle, on the crest of the wave, now persuaded one of the Rexist deputies in Brussels to resign his seat and, in the hope of gaining an overwhelming vote of confidence for his party, presented himself as candidate in the by-election. Premier Van Zeeland, appreciating the significance of the gesture, himself took up the challenge. Supported by the combined Catholic, Liberal, Socialist and Communist parties, he stood against Degrelle. It was a dramatic move. On the eve of the poll two statements were published in the press—one in the name of King Leopold and the other by the Belgian Primate, Cardinal Van Roey—denying that there was any truth in Degrelle's repeated public assertions that he enjoyed the support of the Sovereign and the Primate. It was a memorable election. Van Zeeland defeated Degrelle by over two hundred thousand votes and the Rexist party faded almost as suddenly as it had bloomed. "No man, and certainly not Degrelle," claimed the writer René Hislaire afterward, "could successfully play the role of apprentice dictator in a country so attached to its constitutional liberties as Belgium."

Within a few months, however, Van Zeeland himself was forced to resign because of some financial scandal in which he had played an innocent part, and King Leopold was once more obliged to scratch around for an acceptable prime minister. It took him a month to find one. And for the following two years, while he steadily lost faith in parliamentary procedure, Leopold had to contend with one constitutional crisis after another. These recurring upheavals seem to have had a profound effect on the King's concept of constitutional monarchy; he came to believe, ever more firmly, that the country's stability depended on the strength of his own position. He was fully alive to the fact that in a divided, two-nation state like Belgium, his position as a focal point for national loyalties was an almost indispensable one. The stronger that position, the stronger, surely, would Belgium be. What was needed, he said on more than one occasion, was a more powerful executive: a cabinet of men who would be *his* ministers, rather than a group of individuals taking orders from party organizations. This, he claimed, was how the Constitution should be interpreted. The growing influence of political parties was being substituted for constitutional power; ministers should be "agents of the executive power" instead of being representatives of their parties. Time and again he lectured his ministers on their shortcomings and more particularly on their tendency to act without consulting him. "Those who drew up the Constitution," he once pointed out to his assembled cabinet, "certainly did not wish that the role of the Head of State should be reduced to that of a servile legislator of decisions taken without him by members of his government." He, for one, was going to see that it was not.

That the King's ministers began to resent his independent and badgering tone can be appreciated. Relations between King and cabinets became steadily worse. "There were numerous and sometimes exasperating incidents at the Palace," complained one of Leopold's many prime ministers. More and more did the King seem to be relying on his courtiers rather than on his constitutional advisers. More and more did he come to resent what he considered his government's lack of concern for Belgium as a whole. More and more did he begin to think in terms of a distinction between his two functions—that of the head of the parliamentary executive and that of the Head of State. If Belgium was found to be suffering at the hands of a misguided and irresolute government, might he not one day be able to save her in his extra-parliamentary capacity—as Head of State?

For the moment, however, there was no open break between the monarch and his ministers. When it did come, it was to plunge Belgium, and the dynasty, into the greatest constitutional crisis of its history.

2

If Leopold's public life was stormy, his domestic life was enviably serene. Queen Astrid's buoyancy had proved an excellent foil for his own somewhat serious nature; she was the one person who could shake him out of his absorption in affairs of state. "The Queen," said one observer, "knew how to enjoy life and to make him share her joy." Her frankness, her naturalness and her lightheartedness provided a much-needed relief from the pomposity and the strain of his duties; in her company he could relax completely. Their private life was extremely simple. They still lived in the Chateau de Stuyvenberg. That unpretentious white house in the park at Laeken. Meals at the chateau would be *en famille*, with Astrid serving from dishes on a trolley beside the table. She was often to be seen shopping in department stores or walking with her three children—

Josephine-Charlotte, Baudouin and Albert (who had been born in 1934)—in the public parks. She shared her husband's love of the open air and his enthusiasm for sport—for golf, for swimming, for skiing and for climbing. Like him, she was an indefatigable traveler; together they toured the Dutch East Indies, French Indo-China, Siam, Ceylon and the Congo. In public she eased his way, smiling where he looked grave, speaking where he was shy, charming where he was too preoccupied. With him so handsome and she so radiantly beautiful, they made a striking couple; their popularity, both at home and abroad, was immense. Together, they captured the imagination of the world.

In the summer of 1935, the second year of the reign, the royal couple went south on holiday. They spent a week or so climbing in the Dolomites (where Leopold unveiled a plaque to the late King Albert) and then went to spend a few days in their villa on Lake Lucerne. On the morning of Thursday, August 29, having decided to go climbing, the royal party left the villa in two cars, headed for the little town of Küssnacht. Leopold, with Astrid by his side and the chauffeur in the dickey behind, was driving the first car; the four other members of the party were in the car following. It was a day of golden sunshine. To the left of the wide road lay orchards, to the right glittered the waters of the lake. At about 10 A.M. Leopold, who was not driving particularly fast, turned to Astrid to answer some question about directions; with his attention diverted, he lost control of the car. It mounted the curb, skidded sharply right, shot down the steep embankment and hit a tree. The Queen was flung out against the tree and the car careened on. When it hit a second tree the King was thrown clear, and the car, rolling on, crashed over a low stone wall and plunged into the lake. The chauffeur was flung into the shallow water from which he emerged with a badly cut face.

Dazed, and with his head and right arm injured, Leopold scrambled to his feet. Astrid lay a few yards away. He hurried to her side to find that, in spite of a fractured skull, she was still alive. A member of the royal party had rushed into nearby Küssnacht to fetch help. The doctors could do nothing, but the village cure was just able to administer the last sacrament before Queen Astrid died in her husband's arms.

She was buried, in great state, five days later. The flamboyant hearse, drawn by eight plumed and caparisoned horses, rolled slowly through the crowded streets of the Belgian capital. No sound, other than the clash of the horses' hooves and the steady tolling of the bells, broke the silence. Behind, all alone, walked King Leopold. Wearing a general's uniform, his fair hair uncovered, his face bruised and his arm in a black sling, he paced the four miles from Sainte Gudule to the family vault at Laeken. Obviously in pain, he sometimes swayed as he walked. Now and then he was seen to wipe a tear from his eyes.

How different, one wonders, would Leopold's tragic story have been had the adored Queen Astrid not been killed?

3

It seemed, at one stage, as though Queen Elisabeth would never recover from the death of King Albert. She who had always loved life so much appeared to have lost all further interest in living. For several days after his death she lay alone in a darkened room, and when she was finally persuaded to emerge, she seemed more dead than alive. She gave no thought to what she ate, or what she wore, or what she said. Her health, never really robust, deteriorated still further. Without that nervous energy to keep her going, she looked suddenly old and ill and tired. Nothing seemed to interest her. She would neither play her violin, nor paint, nor sculpt. She made no public appearances. Only once, during this time after Albert's death, did she emerge from her seclusion to appear in public. Veiled, and dressed in deep mourning, she went to console the women whose husbands had been killed in a mine disaster at Pâturages.

As she could not bear to go on living in her old apartments at Laeken, she moved to the little Pavilion des Palmiers in the park.

Here, in the very rooms where old King Leopold II had ended his days, the widowed Elisabeth took up residence. Twenty-five years had passed since the irascible old King, in a long white dressing gown, had married the Baroness de Vaughan in this same glass-domed pavilion; the heady scent of the flowers which he had loved still filled the air of the adjoining hothouses. With three small rooms and a kitchenette at her disposal, the Queen resigned herself to a life of solitude. She ate her meals alone and received few visitors. Her eldest son, King Leopold, came to see her each day and after the death of Queen Astrid the relationship between mother and son, always close, became closer still. When her second son, Prince Charles, still a bachelor and now living in the Brussels Palace, tried to rekindle her interest in music and painting, she remained unresponsive.

It was a visit to her daughter Marie-José, the Crown Princess of Italy, that saw the beginning of Elisabeth's gradual return to normal life. King Victor Emmanuel III had lent her one of the royal villas outside Naples and here, amidst the incomparable beauties of the Sorrentine peninsula, Elisabeth began to revive. She had always loved the sea and the sun; at Naples she could indulge that love to her heart's content. Even if she was not yet reconciled to her loss, her health improved and she regained something of her old zest. Although she was in her late fifties, she learned to dive and to drive; she drove, it was said, with a blithe disregard for the rules of the road. She returned to Laeken after three months, physically if not spiritually restored.

Music, however, was what finally brought her back to life. One of her ladies coaxed her into taking up her violin once more and from this she was drawn back into that world of composers and performers which she loved so well. But it was a slow process. Not until three years after Albert's death—in 1937—did Elisabeth inaugurate one of her most memorable schemes: the *Concours Ysaye*, later to be known as the *Concours Reine Elisabeth*. This was a vast annual international competition for performers and composers who would not, in the ordinary way, have any opportunity of being heard in public. The Queen attended all the eliminating rounds and the winning soloists and composers were granted a special gala performance. In time the *Concours Reine Elisabeth* was to become one of the most important musical festivals in the world, establishing the Queen as one of the last great royal patrons of music.

And after Astrid died, Elisabeth was obliged, willy-nilly, to concern herself in the affairs of family and country once more. There were her three motherless grandchildren—Josephine-Charlotte, Baudouin and Albert—to be cared for, and the King frequently needed a hostess. Elisabeth was once again Belgium's only Queen. And so, through a series of undreamed-of vicissitudes, would she remain for the next quarter of a century.

4

Time and again, during these years before the Second World War, King Leopold III seemed to be taking matters from out of the hands of his ministers and into his own. Of the many examples of his enterprise, that of Belgium's new foreign policy was the most notable.

Belgium, after the First World War, had been obliged to forsake its long-guaranteed neutrality and to seek security in international alliances. It had put its faith in the League of Nations and in the Treaty of Locarno—by which it allied itself with France, Britain, Germany and Italy. During the first few years of King Leopold III's reign, however, both these props tottered to their fall: the League of Nations proved itself to be utterly ineffectual and when Hitler, in defiance of the Locarno Treaty, reoccupied the Rhineland in March 1936, the other Locarno powers raised not a finger to stop him. Once again Belgium found herself face to face with an aggressive and powerful Germany and there was nothing in the irresolute attitudes of either France or Britain to inspire much confidence in their worth as allies and protectors. When Van Zeeland, the Belgian Prime Minister of the day, crossed the Channel to ask the assembled representatives of France, Britain and Italy what they intended doing about Hitler's violation of Locarno, he was sent home with vague promises of a future pact. In the face of this timidity it seemed that the only solution would be for Belgium to look to its own defenses.

But this was easier said than done. Although it was generally accepted that the country must strengthen itself militarily, the Catholic party, made up, for the most part, of Flemings, refused to cooperate while Belgium was still allied—in no matter how tenuous a fashion—to France. While the Locarno Treaty bound France and Belgium together, the Flemings would not hear of rearmament or of a change in the country's conscription laws. It was not that they were pro-German; it was simply that being anti-Walloon, they were anti-French. As a result, the Catholic party stubbornly refused to vote any funds for much-needed military expansion. The only possible way to break the deadlock would be for Belgium to repudiate Locarno and to adopt an entirely new foreign policy. In the autumn of 1936, King Leopold provided her with one.

On October 16 that year, the King called a special meeting of the Council of Ministers. After upbraiding them, in his usual manner, for their continued vacillation in the face of the threatening international situation, the King outlined his ideas on the sort of foreign policy which the country should adopt. Belgium should free itself of all military alliances and build up an army sufficiently strong to dissuade other nations from launching an attack across her territory. The policy, he said, would be "exclusively and wholly Belgian"; it would be a return, in other words, to neutralism.

The King's speech was enthusiastically received by his ministers, and the veteran Socialist leader, Emile Vandervelde, suggested that the King's views be made public. These published views, in fact, were very much in tune with the ministers' own and with the mood of the country as a whole. Leopold's policy, known somewhat grandiloquently as the Policy of Independence-Neutrality, was adopted and Belgium settled back in the fond hope that she would now be left in peace. Six months later France and Britain recognized

Belgian neutrality and declared her released from all obligations undertaken at Locarno. They, however (on the understanding that Belgium would now build up her defenses), would maintain their obligations toward her. In October 1937 Hitler gave a similar guarantee. Lucky Belgium seemed to be both having and eating its cake and it was with considerable gratification that Paul Henri Spaak, the Minister for Foreign Affairs, could announce that he felt "embarrassed at keeping all the advantages without taking any risks." The popular policy of Independence-Neutrality became personally identified with the King, and Leopold once more seemed to have come forward to give his country a lead.

In years to come, the King's enemies were to accuse him of forcing a disastrous foreign policy on an unwilling government. It was simply another instance, ran the legend, of his imperious behavior. The accusation was without any foundation whatsoever. "It is both absurd and unseemly," declared Spaak, who was one day to be Leopold's most bitter opponent, "to suggest that the King had a personal policy.... The truth of the matter was simply that the Head of State, guided by our country's permanent interests, had succeeded in expressing in excellent terms the will of the immense majority."

And the will of the immense majority it remained. Whatever disagreements Leopold might have had with his ministers during this period, they were not about the advisability of Belgium's foreign policy. France and Britain considered the policy at worst pro-German and at best naive, and Germany considered it pro-Allied, but for the Belgian people it represented an opportunity to escape the possibility of a war in which Belgian blood would be spilled and Belgian soil devastated for a cause which would have precious little to do with Belgium itself. Their apprehension was understandable. For centuries foreign armies had battled their way across the Low Countries; the fact that the Franco-Prussian War of 1870 had not been fought on Belgian soil was still talked of as a "miracle." When France and Britain, for not entirely unselfish reasons (they would rather fight in Belgian than on their own soil), exhorted the Belgians to renounce their neutrality, they refused. "No country," said Spaak, "agrees to be a battlefield."

Belgium was prepared, nevertheless, to defend her neutrality to the utmost. On this point King Leopold left no room for doubt. "Twenty-five years ago exactly," he declared in a broadcast to the United States in 1939, "the Belgian Army, under my father King Albert, put a stop to the progress of a cruel invasion. If we are attacked—God preserve us from it—in spite of the solemn and categorical engagements given us in 1937 and renewed on the eve of war—we should fight without hesitation, this time with means ten times stronger, and once more the whole country would be found behind the Army."

As Europe, during the last years of the decade, lumbered ever closer toward war, Leopold again took the initiative in trying to save his country from the impending holocaust. On August 23, 1939, in the name of the Oslo Powers—Belgium, the Netherlands, Luxembourg, Finland and the three Scandinavian countries—the King broadcast an appeal for peace. Five days later, when this touchingly futile plea had gone unanswered, he and Queen Wilhelmina announced that they were prepared "jointly to lend their good offices in the hope of averting war." This, too, was ignored. War broke out on September 3, 1939, when Germany, striking eastward this time, attacked Poland. While France and Britain declared war, Belgium remained neutral; it was now a matter of sitting tight and hoping for the best. With war having broken out on the eastern front, there was a chance that Belgium might yet be spared. That November, in the midst of the unnerving phoney war, King Leopold and Queen Wilhelmina again offered to mediate a peace "before the war in Western Europe begins in full violence." The ingenuous appeal fell, as had all the others, on deaf ears.

In January 1940 the King, constitutionally, overstepped the mark. Early that month two German officers crash-landed just inside the Belgian border and, on being captured, made frantic efforts to burn some papers which they were carrying. The papers were discovered to be Hitler's secret orders for an attack on Holland, Belgium and Luxembourg. Although the documents looked genuine enough, they might have been set as a trap to provoke Belgium into requesting Anglo-French assistance, thereby giving Germany an excuse for attacking Belgium. The government decided to pass the information on to France, Britain and Holland without actually asking for help. This was done. King Leopold, however, seems to have had other ideas. Without consulting, or even notifying, his government, he sent that loyal friend of the dynasty, Sir Roger Keyes, to find out from London and Paris what guarantees Belgium could expect if she entered the war on their side. Quite independently, in other words, the King was preparing to abandon Belgium's neutrality. Although he afterward claimed that he was merely making a general inquiry, both France and Britain assumed that he was asking for help. When the Belgian ambassador in Paris telephoned Spaak, the Belgian Foreign Minister, to ask whether the French could now march in, Spaak was utterly bemused. He tackled the King on the matter and Leopold, blushing crimson, denied that he had approached the Allies. During the night, however, the King had second thoughts, and before dawn the following day he sent for Spaak. Admitting what he had done, Leopold begged Spaak to get him out of a difficult situation. "Spaak," he said, bringing his renowned charm into full play, *"il faut me sauver."* They saved him by getting the long-suffering Keyes to explain to both France and Britain that there had been a "misunderstanding."

Once more, before Germany launched her sudden attack on Belgium, did Leopold make full use of his royal prerogatives. A fortnight after Hitler had invaded Norway and Denmark, leaving Belgium in very little doubt that she would be the next victim, the Prime Minister, Hubert Pierlot, saw fit to offer his cabinet's resignation. The Government had been defeated on some unimportant linguistic reform. Leopold was furious. This really was fiddling while Rome was about to burst into flame. At a time when it was imperative for the country to stand strong and united, he was faced with the prospect of weeks, perhaps even months of negotiation in order to form another government. He refused to accept the resignation. He told Pierlot that he would just have to manage as best he could with the government that he had. The Prime Minister acquiesced and the problem sorted itself out. "One more proof," acclaimed a Belgian newspaper, "that a regime like ours needs the vigor of monarchic institutions.... Like a ship that has gone off course due to an error of its crew, the Government has been put back on the right course by the nation's pilot."

Two weeks later, brutally and without warning. Hitler attacked Belgium. At dawn on May 10, 1940, the Germans invaded the Low Countries, and Belgium, in accordance with the Treaty of April 1937, invoked the aid of France and Britain. German bombs were already exploding over Belgium when the German ambassador presented his country's declaration of war to the Belgian Foreign Minister. As the ambassador launched into the German declaration Spaak cut him short. "Hand me the document," he said wryly, "I should like to spare you so painful a task."

As King Leopold I had done in 1831 and as King Albert had done in 1914, King Leopold III immediately assumed personal command of the army. At seven that morning he took leave of his assembled ministers. "The King was firm, calm and in control of himself," says one of them. "When we parted I felt profoundly moved and tears came into my eyes as I shook his hand." The King rejected his Prime Minister's suggestion that he should appear before Parliament as his father had done in 1914. There was simply no time, in this age of the *blitzkrieg*, for the sedate ride through the decorated streets and the dignified speech from the throne. Over twenty-five years before, as a satin-suited little boy, Leopold had seen his father take leave of Parliament; he now felt, for one reason or another, unable to emulate him. The King, explained Prime Minister Pierlot later to the assembled members, "would have liked to address Parliament, but the rapid unfolding of events has not allowed him to do so; when the battle has started, that is where the Chief must be."

Before very long, this same Prime Minister, backed up by a host of his colleagues and compatriots, would be accusing the King of deliberately avoiding a confrontation of Parliament. They were to claim that Leopold had wished to disassociate himself from any declaration committing him more deeply to the Allied cause than was necessary; he wanted, at all costs, to avoid insulting Germany. It was merely another link, ran the legend, in his long and premeditated chain of treachery.

Chapter Twelve

1

If the opening weeks of the First World War had been the most glorious of King Albert's life, the month of May 1940 proved to be the most inglorious of his son's career. Things went wrong from the start. Although King Leopold's boast that Belgium was now opposing Germany with a force ten times as strong as in 1914 was well-founded, the increase in Belgian strength was as nothing when set against that of Nazi Germany. The enemy onslaught was tremendous. Almost the entire Belgian air force was destroyed before the planes had time to get off the ground and the famous key fortress of Eben-Emael, believed to be all but impregnable, was quickly taken by troops landing on its roof by glider under cover of darkness. However, the Belgian forces, fighting magnificently, held the enemy at the border just long enough (although not so long as had been expected) for the French and British forces to move up and establish themselves along the so-called K-W line. This was a strongly fortified line—the Belgian equivalent of the Maginot line—running from near Antwerp in the north to near Namur in the south. Cutting the country roughly in half, it was looked upon as Belgium's main line of defense and was considered invulnerable. Once the Allies had taken up their position behind it, the Belgians fell back from the border and joined them. On the day of this retreat King Leopold subordinated himself, as his father had done toward the end of the First World War, to the French Generalissimo (in this instance General Gamelin) and the Belgian army ceased to operate as a separate unit. Although the King seems to have been understandably appalled at the ferocity of the German onslaught, the Belgians were now firmly entrenched behind their "iron wall" and there seemed no reason why they should not remain there.

On May 13, the fourth day of the invasion, the Germans, attacking the French through the Ardennes south of the K-W line, broke through their defenses. The disaster occurred at Sedan, and the name of the city became, for a second time, a symbol of French defeat. This breakthrough, at the point where the French defenses were at their weakest (the Ardennes had been considered impassable), had all along been the German intention. Their attack on northern Belgium had been in the nature of a feint; the Allies, expecting a repetition of the 1914 Schlieffen plan, had responded to what Liddell Hart described as the "matador's cloak" only too readily and had allowed themselves to be enticed forward into Flanders. The German *Schwerpunkt*—concentration point—aimed at Sedan since the very beginning, now thrust through. The enemy poured in a relentless torrent across northern France, headed, not southward toward Paris, but westward toward the Channel. They were beginning, in other words, to drive a wedge between the French forces to the south and the Allied forces, in Belgium, to the north. From now on, the fates of both France and Belgium were sealed.

Two days later Holland capitulated. This meant that the troops in Belgium were now all but surrounded by the enemy. Once the thrusting German divisions to the south reached the Channel, the vise-like encirclement would be complete.

To match up with the French retreat after Sedan, King Leopold was ordered by the French commander to abandon the strong and still unbroken K-W line and fall back on the River Scheldt. The order, says General Derousseaux, Belgian Deputy Chief-of-Staff, "came like a shot out of the blue ... the General Staff was stunned by it." Nevertheless King Leopold, with a deep sense of misgiving, complied. His ministers, anxious for the Belgian Army to keep as closely in touch with the French as possible, urged him to retreat southwestward toward France, but he, following orders, retreated westward toward the Belgian coast. These orders, it was afterward suggested, happened to suit him very well.

By May 19 the Germans, somewhat to their own astonishment, had reached the French coast, and the Allied forces in Belgium were well and truly trapped. The French Government, beginning to panic, dismissed Generalissimo Gamelin and brought the veteran General Weygand from Syria to take over command. Here was a name aureoled in glamor! Reputed to be the son of the Empress Carlota, associated with some of the most glorious memories of the First World War, Weygand would be the man to save the situation. Flying over the German "corridor" to Belgium, he conferred with King Leopold. After what Leopold described as "four hours of confused talking," Weygand decided on an offensive. The Allied armies in Belgium would attack southward and the French armies northward, thereby piercing the German "corridor" now stretching from the Ardennes to the Channel. The offensive never materialized. There were no French forces to the south capable of launching an attack, and Lord Gort, commanding the British forces, was beginning to think in terms of evacuating rather than of attacking. The Germans, firmly established on the Channel, were swiftly working their way up the coast toward Belgium; the trap, in fact, was beginning to close. By May 25 Lord Gort had definitely decided to evacuate his troops from Dunkirk and on the following day he received firm orders to do so. The campaign, in Field Marshal Montgomery's trenchant phrase, had been a "complete dog's breakfast."

King Leopold was by now established at the Chateau Blanc at Lophem near Bruges, a stone's-throw from the house where King Albert had taken up residence before his triumphant return to Brussels in 1918. Then the village had been alive with the air of victory; now it was hushed with the atmosphere of defeat. The Belgians, still fighting valiantly, were falling farther and farther back onto an area less than one-eighth the size of their total country; it was an area crammed with panicky refugees and strafed almost continuously by the German air force. Nor were bombs and machinegun bullets the only things with which the enemy was showering the crowded territory: to undermine the morale of the troops, the Germans scattered thousands of leaflets over the area. These leaflets carried a map illustrating, only too accurately, how the Allied armies were surrounded. "Comrades!" ran the accompanying caption. "Here is the situation. In any case the war is over for you. Your leaders are going to escape by airplane. Lay down your arms." To counteract the resulting spread of disillusion among the men, Leopold issued a resounding Order of the Day. After exhorting his troops to keep fighting with customary vigor, he made them a promise. "Officers and Soldiers," he said. "Whatever happens, *I shall share your fate.*"

It was now, when defeat seemed inevitable, that the long-simmering feud between Leopold and his ministers reached its climax. Once that emotional leave-taking at the palace on the morning of the attack was over, the old misunderstandings between Monarch and ministers came crowding back. Throughout the first disastrous fortnight of the campaign, there emerged a strong divergence of views between them. Leopold, backed by his somewhat reactionary entourage, began following one path; his Government, represented by Prime Minister Pierlot, Foreign Minister Spaak, and the Ministers of Defense and the Interior (the rest had already left for France), were following another.

In the first place, the ministers were deeply concerned by what seemed to them the "appalling defeatism" at the King's Headquarters. Being a stage removed from the battle, they did not have the King's appreciation of the military situation. The success of the German attack had convinced Leopold that France would soon be brought to her knees and that the immediate outlook for Europe was hopeless. The ministers could not agree. They considered the setback to be of a temporary nature; the answer, they said, was for the Belgian Army to link itself as closely as possible with the Allied forces. When Leopold, contrary to their urgings, retreated toward the Belgian coastline rather than toward France, they were astonished.

Even though Leopold had sound strategic reasons for his conduct, it was, as far as his ministers were concerned, the first indication that the King was considering a loosening of the ties which bound him to his allies. The duty of the Belgian Army, Leopold now decided, was to defend Belgium only and not to link its fate with that of the French and British troops. With the Allied resistance crumbling, might it not be better, he wondered, to salvage what he could from the debacle?

And as the King's conception of Belgium's role in the struggle began taking shape, so did his conception of his own duty become clearer. If the Belgian Army was forced to capitulate (and the possibility was becoming daily more likely) should he not remain with it, to share its fate? The suggestion shocked his ministers. By invoking the aid of the Allies, they said, by allowing French and British lives to be lost in the defense of Belgium, the King was honor-bound to continue the struggle side by side with his fellow combatants. Even if Belgium were defeated, the King's duty was to go abroad and there become a symbol of continuing Belgian resistance. This is what Queen Wilhelmina had done. That Leopold should ask his ministers whether or not they thought that the Dutch Queen had made a wise move was all but incomprehensible to them. In a memorandum addressed to the King, the Prime Minister made the position crystal clear. In a letter written a day or two later, he reminded the King as tactfully but as firmly as possible that it was for the ministers, and not for the King himself, to decide what course of action he must follow. It was a "general, absolute rule," wrote Pierlot, that "the government alone carries the responsibility for the acts of the Head of State." To these unequivocal instructions Leopold gave an evasive reply. He had not yet made up his mind.

By May 24 the end was clearly in sight. The British were preparing to evacuate and the Belgians could not hold out much longer. The four ministers, having been kept at arm's length by Leopold and his military entourage, had spent the past four days strolling aimlessly around Bruges. They now decided that they must leave the country before it was too late. But the King had not yet given them his decision; in a last desperate effort to get him to accompany them to France, they tracked him down to his new headquarters, the Chateau de Wynendael, and there requested an audience. It proved to be one of the most momentous scenes in the history of the dynasty.

The dawn of yet another cloudless day was just breaking (as in 1914, the weather throughout the campaign had been magnificent) when the four exhausted ministers were ushered into the darkened drawing room of the grim, mock-medieval chateau. Leopold, in general's uniform, received them standing stiffly at attention; he did not ask them to sit down. He looked haggard and disheveled but his jaw was set. Prime Minister Pierlot once again explained to the King exactly where his duty lay. The King must not, for political reasons, be personally associated with the capitulation and once his role as Commander-in-Chief had come to an end, he must continue to play the part of Head of State, side by side with the Allied governments. "This," said Pierlot, "is the duty of the King. The Government unanimously shares this opinion."

For a long time Leopold did not answer. When he did, it was to tell them something of the anguish of the last few days and to let them know that he had decided to remain. His reasons, he said, were sentimental rather than political. To abandon his army would be desertion. "Whatever happens," he said, "I must share the fate of my troops." The decision, he afterward repeated, had been a "horribly painful" one to reach. "I would certainly have an easier life if I retired to France and went to live with my children while waiting for the end of the war. But I believe that when one has the choice of two roads, the road of duty is always the hardest. That is the one I have chosen." He read them a letter which he had just written to King George VI, justifying his behavior. His duty, he pointed out to his fellow Sovereign, was not only to remain with his troops but to try and save his countrymen from the worst rigors of an occupation.

Had the interview ended there, as Leopold wished, much of the ultimate bitterness between the King and his Government might have been avoided. But Spaak was anxious to make one more attempt to change the King's mind. He asked if they could sit down. The King, after a moment's hesitation, agreed. It was now that the ministers, in what Spaak afterward called "stupefaction and terror," realized that the King was contemplating what to them seemed like a change of sides. He was not merely going to remain in Belgium, he was planning to remain there as a reigning monarch. They understood, from the somewhat hesitant answers which he gave to their questions, that he would form a new government, in opposition to them—the elected government—and that he would reign as Hitler's vassal. He would be, in other words, a quisling king. They were astonished; "the horrible words dishonor, desertion, betrayal ... [fell] from our lips in the very presence of him who was going to commit this act," says Spaak. Prime Minister Pierlot made it quite clear that not only would they refuse to sanction the King's decision, but that they were also publicly disassociating themselves from him. "We know that such a thing is without precedent and breaks with the traditions of public laws," said Pierlot. "But we see no other attitude possible...."

Leopold's answer was cold. "I understand your situation. You have your convictions, I know they are sincere. You do whatever they command you to do." With marked formality he shook their hands and strode out of the room. The rift between King and Government was complete.

The ministers fled to France to carry on the business of government and the King returned to the battle. It lasted for three more days. Between May 26 and 27 the Germans smashed the Belgian line in four places. Over three million people—soldiers and civilians—were now wedged behind the lines. Food was giving out, the water supply was contaminated, the enemy planes were continuously strafing the crowded roads. "All along the dunes at Zeebrugge, along the Route Royale," wrote one observer, "the convoys of soldiers and evacuees were being mercilessly bombed. This corner of Flanders, which had seen so much suffering in the last war, had now become the scene of the most hideous carnage." The retreat was rapidly turning into a rout. With all avenues of escape cut off, discipline in the army and self-control among the civilians might snap at any moment and the area become the scene of the most unspeakable savagery. King Leopold, who for the last week had been warning the Allies that the Belgians could not hold out much longer, now decided to put an end to the senseless massacre.

Before sending his envoys to ask the Germans their terms of surrender, the King informed both the French and British missions of his intention. The French mission was able to warn Generalissimo Weygand in Paris, but neither General Blanchard, commanding the French forces in the field, nor Lord Gort, commanding the British, could be contacted. At five o'clock on the afternoon of May 27, the Belgian envoys, carrying a white flag, set out for the German lines. Great scarlet clouds were drifting across the darkening sky when they recrossed the lines some hours later with the German terms: unconditional surrender. After consulting with his staff, the King accepted and a cease-fire was ordered for 4 A.M. the following day.

As soon as the Belgian Government-in-Exile heard of the surrender, they issued a decree.

"In the name of the Belgian people, under Article 82 of the Constitution, considering that the King is under the power of the invader, the ministers united in council state that the King is found unable to reign."

With one storm barely over, the second, and as far as King Leopold personally was concerned, the more violent, was about to break.

2

For Queen Elisabeth, the whole campaign was imbued with a nightmare quality of *déjà vu*. There was the same hurried flight from Laeken, the same heartbreaking journey along refugee-choked roads, the same dispiriting news of defeats and retreats; there was even that same red brick villa on the seashore at La Panne. With events following such a similar pattern, it seemed quite likely that she would be able to establish herself at La Panne once again and there devote herself, as before, to the care of the wounded.

One of the chief differences between the two campaigns was that whereas Elisabeth had been a young woman in her thirties in the First World War, she was now over sixty. Her energy, however, seems to have been unimpaired and the prospect of hard work had never discouraged her. No sooner had she moved into her old villa (within a day or two, finding the absence of King Albert too poignant to bear, she took up residence next door) than she set about organizing things. Her three grandchildren were sent off, in a convoy of cars, to the safety of first France and then Spain. That accomplished, she turned her attention to the hospitals and the refugees. She arranged for a voluntary nursing staff; she opened refugee camps and a missing persons bureau; she set up dispensaries and first-aid posts; she organized urgent treatment for the badly wounded; she opened canteens and arranged for the collection and distribution of milk. She visited the sick, she bandaged the wounded, she comforted the homeless; she once stood for five hours by the roadside, ladling out milk to the hordes of hungry refugees who were shuffling by. Late at night she would be seen amongst the crowds on the shadowy dunes, listening, directing and encouraging, while behind her the sky would be aglow with flame.

Her stoicism was an example to all. In the First World War, in her white robes and floating veil she had been an almost ethereal figure; now, dressed always in black with a Red Cross band on her arm, she looked altogether more businesslike. Although her hair was by now quite grey, her expression was as alert and her figure as slender as ever. Her calm in the face of air raids was remarkable; she never allowed even the most ferocious attack to interrupt her hospital work. "I am a strong man but I thought I should faint," admitted one doctor who had been working side by side with the Queen for several hours, "but she went on, cool, unhurried and efficient." And no matter how anxious or how exhausted she might be feeling, she always presented a cheerful face. "We are in the presence," said one old soldier, "of the heroine of the Yser once again."

But the glory of those far-off days was not to be repeated. This time the enemy was not only in front of, but behind the Yser as well. The Germans were moving swiftly up the Channel toward La Panne. The streams of refugees flowing southward into France were being forced to turn around and come trudging back. On May 24, by which time it was obvious that the fight could not continue much longer, Queen Elisabeth left La Panne and joined the King at his new headquarters in the Chateau of Wynendael. With him was her second son, Prince Charles. It was before dawn the following day that Leopold had his momentous meeting with his ministers. That his decision to remain in Belgium had his mother's full approval there is little doubt. "They ask us to leave?" she is said to have cried out on hearing of the ministers' plans. "How can we leave? Our people are being killed all around us." Always inclined to follow her heart rather than her head, she felt that their place was with their suffering subjects; to her, no less than to her son, flight would have looked like desertion. Yet they must have discussed the decision at great length. Queen Elisabeth, better than anyone, must have known what King Albert would have done in similar circumstances. "Never would King Albert have consented to take refuge abroad," said Leopold to his ministers. "On the contrary, he was determined to remain always on Belgian soil." But the situations were by no means parallel and although King Albert had always shown a certain reluctance to link the fate of Belgium too closely with that of its allies, he might well have followed the advice of his ministers. Unlike his son, he had always had a very deep respect for the Constitution.

Admiral Keyes, who had been with King Leopold as British liaison officer throughout these anguished days, dined alone with the King and his mother on the evening of the day on which Leopold had finally broken with his Government. The King was in a somber mood. With remarkable perspicacity he predicted the collapse of the

French resistance, the change of government in France and the French suit for a separate peace. Both he and Queen Elisabeth spoke of their confidence in the fighting spirit of the British people, and although they did not doubt an eventual British victory, Leopold thought that it might take as long as ten years to achieve it.

Two days later Keyes received a telegram from King George VI for delivery to King Leopold. It was the British Monarch's answer to King Leopold's letter and it advised the Belgian King to leave the country while there was still time. Leopold took it at once to his mother's room. When he reemerged, it was to tell Keyes that both he and the Queen were determined to remain. That afternoon Leopold, having dispatched Keyes earlier with a message to Lord Gort saying that he could not hold out much longer, asked for an armistice.

Keyes was to see the Queen once more during that last chaotic day. Having been instructed by Churchill to make one more effort to persuade the King and his mother to leave for England, Keyes made for the Governor's Palace at Bruges to which the Queen had moved that afternoon. He showed her Churchill's telegram but she remained adamant. She had just seen women and children being bombed in the streets, she said; how could she possibly go? When, toward ten o'clock that night, Keyes delivered Churchill's message to the King himself, Leopold repeated that he must stay with his people. Keyes, his mission over, took his leave and returned, by torpedo boat, to England.

"Misfortune," he wrote later of the King, "has thus overwhelmed his country for a second time in his life, but the Belgians might well be proud of their King, for he has proved himself to be a gallant soldier, a loyal ally and a true son of his splendid parents."

The Germans entered Bruges the following day. King Leopold, Queen Elisabeth and Prince Charles left the city, under escort, for the palace of Laeken. They were to remain there as prisoners. Packed carefully into the back of the Queen's car, as indeed they had been for the whole of the past eighteen danger-fraught days, were four of her most precious possessions. These were her violins—the Amati, the Ruffini, the Guarnerius and the Stradivarius.

3

On the morning of May 28, 1940, a few hours after King Leopold had capitulated, Paul Reynaud, the Prime Minister of France, broadcast to the French nation. His address took the form of a scathing attack on King Leopold. "In the midst of battle," ran the impassioned phrases, "without any consideration, without a word for the French and British soldiers who, responding to his anguished appeal, had come to the rescue of his country, King Leopold III of Belgium has laid down his arms." The King's infamous behavior had opened "the road to Dunkirk to the German divisions"; Belgium's allies, insinuated the French Premier, had been treacherously abandoned. "It is an event," pronounced Reynaud solemnly, "without precedent in history."

At four that afternoon his denunciation was backed up by a broadcast made by Pierlot, the Belgian Premier, now in exile in France. Not only did Pierlot, in the name of the Government, deplore the King's action and disassociate himself from it, but he accused the King of opening "separate negotiations" and "treating with the enemy." Belgium, he declared, could not be held responsible for the sins committed by one man.

Three days later the Belgian Government-in-Exile, meeting at Limoges, gave themselves over to an orgy of vilification of the King. The word "treason" was one which seemed to spring most frequently to the lips of the assembled members, and only the comparative level-headedness of some of the ministers prevented the introduction of a resolution for the deposition of the King. Some even went so far as to demand his execution. The assembly eventually confined itself to a unanimous condemnation of the capitulation and to a declaration of the King's legal and moral *"impossibilité de régner."*

On June 4, Winston Churchill, the British Prime Minister, joined the attack. While his speech to the House of Commons was not nearly so damning as Reynaud's broadcast had been, it endorsed the general opinion of the King's behavior. Churchill's orotund phrases, contemptuously mouthed, were greeted by cries of "Shame!" and "Treachery!" from the more impulsive members of the House. To the British Prime Minister's strictures were now added those of a host of others. "You can rummage in vain," thundered Lloyd George in a Sunday paper, "through the black annals of the most reprobate kings of the earth to find a blacker and more squalid sample of perfidy and poltroonery than that perpetrated by the King of the Belgians. If Belgium ever again tolerates such a monarch, she will share his disgrace." Maeterlinck, Belgium's foremost man of letters, claimed that history had "no example to offer of such treason"; even the name of Judas, he said, was too good for the King.

And so the snowball got under way. Scurrilous cartoons showed Leopold stabbing an amazed John Bull in the back or saying to Hitler, as he leads him to the Channel, "Sorry, Sir, this is as far as I can guide you, Sir." In Paris, to mark the King's perfidy, a statue of his father, King Albert, was draped in black. The ghost of Queen Astrid is said to have appeared to four London spiritualists; the Queen's "distressed condition" was obviously due to her anguish at her husband's "defection." That the King's action was the result of long premeditation there was no doubt. His Hohenzollern blood had proved stronger than his loyalty to his allies; he had been influenced by his German mother or by his "fascist" sister, Marie-José; he was under the thumb of a German girl friend; he was in league with the Rexists; he had always dreamed of being the "dictator-King" of a semi-fascist state; the "thirty pieces of silver" with which he was to be rewarded by Hitler was the crown of a united Holland, Belgium and Luxembourg. He was not, claimed one journal stoutly, the real King Leopold at all; Leopold had been killed beside Astrid at Küssnacht and the man who now sat on the throne was a Nazi imposter named Oldendorff. So convincing was this imposter that he had successfully hidden his identity not only from the King's ministers and entourage, but from his mother, his brother and his children.

In the emotionally overcharged atmosphere of those terrible days between Dunkirk and the fall of France, few men were capable of viewing the capitulation dispassionately. The King's champions were simply howled down and only the very brave dared risk defending his actions. It was to take weeks, months and in some cases even years before the capitulation was regarded as anything other than an act of treachery; of the additional accusations leveled at the King, his name has not been cleared to this day.

What, indeed, was the truth? Paul Reynaud's vehement broadcast, which gave birth to the legend of Leopold's treason, has since been regarded, by the King's defenders, as the act of a desperate man. To excuse the failure of the French resistance, to boost the morale of the French troops, Reynaud needed a scapegoat. If the defeatism sweeping through France could be transformed into a fury against the King of the Belgians, then the Allied cause would be well served. The Belgian ministers, in spite of their break with the King, were appalled at Reynaud's accusations. Reynaud knew, as well as they did, that Leopold had no choice but to capitulate, and Reynaud had received due warning of the fact. It was not the capitulation which had caused the rift between the King and his Government, it was the fact that Leopold seemed to have abandoned his allies by remaining in Belgium. "We listened to Reynaud," reported Premier Pierlot afterward, "with anger and indignation."

Yet, on the afternoon of the very same day, they were backing the French Prime Minister up to the hilt. Reynaud's speech had indeed unleashed a wave of fury against Belgium. And it was against the two million helpless Belgian refugees in France that this fury was directed. They were spurned, insulted, attacked and, in some cases, actually arrested and flung into jail. Pierlot had to do something to save the situation and the only thing to do was to divert the blame from the Belgian people themselves onto the King. And perhaps, after all, Reynaud *did* know more about the circumstances of the capitulation than they did; he might have had good cause for castigating the King. This was why, in his broadcast, Pierlot accused Leopold of dishonoring the Belgian Army and of actually treating with the enemy. And in fact this is what the ministers, who had not seen the King since that dramatic meeting at Wynendael, imagined that he *was* doing. A telegram which they had received from him before the surrender, in which he had asked them to resign and to sign an approval for him to appoint new ministers, had merely confirmed their suspicions. They had refused the request.

By the time the Government-in-Exile met at Limoges, there was no containing the mounting anger against Leopold amongst the assembled senators and deputies. To save the King from possible dethronement, the ministers—Pierlot and Spaak amongst them—allowed themselves to be identified with that resolution stigmatizing Leopold for the capitulation. They were allowing themselves to be caught in a web of compromise.

Churchill, who had at first reserved judgment on the matter, then added his powerful voice to that of the other traducers. It appears that a message from the French Minister of Information had begged Churchill to play down Sir Roger Keyes' stubborn championship of the King. French disgust at Leopold's behavior, claimed the French Minister of Information, had resulted in a marked improvement in the nation's morale. The French request thus led directly, it was claimed, to Churchill's attack in the House of Commons.

That King Leopold was forced to surrender there is now no question. The Belgian Army had fought bravely and to the limits of its endurance. Once the Germans had broken through the French defenses at Sedan, Belgium's fate had been settled. It was easier for Churchill to ask the Belgians to "sacrifice themselves" in the cause of an ultimate Allied victory than it was for King Leopold to expect them to do so. "What was this sacrifice required from King Leopold by his accusers?" asked Emile Cammaerts. "The wholesale massacre of his army and of the two million civilians crammed into West Flanders? And what would have been the supposed result of this sacrifice? Perhaps a short delay in the German advance allowing the British and French more time to embark at Dunkirk. Much more likely a rout jeopardizing the evacuation and converting a more or less orderly operation into a wild scramble."

In the accusation that Leopold had capitulated without a word of warning there was no truth. Almost every day, for the last week of the campaign, King Leopold sent warnings that his army could not hold out much longer. Soon after noon on that last day Leopold warned Lord Gort that he would be forced to surrender, and before sending his envoys to the Germans at five o'clock, he informed both the French and British missions of his intentions. Keyes himself, between five and six o'clock, telephoned Churchill to give him the news and Churchill admitted that, in view of the repeated warnings, he was not surprised. Had Leopold left Belgium, as Churchill had all along urged him to do, the controversy surrounding the capitulation would probably have died away. It would have been recognized for what it was: a regrettable but unavoidable act of military significance only.

In the charge that Leopold intended treating with the enemy there was rather more substance. He had left his ministers with the impression (backed up by his telegram asking for their resignation) that he planned to form a new government and continue his reign by the grace of Adolf Hitler. But by the time he capitulated, he seems to have changed his mind. The reasons for this decision are obscure. Perhaps his ministers' refusal to resign or to sign the necessary permission for him to appoint a new government had had something to do with it. Perhaps the advice of three eminent jurists whom he consulted on the matter had been decisive. Perhaps, with the Germans demanding unconditional surrender, he had no choice. But whatever the reasons, King Leopold III returned to Laeken as a prisoner of war and nothing else.

The King lost no time in answering his accusers. Those three eminent jurists who were said to have advised him against forming a new government now drew up a document in which they set out to clear the King's name.

"Contrary to what has been alleged," they wrote, "the King has not treated with the enemy; he has signed with the enemy neither treaty nor convention. The only order given was to lay down arms, a military order."

Their contentions were supported by a pastoral letter written by Cardinal Van Roey in which the Belgians were informed that the King had signed no peace treaty with the enemy and that his decision to stay with his troops as a prisoner of war was "chivalrous and entirely honorable."

To the championship of the Cardinal was now added that of a host of fellow Belgians. If Leopold was a villain to his ex-allies, he was rapidly becoming a hero to a great many of his own people. Already his officers, in a highly emotional scene at Headquarters ("Many among them had difficulty in restraining their tears," reported one eyewitness), had denounced the "abject accusations of felony leveled against the Chief of the Army," and had renewed their oath of loyalty and obedience to him. Five out of every six Belgian burgomasters signed an address assuring the King of their continued loyalty and fidelity. Messages of goodwill flooded Laeken Palace, and at its gates, guarded now by German sentries, were handed in innumerable bouquets as a tribute to the Sovereign's courage.

And after the fall of France, less than three weeks after Leopold's surrender, it looked as though his most intransigent opponents, the ministers themselves, had come round to his way of thinking.

The collapse of once mighty France had meant the collapse of the Belgian Government's own hopes. Skeptical of Britain's ability to carry on the fight alone, the ministers lost heart. Would it not be better to do not only what Leopold had done—and surrender—but to do what they had originally accused him of doing—and treat with the victorious enemy? In these dispiriting days there seemed no other alternative. They decided to negotiate with the Germans and then resign. Spaak is said to have tried to contact the enemy (who refused to have anything to do with the Belgian Government) while Pierlot tried to get in touch with the King. For in spite of everything they had said about Leopold's inability to reign, they needed his cooperation in the matter. "We wish to do nothing without receiving the advice of the King," wrote Pierlot humbly to Laeken. "If the King thinks that it would be useful and possible to form a new government, naturally we are ready to give our resignation." The Premier also asked whether, despite the by now notorious unpopularity of the ministers in Belgium, they could, return home. The shoe was indeed on the other foot.

But the ministers had reckoned without Leopold's stubborn pride. If they imagined that they could heap insults on his head one moment and come crawling back the next, they were mistaken. So keenly had Leopold felt these insults, claimed one of his entourage, that at times he had seemed almost demented: he had cried, he had torn his hair, he had sat rigid. Now that his ministers were eating humble pie he wanted no truck with them. His reasons for rebuffing their advances were as constitutionally impeccable as they themselves—a few weeks beforehand—would have wished them to be. "The situation of the King has not changed," was the curt reply to Pierlot's approach. "The King performs no political actions and receives no politicians." To this message the head of the King's private office added one of his own. Personally, he wrote, he did not feel that there would be any point in "M. Pierlot and his gang" returning to Belgium.

It was this stand on the part of the King that saved the ministers. Foiled in their attempt to make peace, they were obliged to continue to make war. Although a great many members of the Government, including several ministers, gave up the struggle and returned to Belgium, Pierlot and Spaak took fresh heart. Contrary to their expectations, Britain had not been beaten and from what they had heard, the atmosphere in London was very different from that of Vichy, where they were now headquartered. Might it not be better to clear their lungs of the debilitating fumes of Vichy to breathe in the more invigorating air of the British capital? After yet more vacillations, Pierlot and Spaak left France toward the end of August.

They landed in London, by way of Spain, some two months later. Here, in defiant and embattled Britain, they set up the Belgian Government-in-Exile. From now on they shook themselves free of all previous hesitations, identified themselves wholeheartedly with the British cause and came to be treated with increasing respect by the other Allied governments.

This was all very well, but the chief problem remained unsolved. The breach between King and Government had never been healed. If the Government-in-Exile hoped to restore Belgium's reputation, then it was imperative that they restore King Leopold's reputation as well. They knew, by now, that the majority of the Belgian people had remained loyal to the King; if the Government wished to share this loyalty, they would have to patch up the feud. Unwilling to make a public admission to the effect that they had been wrong in traducing Leopold with such vehemence, they were nevertheless prepared to build him up as the heroic prisoner-King. Toward the end of 1940 Spaak circulated a Note to the Belgian diplomatic and consular agents throughout the world. In it he explained, to the King's advantage, the circumstances of his capitulation, his decision to remain with his people and his present, nonpolitical role. "The attitude of the King, a prisoner," wrote Spaak, "and that of the Government in England, are not contradictory and do not conflict." The Note was backed up a few months later by an equally conciliatory statement by Pierlot. "The attitude of the King," he claimed grandiloquently, "is a symbol and source of encouragement; more and more it becomes a centre of all Belgian resistance." Warming to the task, Spaak, in a broadcast to the Belgian nation, urged them to "close ranks around the prisoner-King. He personifies the battered Fatherland. Be as faithful to him there as we are here." And in their booklet entitled "Belgium, the official account of what happened, 1939-1940," published in 1941, they ended the text with a resounding tribute to the dignified stand of the King.

But they were simply groping in the dark. They had no clear idea of what the King's attitude was or of what he was up to. When Spaak wrote Leopold a respectful letter ("We often think of Your Majesty, of his difficulties, of his burdens, of his painful isolation ...") trying to find out exactly what line Leopold was taking, his letter went unanswered. The King remained obstinately, glacially and regally silent with the result that the ministers became more and more agitated. Was Leopold resisting? Was he following a policy of *attentisme*—of wait and see? Was he collaborating?

What *was* happening at Laeken?

4

"Since May '40," wrote Emile Cammaerts of the prisoner-King at Laeken, "he has led a secluded life in that solemn building overshadowed with old beeches, and in the old-fashioned park which surrounds it. He can wander through these dark avenues, along the damp lawns bordering a lake dotted with white swans, and, occasionally, play a game of golf on that course on which he used to practise regularly in happier days. He is allowed a few friends, but his visitors are met by German sentries at the gate. He cannot leave the grounds without obtaining permission from his gaolers and is naturally reluctant to apply for it...."

The picture, by and large, was an accurate one. The avenues might not have been so continuously dark or the lawns so permanently damp as Cammaerts would have one believe, but that King Leopold was regarded as a prisoner there is no question. There were German soldiers, not only at the palace gates, but within the precincts of the palace itself. On the rare occasions on which King Leopold left Laeken, he left it under guard.

The dreariness of his captivity was greatly relieved by the presence of his mother and his three children. As soon as things had settled down after the fall of France, the royal children returned from Spain and Queen Elisabeth once more took over their supervision. "This hour in the afternoon," it was reported, "when Queen Elisabeth and her grandchildren pay a visit to the royal prisoner, is one of the rare relaxations which the most abused sovereign in history allows himself."

But he was soon deprived of even this solace. Laeken, with its jack-booted German guards, its tense atmosphere and its vulnerability to air attack, was no place for children and early in 1941 the two princes, Baudouin and Albert, were sent to the royal chateau at Ciergnon, in the Ardennes. Princess Josephine-Charlotte went as a boarder to the Institut de la Vierge Fidèle in Brussels. As Leopold was not allowed to visit his sons at Ciergnon, they came to Laeken every alternate Sunday to spend the day with him.

In addition to any personal discomfiture, the King was extremely distressed by what was happening in occupied Belgium. Jews were being persecuted, workers deported, and the country's resources ruthlessly exploited to serve the needs of the Reich. The Rexist leader, Léon Degrelle, now hand-in-glove with the conquerors, had formed an Anti-Bolshevik Legion and gone off to fight for the Germans on the Russian front. As during the First World War, the flame of antagonism between Flemings and Walloons was being skillfully fanned by the enemy: Flemish Nationalists were courted, placed in influential positions and their talk of a new, vast, Dutch-speaking state given a sympathetic hearing. Collaborators flourished and there was a very real danger of the state being split permanently into two irreconcilable parts. Of all this King Leopold was acutely aware but, as a prisoner of war, there was nothing that he could do about it.

The position of Queen Elisabeth was hardly less difficult than that of her son. In some ways it was even more so. All King Leopold had to do was to sit tight and mind his own business; Elisabeth was incapable of doing any such thing. Her heart was too big. She soon discovered, moreover, that although technically she too was a prisoner, the authorities would not object to her leaving Laeken from time to time. Leopold's captivity kept him from playing any part in the life of the country; hers did not. As a Queen, and a German-born Queen at that, Elisabeth was in a position to act as a restraining influence on the occupying power and to alleviate individual cases of suffering. This is what she set about doing. She intervened on behalf of Jews (her lifelong admiration for the Jews was proclaimed by her wearing of a five-pointed brooch when Belgium's Jews were compelled to wear a yellow Star of David), deportees, journalists, and the British wives of Belgian nationals. The well-publicized visit of the Queen to a threatened household was sometimes enough to safeguard it. Whenever she drove out her car would be besieged by supplicants; during the four years of the occupation she received over 30,000 notes, all begging for help. She did what she could, but she had to move cautiously. This was not the time for spectacular gestures. Her position was an extremely delicate one. She was forced to walk a tightrope between open defiance and what could easily look like open collaboration. The Germans might allow her a certain latitude but if her activities went too far, the authorities were quite likely to victimize, if not her herself, then at least the people whom she was trying to help. Hitler might be impressed by royalties but he by no means regarded them as sacrosanct. After all, Princess Mafalda, daughter of King Victor Emmanuel, was to die in Buchenwald.

If, on the other hand, the Queen was successful in eliciting too many favors from the German authorities, she would be accused of fraternization, and her son's enemies would be provided with yet another arrow to store in their already crowded quiver.

It was King Leopold himself, however, who presented them with the next, and possibly the deadliest, arrow.

Leopold, at the time of the capitulation, was still a young man, only just out of his thirties. He had been a widower now for five years. It had been in 1938, three years after the death of Queen Astrid, that he had first met Liliane Baels. Then twenty-two years of age, Liliane was the daughter of Henri Baels, Governor of West Flanders. A Flemish lawyer, Baels had had a distinguished public career; he had served in the Government as Minister of Agriculture and of Public Works and his position as Governor of one of Belgium's nine provinces was one of considerable importance. As a viceroy of King Leopold, his official residence was the Palace of Bruges. The education and upbringing of Baels's children had been commensurate with his standing; his daughter Liliane, who had been born in London in 1916, attended first the College of the Sacred Heart in Ostend and then a fashionable finishing school in Cavendish Square, London. In 1935 she had been presented to King George V and Queen Mary at Buckingham Palace. At the time of her meeting with King Leopold in 1938 she was a young woman of striking appearance. She was tall and dark with a strongly molded face and a frank, steady gaze. Her vitality was exceptional. Like the King she was devoted to sport; she swam, she drove, she played golf. It was, in fact, through a game of golf that Leopold first came to know her. On being introduced to Liliane by her father, the King discovered that she was an excellent golfer; the result was that they played nine holes on the links at Zoute. Not until two years later, however, did they meet again and that was when Queen Elisabeth invited her to luncheon, à *trois*, with Leopold and herself at Laeken, a few weeks before the German invasion.

The war scattered the Baels family and it was not until after the capitulation that they were reunited in Belgium. It was then that Leopold began seeing Liliane more regularly. In the summer of 1941 he asked her to marry him. The prospect, so appealing to the two principals, appalled Henri Baels. He was enough of a politician to see how disastrous such a match could be. With his protestations falling on deaf ears, however, he yielded, but only on the conditions that Cardinal Van Roey, the Belgian Primate, perform the wedding ceremony and that Queen Elisabeth be present to give it her sanction. This was agreed, and in the autumn of 1941, in the private chapel at Laeken, King Leopold III married Mademoiselle Baels. The only witnesses to the secret ceremony were Queen Elisabeth and the bride's father. Liliane was given the title of Princess de Rethy (it was a name which Leopold and Astrid had often used on their private travels) and accommodated in a bungalow in the park. The dynasty had experienced its second morganatic marriage.

But Liliane de Rethy was no Baroness de Vaughan. In no time her charm and high spirits had captured Leopold's three children. Starved of the companionship of a young woman for so long, Josephine-Charlotte, thirteen, Baudouin, eleven, and Albert, six, immediately responded to the beauty and vivacity of their father's new wife. When she asked them to think up a special name by which to call her, they suggested *"maman."* When she protested that only their real mother could be called *"maman,"* they insisted, and *"maman"* from then on she became. This instantaneous and affectionate rapport between Liliane and the children meant that all three youngsters were now able to return to Laeken to live; it marked the beginning of a close and enduring family relationship.

Within three months of the marriage, Liliane became pregnant. The secret could be kept no longer. In December 1941 Cardinal Van Roey, at the request of the King, arranged for the reading of a pastoral letter from every pulpit in the land, in which the King's marriage was revealed to the Belgian people.

The breaking of the news confirmed the worst apprehensions of Henri Baels. The majority of Belgians were stunned by it. The picture of their prisoner-King, heartbroken, alone, bearing up bravely under the trials of the occupation and thinking only of the good of his people, was suddenly shattered. The man who was thought to epitomize the sufferings of his fellow countrymen was now revealed as being selfishly concerned with his own happiness. "Sire!" admonished one Brussels newspaper. "We thought you had your face turned toward us in mourning; instead you had it hidden on the shoulder of a woman."

Nor was this the only image to be tarnished by the marriage. The Belgians, who had loved Queen Astrid during her lifetime, by now idolized her memory. Leopold's remarriage seemed to make a mockery of this adulation. Resentment was particularly acute among women—hitherto Leopold's most ardent admirers. They say that there was a noticeable drop in morale among those women whose menfolk were prisoners of war. As more Walloons than Flemings were prisoners (to sow further discord between the two races, the Germans had released large numbers of Flemish prisoners) it was in Wallonia that the disenchantment was more prevalent.

And then the King's choice of bride was severely criticized. The Belgians might be a bourgeois people but they liked their kings on pedestals. When Liliane Baels, on being asked by the King to marry him, protested that "kings marry princesses," she was merely expressing what most Belgians felt was right. "The people do not accept such a marriage," said the Socialist Prime Minister, Achille Van Acker, after the war. "They accept it in a film, in a novel, in some other country, or in a history book...." As a Flemish commoner, Liliane was especially resented by the bourgeoisie in Wallonia. She was looked upon as an *arriviste*, an adventuress, and whether the bourgeoisie looked in disapproval or in envy was neither here nor there.

Further fuel was heaped onto the blaze of animosity by the behavior of Liliane's family. Her father, Henri Baels, Governor of West Flanders, had fled before the advancing Germans and, after a short visit to Belgium after the capitulation, had decided to sit out the rest of the war in the south of France. Her brother Walter was guilty of evading military service, having refused to answer the exiled Government's call to all eligible young Belgians in unoccupied countries to join the special Belgian units of the British armed forces. He was to be prosecuted and sentenced for this omission after the war.

And finally there was the somewhat less emotional but no less significant aspect of the marriage: it was unconstitutional. Not for the first, and certainly not for the last time had Leopold been hamstrung by the Belgian Constitution. Under Article 64 the marriage required ministerial approval. This, of course, it did not have. Belgian law, moreover, demands that the civil ceremony precede the religious ceremony and not vice versa, as was the case with the King's second marriage. And then it was Leopold himself who decided that it would be a morganatic union; this decision also was subject to, and did not get, ministerial sanction.

The King's reputation, which had stood so high among his people after the capitulation, now started to deteriorate. The image of the handsome, misunderstood hero began to fade and some of his subjects started wondering whether the King's behavior was as blameless as they had at first imagined it to be. And as the tide of war began turning, and the Belgian Government-in-Exile was found to be on the winning side after all, so did the scrutiny of the King's behavior—the so-called Policy of Laeken—intensify. It could not, it was now claimed, stand up to any such examination.

5

King Leopold III always claimed that his wartime policy, the Policy of Laeken, was one of strict neutrality. He had remained in Belgium with the express purpose of sharing his people's sufferings; it had never been his intention either to defy, or to collaborate with, the enemy. His defenders called it a policy of withdrawal, of passive resistance almost. His accusers called it one of *attentisme*, of wait-and-see or even wait-and-profit. His friends considered his behavior to be innocently impartial; his enemies dubbed it blatantly opportunistic. To those who claimed that his presence in Belgium prevented the establishment of a pro-German government, there were others who answered that the King would be ready enough to head such a government himself if Germany were to win the war. If she did not, then he would still have allowed himself enough leg room to climb onto the Allied bandwagon. While he himself was busily consolidating his position amongst the Axis powers, said his accusers, the Government-in-Exile guaranteed him a place among the Allies. Whichever way the cat jumped, Leopold would be safe.

Leopold's traducers had some reason for their suspicions. Throughout his captivity, the King seemed more intent on currying favor with the occupying power than on defying, or even ignoring, it.

For one thing he was said to believe that as far as Belgium was concerned, the war was over. In the autumn of 1940, in answer to a statement that the resources of the Congo should be used to aid the British war effort, a message from Laeken let it be known that Belgium was no longer at war with Germany. She had undertaken, vis-a-vis her guarantors, to defend Belgian soil only; this she had done to the best of her ability. If the Belgian Government-in-Exile wished to carry on the war, that was their business; their decision did not have the sanction of the King.

And not only did Leopold appear to have resigned himself to a German victory but he was surrounded by men whose sympathies were said to be actively pro-German. His closest associate, the onetime president of the Socialist party, Henri De Man, openly welcomed the Nazi conquest as a means of ridding Europe, and Belgium, of decayed parliamentary regimes and "capitalist plutocracy" and of introducing an authoritarian "nationalist-socialist" state. The King's private secretary, Robert Capelle, and his *chef de cabinet*, Louis Frédéricq, were accused of being hand-in-glove with the editors of various pro-German newspapers. The King, in fact, seems to have been particularly friendly with one of these pro-German editors, Robert Poulet, himself. There were even rumors that Leopold, encouraged by this reactionary entourage, was planning to set up a royal dictatorship under the aegis of Hitler.

A meeting between King Leopold and Adolf Hitler at Berchtesgaden, in the winter of 1940, seemed to confirm the rumors. Whether Leopold solicited the audience or whether he was ordered to Berchtesgaden no one seemed to know, but the King, wearing dress uniform, was accorded full honors and, after a two-hour meeting, he and the *Führer* had tea together. They were known to have discussed the food situation in Belgium, the repatriation of refugees and prisoners of war, and the relationship between Germany and Belgium. In answer to Leopold's question on the future independence of his country, Hitler launched into a rambling monologue about his plans for a new Europe. Although he promised that he would not touch the Coburg dynasty, the *Führer* remained vague on the matter of Belgium's future. Had Leopold, it was wondered, hoped to discuss the possible setting up of a royal dictatorship?

Nor was this trip to Berchtesgaden the King's only journey to the Reich. He traveled to Austria where he visited Vienna and Salzburg. Few were convinced by the explanation that he had gone to consult a dentist; nor was the rumor that he had been the guest of Count Kuehn, a notorious Austrian Nazi, likely to calm an uneasy public opinion.

And there were more tangible proofs of his contacts with the Axis powers than this. In the spring of 1941 a telegram reached Laeken thanking Leopold for his good wishes on the occasion of Hitler's birthday, and a year later Leopold sent a telegram of condolence to King Victor Emmanuel on the death of his son, Prince Amadeo—"a great patriot and a brilliant military chief."

Yet on the rare occasions that the Belgian Government-in-Exile attempted to contact the King, their approach was met with stony silence. Once, when they sent him a message asking him to make a public protest against the deportation of Belgians to forced labor camps in Germany ("the future of the dynasty would be better assured if the King did not shrink from any of the risks of the exercise of his high function") Leopold did not reply. He did, however, make a private approach to Hitler on the matter. The *Führer's* answer was very much to the point. If there was any repetition of such a "monstrous" protest, threatened the *Führer*, the King would be removed from Belgium. Leopold at once drew in his horns.

As the graph of Leopold's popularity fell, so did that of the Government-in-Exile begin to rise. The Belgian people, quite naturally, wanted to be on the winning side, and it was becoming increasingly obvious that it was "Pierlot and his gang" who would be coming home with the laurels. That the Government itself was alive to this shift of loyalties was made only too clear by a letter which they wrote to the King toward the end of 1943. The letter was taken to Cardinal Van Roey by Francois De Kinder (brother-in-law of Premier Pierlot) who had been dropped into Belgium by parachute; the Cardinal then delivered it to the King.

In this letter the Government pointed out to King Leopold, in no uncertain terms, exactly what was expected of him on their return to Belgium. Immediately after his liberation, he was to inform his subjects that, among other things, Belgium had never ceased to be at war with Germany and that all collaborators, and those who had planned to set up a dictatorship, would be repudiated. The Government assured him that they were anxious for him to resume his constitutional prerogatives but they believed—and here was the rap over the knuckles—"that the best way to carry out this objective would be for the King to follow the respectful advice that we have permitted ourselves to give him."

They should have known Leopold better than that. If they imagined that this proud, headstrong, sensitive man could forget the insults which they had heaped on his head after the capitulation and meekly carry out their suggestions, they were wrong. He had never been one to knuckle down under his cabinet; still less was he likely to do so now that the cabinet was using such an imperious tone. Ignoring their "respectful advice," he answered one point only. This was their insinuation that he had encouraged the setting up of a dictatorship. "The King, following the example of his predecessors, has always maintained a respect for the Constitution," he wrote. "He has never considered violating it.... The alleged reports which tend to throw doubt on those points are completely groundless and whoever is circulating them is committing a crime against the dynasty and against Belgium."

Having sent off this glacial reply, the King sat down to draw up a memorandum which was, in effect, the real answer to the Government's letter. It was to become known as Leopold's Political Testament. In it, along with a rationalization of his wartime conduct and his plans for postwar Belgium, the King gave vent to his long pent-up fury against his ministers. He had forgotten, and forgiven, nothing. Far from showing any contrition for his behavior, he demanded that the Government apologize to him before they be allowed to resume power in Belgium. Until they did this, he would refuse to work with them and, as he took pains to remind them, no act of the Government was valid without his signature. The Testament was addressed, not to the Government-in-Exile, but to whoever would be holding interim power after the liberation. It was an astute move. Leopold suspected that when Belgium was liberated he himself would have been deported by the Germans; his absence would be his trump card. Without him the Government would not automatically be able to resume power and he was now leaving instructions to the effect that if they *did* wish to do so, they must apologize to him first. This way he would be vindicated and would emerge as the master. If, on the other hand, they refused to apologize and simply took over the business of government, Leopold would repudiate them and, in the terms of the Constitution, the matter would be taken before Parliament. If Parliament was unable to settle the dispute, then it would be dissolved and the electorate would have to be consulted. And the electorate, reckoned Leopold, would be on his side.

The controversy, henceforth to be known as the Royal Question, was beginning to take its final shape.

In June 1944, when the Allied armies landed in France, Leopold was deported to Germany. To some, the deportation seemed to suit the King's plans rather too well for it to be as unwelcome as was later protested. Leopold was taken away in one car, Liliane and the children (she by now had a two-year-old son of her own, Alexander) in another. Queen Elisabeth and Prince Charles remained, under guard, in Brussels. Despite the fact that Prince Baudouin was just recovering from measles and that Prince Albert had mumps, the royal party were driven for three days across Germany until they reached the fortress-castle of Hirschstein, overlooking the River Elbe near Dresden. For almost a year, guarded by storm troopers and police dogs and confined by barbed wire fences, the King and his family remained at Hirschstein. With the fate of the Russian Imperial family at Ekaterinberg twenty-five years before constantly in mind, their imprisonment was anything but reassuring. During the day Leopold and Liliane walked, read, played cards and helped the children with their lessons. At night they tried to tune into the B.B.C. on the little bedside radio which Liliane had managed to conceal in her luggage. There is no doubt that the isolation, the privations and the anxieties of these months at Hirschstein brought this already closely knit family group even more firmly together.

In the spring of 1945, with the Allied forces drawing ever closer, they were moved once more. This time they were taken to Strobl, near Salzburg, in Austria. Their prison was now a shooting box, a wooden chalet enclosed by a twelve-foot-high fence. The tedium of their lives was one day disturbed by the frightening stampede of the German guards into their rooms. Expecting murder, the King was in fact being asked to provide protection: the American Seventh Army was approaching. A member of the suite slipped out to warn the advancing columns that the chalet housed the Belgian royal family and the American tanks came crashing through the barbed wire barricade to liberate them. "It was the most beautiful mess I've ever seen," Princess Liliane afterward exclaimed. Within two minutes the German guard surrendered. The King was free.

6

It was the British who liberated Queen Elisabeth. The Germans had marched out, leaving the great palace at Laeken all but empty. Prince Charles, King Leopold's brother, who during the occupation had lived in his old quarters in the Brussels palace, had since escaped to join the Resistance fighters in the Ardennes. Elisabeth was thus the only member of the royal family still at Laeken.

One day her lady-in-waiting, looking idly out of the window, saw a crowd of men marching along the roadway which ran through the public part of the park. Looking more intently, she realized that they were wearing British uniforms. She rushed to tell the Queen. Together they hurried down the echoing staircases and out into the sunshine. Hatless, and in a frenzy of excitement, the two grey-haired old ladies ran on and on down the long, deserted driveway until they reached the gates. Flinging them open, a breathless Queen Elisabeth invited the somewhat startled company of British troops into the palace to stay.

Chapter Thirteen

1

For six years, from the liberation in September 1944 until the summer of 1950, the Royal Question dominated the political life of Belgium. Starting as a relatively dignified and, for the most part, personal quarrel between the King and his ministers, the Royal Question spread and gathered momentum until it brought the country to the very brink of civil war. A controversy that might at one stage have been settled by two men—Paul Henri Spaak and King Leopold himself—was taken up by party politicians, party members and sympathizers and finally by almost every adult in Belgium. The original problem, that of defining the Sovereign's powers under the Constitution, was lost under a passionate wave that crashed across the country. It was a wave compounded of generalizations, irrelevancies, misunderstandings, innuendos, accusations, half-truths, insults and some sincerely held convictions. It was a wave that all but split the country into two irreconcilable halves.

In Parliament it was the Left, the Liberal-Socialist-Communist bloc, that was against Leopold, and the Catholic Right that was for him. In the country itself, most of his opponents were to be found in industrial Wallonia and l'*agglomération bruxelloise*—the metropolitan area of Brussels—and his supporters in pastoral Flanders. Within each of these geographical areas, however, he had both friends and enemies. Even families were divided, with fathers pitted against sons and brothers refusing to have anything to do with each other. What the Dreyfus Affair had been to France half a century before, the Royal Question was to Belgium during the second half of the 1940's.

When Pierlot and Spaak, in the full flush of their triumph, returned to Belgium after the liberation, they were duly presented with the King's Political Testament. His demand that they make him a public apology before he agreed to recognize and work with them had a distinctly sobering effect. For the moment, however, they kept the King's demand secret; with Leopold still a prisoner at that stage, the issue could be avoided until his release. In the meantime, the Government's original declaration of the King's "impossibility to reign" owing to the fact that he was a prisoner still held good, and the Government simply continued to govern as they had been doing for the last four years. In September 1944 Parliament, leaning heavily to the Left, gave them an overwhelming vote of confidence and elected the King's brother, the tall, hatchet-faced Prince Charles, as Regent. The Government took care, however, not to close the door on Leopold completely. What they were hoping for was that the King, on his release, would swallow his pride, forget his demand for an apology, and simply return on their conditions. But if he insisted on championing his Political Testament and on reviling the wartime Government, then he would have to abdicate.

By the time that Leopold was released from that wooden shooting box in Austria in May 1945, Parliament was definitely in favor of abdication. They were determined that Leopold should not return and, until the situation had been clarified, Leopold was to remain in Austria and his brother Charles to continue as Regent. Pierlot had by now resigned and the new Prime Minister was the Socialist Achille Van Acker. The only member of the wartime cabinet to remain in the Government was Leopold's chief opponent, the portly, warmhearted but intransigent Spaak. Between them, Leopold and Spaak might have come to some agreement, but neither man seemed capable of forgetting the past. When they met in Austria, for the first time since that bitter dawn at Wynendael four years before, the King refused to shake Spaak's hand. "What have you come here for?" he asked icily. Spaak, who was to suffer his full share of royal snubs (Queen Elisabeth turned her back on him at their first meeting after the war) soon charmed his way back into the King's good graces, but even if he had been able to work out some solution, the matter was already slipping out of Spaak's hands and into those of his less diplomatic supporters. Parliament was resolved by now on nothing less than abdication. Not wishing, however, to be responsible for dethroning the King, they were anxious for the offer of abdication to come from him. And the King, of course, was equally anxious that it should not.

For five weeks after the King's liberation, during a series of visits which Prime Minister Van Acker paid to Austria, Sovereign and Premier wrestled with the problem. When Leopold finally, and somewhat to Van Acker's discomfiture, agreed to do what was being asked of him—that is to forget about his Political Testament and to make a statement to the nation along the lines originally demanded of him by the Government-in-Exile—the new Government, still determined to force his abdication, refused to accept his sacrifice. They handed in their resignations. They could not be responsible, they declared, for the civil disorders which would follow Leopold's return; in other words, they were refusing to maintain order if Leopold came back. There is a theory that this stand was instigated by Spaak. In the speech which Leopold intended broadcasting to the nation, the King made mention of the wartime Government's willingness to make peace with the Germans at one stage; this was a public rebuke which Spaak was not prepared to tolerate.

The Government having resigned (and having suggested that the King form an alternative one) Leopold set about trying to do so. It was impossible, and the previous Government resumed office. Still Leopold refused to abdicate. The Government, getting desperate, now threatened a parliamentary debate in which Leopold's behavior during the occupation would be made public. They had facts in their possession, they said, which would shock the Belgian people. Even this did not weaken the King's tenacity. After consultation with his mother and his brother, he let it be known that he would wait until the next general election had shown whether or not the Belgian people wanted him to return; this was tantamount to saying that the Government could go ahead and make public whatever it liked. In the face of this obstinacy, there was nothing for it but for the

Government to carry out its threat and expose the King's wartime activities.

Just before doing so, however, there was one point to be cleared up. As the King was not still a prisoner, the "impossibility to reign" clause no longer held good. To make it good, Parliament passed a bill in which the King could only resume his powers if invited to do so by the two Houses of Parliament sitting in joint session. That particular end tied up, Premier Van Acker opened his attack on the King before Parliament on July 20, 1945.

Van Acker's aim was to prove to the Belgian people that Leopold had believed in, and accommodated himself to, a German victory and that he was thus morally unfit to resume power. With feeling against all who had collaborated with the enemy at fever pitch, the atmosphere in which the attack opened was anything but favorable toward the King. In his indictment, the Prime Minister was backed up, every inch of the way, by Spaak. They spoke of the King's wartime entourage, of the pro-Nazi one-time Socialist leader Henri De Man, of the friendship between the King's secretaries and the fascist editors of various newspapers. They accused the King of maintaining that Belgium was no longer at war with Germany; this was why he had forbidden the wealth of the Congo to be used to further the Allied cause. They claimed that the King sought the interview with Hitler at Berchtesgaden and that their meeting, at which Leopold had brought up various political issues, was tantamount to collaboration. They spoke of Hitler's telegram of thanks to Leopold for his birthday greetings and of Leopold's telegram to the King of Italy on the death of Prince Amadeo. ("Did the King of England, during the war, telegraph the King of Italy when the Duke d'Aoste [Prince Amadeo] died?" cried Spaak. "It is very indicative of a state of mind.") They mentioned his trips to Austria. ("We would have nothing to say if he had remained in Belgium or if he had attempted to reach an Allied country," said Van Acker.) They accused him of engineering his own deportation in order that the Government-in-Exile be forced to eat humble pie and beg him to come back. They discussed the inadvisability and the illegality of the King's second marriage.

Around Van Acker's somewhat dryly voiced charges, Spaak created a more emotional atmosphere. Although Spaak's attack was considered rather muddled, on what was probably the main issue he was crystal clear. If Leopold came back, said Spaak, he would be coming back, not as King of all the Belgians, but as the King of the Flemings and the Catholic Party. He would be King of one part of the country against the other. The cry of "Long live the King!" would be an appeal for discord rather than an appeal for unity. "We cannot say with you 'Long live the King,'" said Spaak to his Catholic opponents, "but, quoting Châteaubriand's words to the Duchess de Berry, I am ready to say 'Sire, your son is our King.'"

It needed more than Spaak's impassioned speeches, or even Van Acker's grave accusations, to budge King Leopold. He would wait, he repeated, until the electorate had given its verdict. This it did in February 1946. But the results of the election were inconclusive: the Left lost some support but still outnumbered the Catholic Right by seventeen votes, and the cabinet had, of necessity, to remain tripartite—Catholic, Liberal and Socialist. Van Acker was again Prime Minister and King Leopold had come no closer to, or farther away from, regaining his throne.

In answer to the Government's attack, however, Leopold now prepared his defense. He appointed a commission to examine all his private papers and to publish a report on their findings. The report, which took a year to compile, dealt with each of the Government's charges and dismissed them all. The report claimed that the King's controversial statement on the use of the Congo resources had been misinterpreted and that he had not urged "absolute neutrality." Working from the King's own account of the Berchtesgaden interview (the Government had used the account of Hitler's interpreter) the report denied that the King had solicited the audience or that he had raised any political questions with Hitler other than that of Belgium's future independence. Ignoring the telegram to the

King of Italy, they claimed that someone else was responsible for sending the birthday greetings to Hitler. The trips to Salzburg and Vienna were also ignored as was, very largely, the business of the King's entourage. They set out to prove that the King's marriage was indeed constitutional and maintained that the fact that the King and his wife had made official protests at his deportation was proof that he had not engineered it. Finally, the commission protested that the Policy of Laeken, far from being one of *attentisme* or opportunism, was one of rigid neutrality. There was no substance whatsoever, they said, in the Government's hints at collaboration; the King had simply seen his constitutional duties in one light, the Government in another.

The report, whatever its merits, was of very little practical value. Leopold's supporters believed that it cleared his name and his opponents believed that it did not. Impartiality had long since been thrown out of the window. The emotional battle lines had been firmly drawn and no amount of argument in Parliament, in the press or in private was able to make a scrap of difference. There seemed to be no way out of the impasse. In March 1947 Spaak became Prime Minister, heading a Socialist and Catholic coalition, and on his suggestion, the Royal Question was shelved for the time being. "No fundamental agreement can be reached on the Royal Question," explained Spaak on taking office. "Each of the two parties maintains its position. Neither of the two asks the other to abandon any of its convictions."

So while Prince Charles continued to play the part of Regent with confidence and dignity, his proud and tenacious brother, now living with his family in the Château Le Reposoir by the Lake of Geneva, was forced to cool his heels. Not for one moment, however, did King Leopold III lose sight of his objective; he was determined to regain his throne and with it the opportunity to exercise his royal powers to the full.

2

Life for King Leopold's sister, Marie-José, Princess of Piedmont, had not been easy. Her marriage to the debonair Prince Umberto had never been particularly happy and for someone of her liberal and democratic sympathies, life in Fascist Italy had been fraught with difficulties. Although, under Mussolini, the royal family had played an increasingly negative and inglorious role, its members had nonetheless been identified with the regime: King Victor Emmanuel and his sons had worn Fascist uniforms and Princess Marie-José had herself nursed the wounded in the Abyssinian campaign. Italy's entry into the Second World War had heightened Marie-José's dilemma considerably. Her anti-Fascist sympathies had infuriated one section of the population and her efforts on behalf of her much maligned brother Leopold had alienated another. The fall of Mussolini in the summer of 1943 and the undignified flight of the King from Rome to join the advancing Allies had merely underlined the royal family's reputed spinelessness; even though Marie-José had been in Switzerland at the time of the flight, she too had suffered from the general condemnation. By now neither Right nor Left seemed to want to have anything to do with her.

With the monarchy clearly in need of a new image, the discredited King Victor Emmanuel, during the last year of the war, decided to retire from public life and to hand over his duties to his heir, Prince Umberto. Although Victor Emmanuel remained King, Umberto, as Lieutenant-General of the Realm, took over his powers. With his wife Marie-José once more by his side, Umberto carried out his difficult task with his customary good nature. But it needed more than a display of his renowned charm to ensure the continuance of the dynasty. These postwar years were hardly conducive to the refurbishing of the monarchy's badly tarnished reputation. In the face of mounting dissatisfaction with the regime, it was agreed to hold a referendum at which the Italian nation would decide whether the country would continue as a monarchy or become a republic. To improve the dynasty's chances, King Victor Emmanuel finally abdicated and retired to Egypt. On May 9, 1946, Umberto and Marie-José became King and Queen of Italy. The date of the plebiscite was set for June 3, less than a month away.

The new King and Queen, Umberto at forty-one and Marie-José at thirty-nine, made an attractive couple. He, although balding, had retained his dark good looks and athletic build, and she was as soignée as ever. Of the two, she seems to have had the more forceful character. "Once more I noticed how our Queen's personality effaces that of everyone else," claimed Dr. Castellani, who knew her well; "even when she is silent she outshines them all. In her nature are combined a powerful, almost masculine intellect, a vivid mind...." It was Umberto, however, who had the most appeal; Marie-José's composure gave her a withdrawn, almost forbidding quality whereas Umberto's warmth of heart was apparent to all. On more than one occasion the new King was all but suffocated by a surging crowd of women, eager to embrace their gallantly smiling Monarch.

Yet Marie-José was anything but severe. She had, said her intimates, "a deep kindliness of heart." As soon as the war was over she turned one of the royal villas into a hospital for maimed children and organized an outdoor dispensary on the grounds of the Royal Palace in Rome. Dr. Castellani tells the story of how one night, when she was already dressed to attend a gala dinner, Marie-José received a message to say that the son of a poor woman who had been attending her dispensary had been wounded and was dying. The woman begged the Queen to visit the boy. During the Abyssinian campaign a legend to the effect that the Queen had a healing touch had grown up amongst the soldiers; only the touch of the Queen's hand, the distracted mother now claimed, could save her son's life. Without hesitation Marie-José took off her jewels and changed into a simple dress. Then, accompanied by Dr. Castellani, she made for the hospital. By the time she arrived, the boy was dead. Determined to console the mother, the Queen, escorted only by the aging doctor, walked through the dark, narrow streets of the rough Trastevere district; the local population, volubly republican, was anything but welcoming. Having found the dingy apartment in which the woman lived, Marie-José comforted her as best she could. When she left, she was greeted with cheers by the crowd that now blocked the little street.

Given time, and by gestures such as this, Umberto and Marie-José might well have won the hearts of their subjects. Umberto, claimed one admittedly partisan witness, "endowed with all the qualities that go to make a great king, had made himself extremely popular during the few weeks he was on the throne, and his popularity was increasing daily by leaps and bounds among all classes of the population." Whether Marie-José was equally anxious to win such popularity is open to doubt; she is said to have had very little taste for her position. There was a story, possibly apocryphal but none the less revealing, that she was once seen, late at night, tearing down the monarchist posters that had been put up in preparation for the plebiscite.

At the Referendum, held—claimed the monarchists—at the worst possible time for their cause, some twelve million voted for a republic and some ten million for the monarchy. It had been a close thing but when Umberto was urged to make some sort of stand he refused. "I will not allow my hands to be stained with a single drop of Italian blood," he said to his more impetuous supporters. And in a dignified statement to the nation he declared: "I believe it to be my duty to do everything still in my power to spare Italy further grief and tears after it has suffered so much." With that, he prepared to go into exile.

Marie-José and her four children left the Quirinale on the afternoon of June 5, two days after the Referendum. They were bound for Portugal. Looking "tall and regal, composed and smiling sadly," the Queen entered the royal car and was driven to the airport. From here she flew to Naples and then embarked on a cruiser for Lisbon. She was joined there, ten days later, by Umberto.

"Yesterday," said the King on his arrival in Portugal, "was the saddest day of my life. I wept when I left Rome."

Their reign had lasted for twenty-five days. Their exile, a great deal of which they have spent apart, has lasted for almost as many years.

3

For year after year King Leopold waited by the shores of Lake Geneva. His home, the Château Le Reposoir, was a comfortable old villa set in a large garden with lawns that sloped down to the lake. On clear days the distant, snow-tipped summit of Mont Blanc could be seen sparkling in the sunshine. Visitors to Le Reposoir were always impressed by the evident harmony of the household. King Leopold, Princess de Rethy, Princess Josephine-Charlotte, Prince Baudouin, Prince Albert and little Prince Alexander made a devoted family group. Although in his late forties, the King had kept his lean good looks and appeared no more than thirty-five. Princess Liliane, noted a guest, "is a beautiful woman of twenty-eight, with dark hair and luminous eyes, a matte-white complexion and a willowy, sinuous figure." It was she who kept up the family's spirits; her manner was cheerful, her conversation amusing and her talent for after-dinner charades and *jeux de société* considerable. Princess Josephine-Charlotte, now in her late teens, was blonde and attractive; Prince Albert, seven years younger, was an "intelligent-looking boy, rather shy"; Prince Alexander, Liliane's own son, was hardly more than a baby. Prince Baudouin, Leopold's heir, was a tall, scraggy, bespectacled youngster, with delightful manners and a serious expression. He was a part-time student at the College of Geneva. "He adores his father," noticed one eyewitness, "and constantly gazes at him with respect and admiration."

In 1949 Leopold, Liliane and Baudouin visited the United States via the Antilles. They were away for several months. It was one of the very few diversions to break the tedium of King Leopold's exile. For a man of his temperament, these years of waiting must have seemed interminable; he must have come, at times, very close to despair. How much more of his life was to be fretted away in this idleness? Yet he never once considered giving up the fight, not even when the fight seemed to be hopelessly one-sided. He knew what was being said about him in Belgium—that Huysmans, a Socialist Prime Minister, had dismissed him as a "fascist"; that ex-Premier Pierlot, in a series of articles entitled *Pages d'histoire*, was enlightening his readers on the subject of their Sovereign's imperiousness; that Victor Larock, a Walloon member of Parliament, was castigating him, for week after week, in the pages of *Le Peuple*; that he was being accused of planning to set up a dictatorship on his return. He felt these insults keenly. To a group who came to Geneva to urge him to resume contact with the Government, Leopold's answer was as defiant as ever. He would do so, he said, when "it has been publicly declared that nothing has ever stained the honor of the Head of the Dynasty." Spaak, the new Prime Minister, was by now just as anxious as the King to remove these stains; their reasons, however, were very different. Leopold reckoned that once his name had been cleared he would be able to return; Spaak hoped that once the King's reputation had been restored, he would be ready to abdicate with honor. The first meeting between the two men since Spaak's scathing attack on the King in Parliament some two and a half years before was in January 1948. Spaak came to Le Reposoir and, in an atmosphere of surprising cordiality (Leopold could still be charming and Spaak was a man with a warm heart) the two men discussed the situation. But neither then, nor at any of the subsequent meetings, could they discover a means of breaking the deadlock. Spaak was hoping that the forthcoming elections would settle the matter. Leopold had by now decided against making the Royal Question an electoral issue. An electoral campaign against his person, he said, would be an attack on the monarchy as an institution; there were, moreover, far too many other issues involved in an election. He now favored a referendum. This way the people could make their choice on the single issue of his resumption of power. But the Belgian senate rejected the idea of a referendum and the stalemate continued.

Not until the elections of June 1949 was the deadlock broken. From then on things moved swiftly to their climax. Despite Leopold's refusal to participate, the Royal Question had been a predominant issue in the election, with the results favoring the King: the Catholic Right emerged with a small majority. The Liberals, who had hitherto been firmly anti-Leopold, now began to have second thoughts. The election had shown that although their supporters in Wallonia remained anti-Leopold, Liberals in Flanders were undecided. Anxious to put an end to the lingering controversy, the Liberal Party issued a manifesto supporting the Catholic demand for a national "consultation." In August Catholics and Liberals formed a coalition Government and agreed to hold a referendum. As Leopold refused to accept the Liberal proposal for a vote of two-thirds in the King's favor and declared a simple majority to be sufficient, the matter was left open. Not until October 1949 was a joint communiqué issued by Leopold and Gaston Eyskens, the Catholic Prime Minister, stating that if less than fifty-five percent declared in the King's favor, he would not resume the exercise of his powers. Nowhere, however, did the King say that he would abdicate if the vote were unfavorable.

With the date of the referendum fixed, the political atmosphere, never very edifying where the Royal Question was concerned, deteriorated still further. Right and Left sprang to each other's throats; every cupboard was ransacked for skeletons. Ex-Premier Pierlot was accused of having "crawled on his belly for the Huns" in the days after the fall of France. Posters showed King Leopold shaking hands with Hitler. Spaak was called chicken-livered, hypocritical, stupid and treacherous. Leopold's policy of *attentisme*, it was claimed, had disgusted every member of the Resistance. The King did not want advice, declared Spaak, "he thirsts only for praise and flattery."

Such was the poisonous climate in which, on March 12, 1950, approximately five and a half million Belgians went to the polls to decide the fate of their King. Balloting was secret and compulsory.

The question which the electorate was asked to answer was somewhat ambiguous: "*Etes-vous d'avis que le Roi Leopold III reprenne l'exercise de ses pourvoirs constitutionnels?*" If one did favor his resumption of power then well and good; if one did not, then what did one favor? Abdication? Postponement of the question? The abolishment of the monarchy? Not all the voters were very sure of the answer and the governing Catholic Party did very little to enlighten them.

King Leopold had declared that he would consider a fifty-five percent vote in his favor to be decisive. In the final count 57.68 percent of the population voted for his return and 42.32 percent against it. In Flanders the pro-Leopold vote was 72 percent, in Wallonia the anti-Leopold vote was 58 percent, and in Brussels the vote against him was 53 percent. Although the result could hardly be considered an overwhelming victory, Leopold declared the national will to have been "clearly expressed" and made ready to return to his kingdom. All that remained was for a joint sitting of both Houses of Parliament to implement the law of July 19, 1945, whereby the "impossibility to reign" would come to an end and to invite the King back to Belgium.

But it was not going to be quite so easy as that.

The Liberal Party, whose cooperation had made the referendum possible, now declared that they considered the majority too small to satisfy their requirements. They therefore refused to vote with the Catholics in the joint sitting. When Premier Eyskens went to Geneva to report on this latest impasse, Leopold, refusing to take any action himself, declared that it was up to Parliament to resolve the matter. Eyskens and his coalition cabinet were forced to resign and for the following five weeks there was the usual desperate scrabble round by various ministers to form a government. With all attempts proving fruitless, the Regent, Prince Charles, was obliged to dissolve Parliament and call for yet another election.

This was held on June 4, 1950, and resulted, at last, in an absolute majority for the Catholic Party. It was a small majority but it was enough. In a joint sitting held on July 20, the Catholic Right outnumbered the Liberal-Socialist-Communist Left (for by now the Liberals had again come down, squarely, on the side of the anti-Leopold faction) by a dozen members. They could now vote for the King's return. Just before the final count was made, Spaak addressed the assembled members. "In a few minutes," he said prophetically, "you will have called Leopold III back to the throne and given the signal for troubles that will tear Belgium apart from one end to the other. Ladies and gentlemen, so much the worse for you. We shall leave this chamber before you vote. You will remain alone to accomplish one of the gravest and most disastrous acts of our history."

With that Spaak led the members of the three parties out of the chamber and into battle. From now on, it was to be a very different sort of battle from that which had raged across the floor of the House for the last half-dozen years.

Ever since the result of the referendum had been announced, tension had been mounting throughout Belgium. The relationship between Flemings and Walloons, always uneasy, was now becoming explosive. Walloon separatist organizations were threatening a break-up of the country if the King returned; they accused Cardinal Van Roey of being in league with the King to set up a Salazar-like regime. Early in July there were strikes by mine workers at Charleroi and at Liège. Three days later over 80,000 workers marched on Brussels and there, led by Spaak, paid tribute to the Regent for his efficiency, his patriotism and his unquestioning loyalty to the Allied cause during the war. One would have had to have been very naive indeed to take this fulsome praise of the Regent at face value. During the next three days there were strikes and demonstrations against the King at Antwerp, Ghent, Namur, Mons and throughout the coal-mining "black country" around Charleroi. On Bastille Day, July 14, ten thousand workers flooded into La Louvière screaming for Leopold's abdication. "Leopold to the gallows!" they shouted. "Hang him, hang him!"

In contrast to these frenzied protests, Spaak's appeal to the still-absent Monarch was commendably dignified. Spaak, so alive to the fact that the Belgian monarchy must be a patriotic focal point, was determined that the country should not be saddled with a king who was acceptable to the Catholics and the Flemings only. "Sire," he said in an open letter to the King after the results of the referendum had been announced, "Belgium's unity and prosperity are in danger. Everything the majority wants is not necessarily good, everything that is legal is not necessarily to be recommended.... May Your Majesty, whose policy and conduct have now received the approval of the majority of the Belgians, content himself with his victory. May you send us your son."

But Leopold remained deaf to all protests. All he knew was that after ten years of waiting he had been vindicated. On July 22, 1950, two days after the joint sitting of Parliament had voted for his return, King Leopold III arrived home.

This was no *joyeuse rentrée*. The King, accompanied by the nineteen-year-old Prince Baudouin and the sixteen-year-old Prince Albert, arrived by air from Geneva at a quarter past seven in the morning. The Government could not risk his arrival at a busier time than this. There were less than three hundred people at the airport to welcome him home; standing bareheaded in the pale sunshine, they made a very thin crowd indeed. The royal party entered a closed car and, preceded by four armored vehicles, were driven swiftly through the deserted streets to Laeken. Once the King had passed through the heavily guarded gates, they were clanged shut. Leopold was home once more but he was hardly less of a prisoner now than he had been when he left, over six years before.

4

On the afternoon of his return to Belgium, King Leopold III broadcast an address to the nation. Even now, in a speech calling upon his subjects to unite and to forget past dissensions, the King could not resist a dig at his opponents. "Like my predecessors, who were cruelly attacked at certain times of their reign," he said, "I shall forget the polemics of which I have been the object, to think only of the future."

If the shaft was aimed at Spaak, it hit home. As proud a man as was his Sovereign, Spaak looked upon King Leopold's triumph as his own humiliation. That night Spaak addressed a vast crowd gathered in the Place des Martyrs. Here, where those citizens of Brussels who lost their lives in expelling the Dutch in 1830 are buried in a common grave, Spaak rallied his supporters. "We Socialists have decided to continue the fight," he shouted to his cheering audience. "Perhaps we will lose this or that battle, but because we represent political honor and the memory of the Resistance, and because our cause is fine and just, we will eventually win." Nor was this mere rhetoric on the part of Spaak; the weapon which he had chosen for the fight was the strike. Five days later the first strikes, designed eventually to paralyze the entire national economy, got under way. There was nothing more, Spaak said frankly to his horrified opponents in the House, that could be done by parliamentary means. "Call it a threat, call it blackmail if you like, I call it a fact that the strike that has begun will develop.... Whatever you do it will extend and grow worse. And I will make you another prophecy. Up to now it is an insurrectionary strike against King Leopold. If you let it continue ... this insurrectionary strike will prove the beginning of a revolution."

On the afternoon of July 27, a hot summer's day, thousands upon thousands of demonstrators, led by the bulky figure of Spaak himself, marched from Parliament to the Palace of Laeken. Singing *La*

Marseillaise and *L'Internationale* and shouting "Leopold to the gallows," the great crowd converged on the palace. Here they were met, not only by locked gates and mounted police, but by an angry force of Royalists. Opposing battle cries led first to fistfights and then to the ripping up and flinging of paving stones. It needed a charge of mounted police, with sabers drawn, to clear the battlefield.

By the next day there were over 500,000 strikers out in Wallonia and by the end of the week strikes were almost total throughout the Walloon provinces. In Flanders, the port of Antwerp was paralyzed, trains were held up at the frontier, public transport in Brussels was at a standstill and barricades were going up in the streets of Liège. And then, on Sunday, June 30, at Grâce-Berleur, near Liège, the police, trying to break up an anti-Leopold meeting, panicked and killed three demonstrators. With this, the strike turned into an insurrection: 100,000 demonstrators started to march on Brussels. Civil war seemed inevitable.

Only now did that unhappy, obstinate man lurking behind the drawn blinds at Laeken consider abdicating. At one o'clock on the Monday morning after those three men had been killed, an anxious delegation, representing the three major political parties, waited on the King. Abdication, they told him, was the only possible solution. But still the King seems to have remained undecided. The day was spent in feverish consultation and not until eight o'clock that evening did Leopold agree to step down. He would delegate immediate power to his son Baudouin, who would be known as Prince Royal until his twenty-first birthday (just over a year from then) on which date he would assume the crown. The communication announcing the King's decision, however, was delayed until the following morning. By then the defiant King had decided to have one last try. Rather than abdicate, he wanted to hand over power to Baudouin for an indefinite period, leaving the door open for a possible return. But the Government was not having any of it. On the threat, it was said, of defection by several members of the Government, Leopold was induced to agree to his abdication. At dawn on August 1, 1950, the message of abdication was read to the press. Eleven days later, Prince Baudouin, now Prince Royal, took the oath of office.

The King had lost his battle, but the dynasty had been saved.

Epilogue
The Reluctant King

1

Seldom has a monarch assumed his responsibilities with less enthusiasm than did young King Baudouin. Seldom, too, has a monarch made this lack of enthusiasm more apparent. The new King felt, quite simply, that he had been forced into usurping his father's throne, and he was determined to make the entire country aware of his feelings.

A shy, awkward youth who had known only imprisonment and exile for the last decade, Baudouin was devoted to both his father and his stepmother. Those ten troubled years had drawn the royal family ever more closely together and the sensitive Baudouin had always felt the insults which had been heaped upon the heads of his father and Princess Liliane. Now that he was King, he was determined to make amends. His father would be compensated not only for the loss of his throne, but for the treatment which he had suffered at the hands of his enemies. When in July 1951 Baudouin took the constitutional oath as Sovereign, he made a point of promising to do all in his power to prove himself worthy, not of Belgium or its people, but of his father. Ex-King Leopold was allowed to remain at Laeken in the very apartments which he had occupied as King, while Baudouin continued to live in the rooms in which he had spent his childhood. When the family sat down to eat, Leopold kept his place at the head of the table. The son inherited his father's entourage and followed his advice in everything; he even took over his quarrels. Remembering the British attacks on his father at the time of the capitulation, Baudouin would not attend the funeral of King George VI. Resenting the way certain Catholic members of Parliament had forsaken

Leopold at the time of his return, Baudouin refused to have any truck with them. It soon became clear to the Belgian people that if it was Baudouin who reigned, it was Leopold who ruled.

Determined to find a scapegoat for this unsatisfactory state of affairs, the Belgian press, always outspoken, turned on the Princess de Rethy. Hardly a day went by without some scurrilous reference to the new King's stepmother. She was accused of being, if not exactly the power being the throne, at least a malign influence on it. She was said to be flighty, meddlesome and indiscreet. It was rumored that she had been pro-Nazi; it was suspected that she was causing a rift between ex-King Leopold and his mother; it was known that her father had spent the war years in the comfort of the south of France and that her brother had evaded military service. When low-lying areas of Britain, Holland and Belgium were devastated by floods in 1953 and the Queens of England and Holland rushed to the scenes of disaster, King Baudouin was discovered to be sunning himself on the Riviera in the company of his father and stepmother. He hurried home, came down with influenza before he had time to make his presence felt and promptly arranged to go back to the Riviera to recuperate. It was the Princess de Rethy, decided *Le Peuple*, who was to blame for the King's selfish behavior. When Baudouin, without consulting his Government, announced that his brother Albert was to marry the Italian Princess Paola Ruffo di Calabria, in the Vatican and not in Brussels, the infuriated Belgian public claimed that Liliane had had a hand in the arrangements. So violent was their opposition to the Vatican ceremony that Baudouin was obliged to change the venue to Brussels. Liliane was accused, moreover, of discouraging the King himself from marrying; she was determined to remain first lady of Belgium, they said.

Baudouin felt these criticisms of his father's wife as keenly as if they had been directed at himself. On one occasion, having read yet another venomous attack, he is said to have flung the newspaper to the floor and to have stalked out of the room. When he returned a few minutes later he seemed in control of himself once more but canceled all official duties for the day. "I don't know how that boy can carry on," remarked one observer.

But carry on he did and as year followed year, so did the Belgians come to realize that there was far more to their King than they had at first imagined. From a sullen and stubborn youth, obsessed with the idea of fighting his father's battles, he developed into a man of considerable character. He began to look more assured, more relaxed; he applied himself to his job with more zest. When he visited the United States in 1959, the Belgians were surprised to see photographs of their normally unsmiling King looking unusually confident and happy. When he arrived home he was given the first really heartfelt reception of his reign. He met Queen Elizabeth of England and from then on worked toward a renewal of the ties which had once bound the two countries so closely together. In the affairs of the Belgian Congo, a sphere in which the Kings of Belgium have always been allowed to play a prominent role, he showed an unsuspected (and some say ill-timed) boldness of touch: he was the one to announce the need to give the Congo its independence and who, despite his Government's apprehensions, insisted on flying to the Congo to judge the situation for himself. Those who had dealings with him found him becoming increasingly conscientious, constructive and shrewd. Like his grandfather, King Albert, he revealed himself to be a man of few words and much good sense. He was developing into a skillful mediator.

And so, through the years, the criticism died down. The charge that Baudouin was interested solely in avenging his father's name was forgotten; the suspicion that he planned to abdicate in favor of his brother Albert and become a Trappist monk faded. Leopold and Liliane moved out of Laeken to a home of their own—Leopold to interest himself, to an ever-increasing extent, in travel and exploration, and Liliane to devote herself, with what the Belgians at last recognized as extreme good nature, to the wellbeing of her family. She and Leopold had three children of their own: Prince Alexander and two daughters.

It was King Baudouin's continuing bachelorhood that now began to bother his subjects. The dynasty, never a large one, had always been thin on princes; as usual it was down to two and as by the year 1959 neither of these was married, the old anxiety that the dynasty might die out made itself felt once more. In July that year, however, the twenty-five-year-old Prince Albert married Princess Paola. The wedding provided Brussels with its first royal spectacle since the marriage of ex-King Leopold to Princess Astrid over thirty years before and the dynasty gained a princess of exceptional beauty, elegance and vivacity. This lively and hardworking couple have three children at present—Prince Philippe, Princess Astrid and Prince Laurence.

Not until he married, Queen Elisabeth once said to the new King, would he become Baudouin I; until then he would always be looked upon as "the son of Leopold III." But Baudouin, like Albert I, was not going to be hustled into an arranged match. Not until he was over thirty, in December 1960, did he marry. His bride was Dona Fabiola de Mora y Aragon, a Spanish aristocrat of quiet beauty, warm heart and wide culture. By the smiling sincerity of her manner, she quickly won the approval of her husband's subjects. But the tragedy which has so often left its mark on those connected with the Belgian throne has touched her, too: her three miscarriages have left King Baudouin without a direct heir. If the royal couple remain childless, the succession will pass to the King's brother, Prince Albert of Liège. Albert remains the heir to the throne and his eldest son, Prince Philippe, is already being referred to as "the little King."

Thus through five generations has the pattern been repeated. There have always been two royal brothers and if the succession passes from Baudouin to Albert, it will have passed as often through brothers as it has from sovereign to eldest son. King Leopold I had two sons and the crown passed from the elder, Leopold II, through the younger, Philip of Flanders, to *his* second son, Albert I. Leopold III had two sons and the crown may well pass through the second son, Albert, to his sons. And there is another pattern. Leopold I's first-born son died in infancy; Leopold II's only son died in childhood; Philip of Flanders's eldest son, Baudouin, died in his teens; Albert I's eldest son, Leopold III, lost his throne; Leopold III's eldest son, Baudouin, remains childless. Is there indeed some sort of curse on the first-born sons of the dynasty?

2

With the exception of those eighteen months during which Astrid had been Queen and until King Baudouin married Fabiola in 1960, Elisabeth was the only queen in Belgium for over half a century. In fact, for many years she was the only female representative of the dynasty in the country. Ex-King Leopold's wife, the Princess de Rethy, played no part in public affairs; Prince Charles, the ex-Regent, had never married; Marie-José, ex-Queen of Italy, lived in Switzerland; Leopold's eldest daughter, Josephine-Charlotte, married Prince Jean, Hereditary Grand-Duke of Luxembourg, not long after her brother Baudouin had become King; Leopold's second son, Prince Albert, did not marry until the year before Baudouin himself married. It was thus on Queen Elisabeth's slight but still erect shoulders that a great many royal duties devolved. She carried them out with customary enthusiasm, vigor and charm. In a dynasty racked by change and controversy, Queen Elisabeth remained the one constant element. By the end of her long life there were few Belgians who could remember a time when that small, graceful figure was not a part of the Belgian scene. However, it was the twenty years between the end of the Second World War and the end of her own life that saw that complex personality in full flower; this was indeed Elisabeth's Indian summer.

In some ways King Albert's death had released her. His circumspection and his strong sense of duty had tended to keep her own far more capricious nature in check. Now that she was free to do whatever she pleased, she gave her inclinations full rein. As she grew older so did the Wittelsbach strain—the surging, unorthodox strain of her father's family—become more apparent. To the bourgeois life of postwar Belgium, the aging Queen Elisabeth brought a gust of nineteenth-century Bavarian waywardness. The willful, unconventional spirit that had characterized the Empress Elizabeth, King Ludwig II and her own father Duke Charles Theodore lived on in Queen Elisabeth of Belgium. But although she too could be self-willed, her altruism prevented her from ever being self-obsessed. When people spoke of the Queen's eccentricity, they often forgot those less publicized activities—in the realms of medicine and music—that were a direct result of her practical interest and her warm heart.

"I always do what I wish," she would proclaim with a touch of imperiousness, and what she wished seemed, to some of her subjects, to be very strange indeed. They found her leftwing views embarrassing and some of her enthusiasms decidedly cranky. Like the late King Albert, Queen Elisabeth took excessive care of her body. In her seventies and eighties she was still sunbathing, swimming, taking cold baths and going for long walks. She did yoga exercises every morning. When she discovered that one of her luncheon guests, the conductor Erich Kleiber, was interested in yoga, she insisted that the two of them sit cross-legged on the floor, there and then, to practise breathing and muscular control. Passionately interested in birds, she collaborated with Professor Koch in recording the bird song in the park at Laeken. She would be up for hours after midnight and long before dawn, tiptoeing among the trees with a microphone in her hand; she was once able to approach within three feet of a nightingale by whistling in imitation of its song. She practiced the violin tirelessly. She was discovered at six o'clock one morning at the bottom of an old bomb crater in the park, playing for all she was worth. "It's such a lovely morning," she explained, "and the acoustics in this crater are perfect." On another occasion she talked three fellow performers into playing Brahms and Schubert Quartets on the golf course outside her studio; when night fell, they played on by the light of the moon. Elisabeth would not think of stopping for food or rest; she was transported. Her maid, bringing in her breakfast the following morning, was startled to find the bed not slept in. "It's all right," explained a fellow servant, pointing out of the window to the little group still playing away in the morning sunshine, "they are at it again."

"At it *again?*" exclaimed Elisabeth on hearing of the remark. "Not at all! We never stopped."

She would travel any distance to hear good music. She attended the Edinburgh Festival and went to Alsace to hear Doctor Schweitzer play Bach, and to Puerto Rico to hear Casals play the cello. She traveled to Communist Poland for a Chopin Festival in 1955 (she had just turned down an invitation to a royal wedding on the grounds that it would be too tiring); she visited Soviet Russia in 1958 to attend a Tchaikovsky competition and three years later, when she was eighty-six years old, she again accepted an invitation to Moscow. She would not hear of Russian performers being excluded from the international competition which bore her name. When a Russian violinist once won the first prize, she made a point of attending a reception at the Soviet Embassy in order to congratulate him. Nor were musical festivals the only reasons for her visits to Communist countries. In 1961 (in spite of press grumblings at this "flirting behind the Iron Curtain" and of quips about "the Red Queen") she attended the Chinese National Day celebrations in Peking, and on May Day the following year she laid a wreath on Lenin's tomb in Moscow. In a changing world, Queen Elisabeth moved with all the authority, the internationalism, the blithe disregard of public opinion that had characterized royalty in a time long past. In an age grown self-conscious and restricted, she ranged like a free spirit.

Her dynamic personality never ceased to amaze those who encountered her for the first time. Dr. Castellani, on being introduced to her in Portugal, noted that, other than looking fifteen years younger than her age, there was nothing exceptional about her appearance; she could easily be mistaken for a neatly dressed, self-composed schoolteacher. "But the moment she starts talking," he said, "a transformation comes over her, and her magnetic personality manifests itself—the personality that has fired to greatness the imagination of writers and famous men of art and science." Noticing that her daughter's Court-in-Exile seemed to be sinking into lethargy, Elisabeth whisked them off on a tour of the Moorish cities of Spain; her vitality and her enthusiasm were an example to them all.

But for all her vagaries, there was no member of the dynasty who had done more for the Belgian people. The full extent of Queen Elisabeth's contribution to the medical and cultural life of the country is probably incalculable. In the mid-1950's her work received official recognition by the inauguration of the *Front Blanc de la Santé* and by the award of an Honorary Degree by the Royal Academy of Belgium. The *Front Blanc de la Santé* was the name given to the organization in which were united the Queen's four great foundations—the Braille League for the blind, the Anti-Polio League, the Anti-Cancer League and the Anti-Tuberculosis League. The great ceremony marking the amalgamation of the Queen's chief medical *oeuvres* brought home to many Belgians, for the first time, the magnitude of the Queen's life-long concern for the sick. When she received her honorary degree from the Royal Academy, an academy in whose three branches—the Sciences, the Fine Arts and Letters—she was vitally concerned, the President aptly summed up her achievements with these words: "The Queen looks high and far. Rising above the littleness of this world, she practices an idealism which she knows how to synchronize with the practical realities of this complicated life."

This was indeed her secret. An idealist, a philanthropist, the Queen was nonetheless an essentially practical woman. The last of the great royal patrons, her patronage was of a positive, realistic variety. At a time when other royalties had grown passive and overcautious, Queen Elisabeth flung herself with businesslike ardor into whatever happened to interest her. Here was no tame, pliable figurehead, afraid to step out of line. In her eighties she was in Israel for the inauguration of the Queen Elisabeth Archeological Institute; in her eighty-ninth year, glitteringly dressed and with the usual outsize orchid pinned on her shoulder, she was attending what was probably her most famous institution—the *Concours Musical International Reine Elisabeth de Belgique*. When she died in her ninetieth year, in November 1965, Belgium lost not only its most memorable Queen, but a woman whose great qualities of mind and heart had always been at the disposal of her subjects. "The crown has no meaning," she used to say, "unless it is a symbol of service." And this is what, for over fifty years, in her bold, inimitable and unself-conscious fashion, Queen Elisabeth had made of her own crown.

3

"Belgium," the Socialist Prime Minister Achille Van Acker once said, "needs the monarchy like it needs bread." This was as true then—in the 1940's—as it had been a century before and it is hardly less true today. In a bitterly divided, two-nation state like Belgium, the monarch is a very necessary focal point for national loyalties and the fact that the Belgian monarchy has always been, and remains, an extremely influential one makes it doubly necessary. Of all the monarchies of Europe, none is more powerful nor more involved in the political life of the country than is the Belgian monarchy.

Yet it was never meant to be such a force. The Constitution-makers of 1830, republican in spirit, had intended that the King should be nothing more than a figurehead, and it was due almost entirely to the personalities of the Belgian kings that the monarchy became steadily more powerful. Each monarch, in his own way, was a remarkable man, and whatever their faults might have been, the Kings of Belgium gave their country an importance out of all proportion to its size. They were all men with a strong sense of duty who tended to take themselves, and their mission, very seriously. Belgium has never had a passive or an irresponsible or a frivolous king. Some of them might have been misguided but none of them has been weak.

This strengthening of the monarchy began within a few days of the inauguration of King Leopold I. As a king, Leopold was able to command a respect denied to mere parliamentarians and the sudden Ten Days War allowed him—in terms of the Constitution—to assume supreme command of the army. From this position of strength Leopold went on to take over complete control of Belgian foreign policy. As, by way of astute diplomacy and judicious dynastic alliances, his prestige grew abroad, so did it increase at home until his authority was all but unassailable. He came to exercise, in all spheres of national life, a direct and personal influence. He might not have been particularly interested in domestic politics but he kept them firmly under his control. He was extremely jealous of his prerogatives. "In everything, however unimportant," he once said to a minister, "it is the duty of the minister before committing himself to a definite policy, to report to the King in order to learn his opinion. The minister has authority only in that he is a minister of the King." If Leopold I was a model constitutional monarch, he was one to the very limits of his powers.

Leopold II thus inherited from his father an extremely strong position. For so authoritarian a nature as his, however, it was not nearly strong enough. Unable to extend his constitutional prerogatives (and too wise to try) he found other ways of aggrandizing the monarchy. By founding and developing the vast Congo Empire and by making himself, and his dynasty, rich beyond compare, Leopold II won the power and importance denied him by his governments. In an age in which his fellow sovereigns were gradually losing their influence, King Leopold II was reversing the trends of history and increasing his.

But his ambitious schemes did not outlast him. For all his complicated financial maneuverings, his wealth was not transmitted to his descendants and his successor, King Albert, seemed unlikely to be interested in any further augmenting of monarchial power. But as had happened to King Leopold I in 1831, King Albert became Commander-in-Chief of the army in 1914 and his courage and tenacity raised the prestige of the monarchy to heights quite different from those envisaged by Leopold II. The end of the First World War found Albert endowed with immense authority and at a time when thrones were collapsing like ninepins, his stood secure. The timely introduction of universal suffrage raised the monarchy above the political parties once and for all and from then on the King, by his conscientiousness, his skill and his wisdom, ensured that it remained an institution of unquestionable importance.

King Leopold III, inheriting a set of executive powers and a tradition of strength wholly out of tune with accepted twentieth-century monarchial practice, was determined to make the most of them. As had happened twice before in the history of the dynasty; he was given supreme command of the armed forces; as Commander-in-Chief of the army—as opposed to head of the parliamentary executive—he felt himself compelled, in May 1940, to reject the advice of his ministers and thus to make the first break between King and Constitution. The Royal Question, in some ways, was a last-ditch stand on the part of the monarchy, a final test of strength between King and Parliament, and it was the King who lost.

But the Belgian monarchy remains, for all that, a powerful institution. Although King Baudouin will probably never defy his Government to the extent to which his father did during the 1940's, his prerogatives have been in no way curtailed since then. He could, in theory, be as strong a monarch as any of his predecessors. His court remains actively concerned in political affairs and he is constantly being called upon to settle national disputes. Unlike the Bicycling Monarchies to the north, the Belgian monarchy is still very much involved in the day-by-day workings of the country.

Yet, in the final reckoning, the main strength of the Belgian monarchy lies in the constitutional behavior of its sovereigns. It is this behavior, more than anything, that has kept them on their thrones. With the exception of King Leopold III (and his was a special case) their respect for the Constitution has always been unimpeachable. Leopold I, who considered the Constitution to be far too liberal, adhered to it, he once told his daughter Charlotte, "with a scrupulous fidelity, not only as a whole but also to the very letter. Never has the least article been transgressed...." And this was true. Leopold II, too, was careful not to rock the constitutional boat; his only long-standing disagreement with his governments was on the question of Belgium's defenses, and his only attempt to increase his constitutional authority—by the demand that in the revised Constitution of 1893 he be allowed to call referenda—came to nothing. King Albert, at a time when kings such as Alfonso of Spain and Victor Emmanuel of Italy were becoming ever more closely identified with dictatorships, remained—for all the strength of his position—resolutely democratic. Whether Leopold III, had he not been faced with that agonizing choice in 1940, would ever have violated the Constitution is doubtful; but when he did, he paid for it. His son Baudouin still plays an important and influential role but remains well within the prescribed limits. The courage, the resolution, the stubbornness which has so often characterized the monarchs of Belgium has never—always excepting Leopold III—been pitted against their country's constitutional laws, and even Leopold III was convinced that he was acting in the spirit of the Constitution.

"The great thing," King Leopold I used to say, "is success." By a blend of defiance abroad and flexibility at home, his dynasty has proved itself surprisingly successful. Whether, in an age in which other monarchs have become little more than symbols, the more politically involved Belgian monarchy will continue to be so successful remains to be seen. It might not always be as necessary to Belgium as bread.

Bibliography

I would like to express my thanks to the authors, editors, copyright owners and publishers of those of the books listed below from which short extracts have been reprinted in *The Coburgs of Belgium*.

ALBERT I, KING OF THE BELGIANS. *The War Diaries of Albert I.* Edited by R. Van Overstraeten. Translated by Mervyn Savill. William Kimber, 1954.

ANONYMOUS. Recollections of a Royal Governess. Hutchinson, 1915.

ARANGO, E. RAMON. Leopold III and the Belgian Royal Question. Oxford University Press, 1964.

ASCHERSON, NEAL. The King Incorporated. New York: Doubleday, 1964.

ASPINALL-OGLANDER, CECIL. *Roger Keyes*. The Hogarth Press, 1951.

ASQUITH, MARGOT. *More Memories*. Cassell, 1933.

BARKELEY, RICHARD. The Road to Mayerling. Macmillan, 1958.

BARTHEZ, A.C.E. The Empress Eugénie and Her Circle. T. Fisher Unwin, 1912.

BAUER, LUDWIG. *Leopold the Unloved*. Translated by Eden and Cedar Paul. Boston: Little, Brown, 1935.

BELGIAN MINISTRY OF FOREIGN AFFAIRS. Belgium; the Official Account of what happened 1939–1940. Evans, 1941.

BIERME, MARIA. La Famille Royale de Belgique 1900–1930. Bruxelles: Libraire Albert Dewit, 1930.

BLASIO, JOSE LUIS. *Maximilian. Emperor of Mexico*. Translated by R. H. Murray. New Haven: Yale University Press, 1934.

BOCCA, GEOFFREY. *Uneasy Heads*. Weidenfeld & Nicholson, 1959.

BOIGNE, COMTESSE DE. *Memoirs 1781–1830*. New York: Scribner's, 1907–08.

BOULGER, DEMETRIUS C. *The History of Belgium.* London: Published by the Author, 1909.

BRONNE, CARLO. *Leopold Ier et son temps.* Bruxelles: Les Oeuvres, 1947.

BUFFIN, BARON C. *La Tragédie Mexicaine; Les Impératrices Charlotte et Eugénie.* Bruxelles: A. Dewit.

BULOW, PRINCE VON. *Memoirs 1897-1909.* Boston Little, Brown, 1933.

BURY, LADY CHARLOTTE. *The Diary of a Lady-in-Waiting.* John Lane, 1908.

CAMMAERTS, EMILE. *Albert, King of Belgians.* Nicholson & Watson, 1935.

———. *The Keystone of Europe; History of the Belgian Dynasty.* Peter Davies, 1939.

———. *The Prisoner at Laeken.* The Cresset Press, 1941.

CAPELLE, COMTE. *Au Service du Roi 1940-1945.* Bruxelles: Charles Dessart, 1949.

CASTELLANI, ALDO. *Microbes, Men and Monarchs.* Gollancz, 1960.

CHRISTOPHER, H. R. H. PRINCE OF GREECE. *Memoirs.* Hurst & Blackett, 1938.

CHURCHILL, WINSTON S. *The Second World War.* 6 vols. Cassell, 1948-54.

COOPER, LADY DIANA. *The Rainbow Comes and Goes.* Rupert Hart Davis, 1958.

COPE, ZACHARY. *The Versatile Victorian.* Harvey & Blythe, 1951.

CORTI, EGON CAESAR, COUNT. *Leopold I of Belgium.* Translated by Joseph McCabe. New York: Brentano's, 1923.

———. *Maximilian and Charlotte of Mexico.* 2 vols. Translated by C. A. Phillips. New York: Alfred A. Knopf, 1928.

DAWSON, DANIEL. *The Mexican Adventure.* Bell, 1935.

DE FLEMALLE, CAPITAINE GABRIEL DE LIEBERT. *Fighting with King Albert.* Hodder & Stoughton, 1915.

DE LICHTERVELDE, LOUIS, LE COMTE. *La Monarchie en Belgique.* Bruxelles: Librairie Nationale d'Art et d'Histoire, G. van Oest et Cie. Editeurs, 1921.

———. *Léopold II.* Bruxelles: Editions Universitaires, Les Presses de Belgique, 1926.

———. *Metier de Roi: Léopold II, Albert I, Léopold III.* Bruxelles:

———. *Metier de Roi: Léopold I, Léopold II, Albert I, Léopold III.* Bruxelles: Editions Universitaires, Les Presses de Belgique, 1945.

———. *Léopold, I.* Bruxelles: Librairie Albert Dewit, 1929.

DELMARCELLE, ROBERT. *Baudouin.* Bruxelles: Lucien de Meyer, 1953.

DE MEEUS, ADRIEN. *History of the Belgians.* Translated by G. Gordon. Thames & Hudson, 1962.

DINO, DUCHESSE DE. *Memoirs.* 3 vols. Edited by Princesse Radziwill. NEW YORK: SCRIBNER'S, 1909-1910.

DUMONT, GEORGES H. *Leopold III, Roi des Belges.* Paris: Charles Dessart, 1946.

———. *La Dynastie Beige.* Bruxelles: Elsevier, 1959.

ERNEST II, DUKE OF SAXE-COBURG-GOTHA. *Memoirs of Ernest II.* 4 vols. Remington and Co., 1888–1890.

EULALIA, H. R. H. THE INFANTA. *Court Life from Within.* Cassell, 1915.

———. *Courts and Countries After the War.* Hutchison, 1925.

———. *Memoirs of a Spanish Princess.* Translated by Phyllis Megroz. New York: Norton, 1937.

FLEURY, COMTE. *Memoirs of the Empress Eugénie.* New York and London, D. Appleton and Co., 1920.

FORBES, ROSITA. *These Men I Knew.* New York: Dutton, 1940.

GALET, EMILE JOSEPH. *Albert, King of the Belgians in the Great War.* Translated by E. Swinton. Putnam's, 1934.

GAYRE, GEORGE ROBERT. *A Case for Monarchy.* Edinburgh: The Armorial, 1962.

GERLACHE, COMMANDANT DE GOMERY DE. *Belgium in War Time.* New York: G. H. Doran Company, 1917.

GOFFIN, ROBERT. *Was Leopold a Traitor?* Translated by Marjorie Shaw. Hamish Hamilton, 1941.

GORIS, JAN-ALBERT (ed.). *Belgium.* Berkeley: University of California Press, 1945.

———. *Strangers Should Not Whisper.* New York: L. B. Fischer, 1945.

GRANT, HAMIL (ed). *The Last Days of the Archduke Rudolph.* New York: Dodd, Mead, 1916.

GREENWALL, HARRY J. *Round the World for News.* Hutchinson, 1955.

GREVILLE, CHARLES. *The Greville Diary.* New York: Doubleday Page, 1927.

GREVILLE, HENRY. *Leaves from the Diary of Henry Gréville.* 4 vols. Edited by The Countess of Strafford. Smith, Elder, 1905.

GRISCOM, LLOYD C. *Diplomatically Speaking.* Little, Brown, 1940.

HALL, FREDERIC. *Mexico and Maximilian.* New York: Hurst, 1909.

HARDING, BERTITA. *Phantom Crown.* Harrap, 1934.

HASLIP, JOAN. *The Lonely Empress.* Weidenfeld & Nicolson, 1965.

HAYWARD, ABRAHAM. *Biographical and Critical Essays.* Longmans, Green, 1873.

HOHENLOHE-SCHILLINGSFURST, PRINCE CHLODWIG. *Memoirs.* New York: The Macmillan Co., 1906.

HOLDEN, ANGUS. *Uncle Leopold: A Life of the First King of the Belgians.* Hutchinson, 1936.

HOWARTH, T. E. B. *Citizen-King.* Eyre & Spottiswoode, 1961.

HUIZINGA, J. H. *Confessions of a European in England.* Heinemann, 1958.

HYDE, HARFORD MONTGOMERY. *Mexican Empire.* Macmillan, 1946.

JERROLD, BLANCHARD. *The Life of Napoleon III.* 4 vols. Longmans, Green, 1874-82.

JUSTE, THEODORE. *Memoirs of Leopold 1.* 2vols. Translated by Robert Block, M.A. Sampson Low, Son and Marston, 1868.

KENNEDY, AUBREY LEO. *My Dear Duchess; Social and Political Letters to the Duchess of Manchester, 1858-1869.* John Murray, 1956.

LARISCH, COUNTESS MARIE. *My Past.* Putnam's, 1913.

LAROCHE, LOUIS. *Louise d'Orleans; Premiere Reine des Beiges.* Paris: Imprimerie des Orphelius-Apprentis, F. Bletit, 1902.

LEGGE, EDWARD. *The Comedy and Tragedy of the Second Empire.* New York: Scribner's, 1911.

LEOPOLD I, ROI DES BELGES. *Lettres de Leopold I.* Edited by Carlo Bronne. Bruxelles: Charles Dessart, 1943.

LIEVEN, PRINCESS. *The Unpublished Diary and Political Sketches of Princess Lieven.* Edited by Harold Temperley. Cape, 1925.

——. *The Private Letters of Princess Lieven to Prince Metternich 1820-1826.* Edited by Peter Quennell. John Murray, 1946.

——. *The Correspondence of Lord Aberdeen and Princess Lieven.* Edited by E. Jones Parry. London: Offices of the Royal Historical Society, 1938-39.

LONDONDERRY, THE MARCHIONESS OF (ed.). *Letters from Benjamin Disraeli to Frances Anne, Marchioness of Londonderry 1837-1861.* Macmillan, 1908.

LONGFORD, ELIZABETH. *Queen Victoria.* Weidenfeld & Nicolson, 1964.

LONYAY, KAROLY. *Rudolph, The Tragedy of Mayerling.* Hamish Hamilton, 1950.

LOUISE, PRINCESS OF BELGIUM. *My Own Affairs.* Translated by Maud M. C. ffoulkes. Cassell, 1921.

LUCAS, NETLEY (Pseud. Evelyn Graham). *Albert the Brave, King of the Belgians.* Hutchinson, 1934.

LYTTLETON, LADY SARAH SPENCER. *Correspondence 1787-1870.* John Murray, 1912.

MACDONNELL, JOHN DE COURCY. *King Leopold II.* Cassell, 1905.

MALORTIE, BARON DE. *Here, There and Everywhere.* Ward and Downey, 1895.

MARTIN, PERCY F. *Maximilian in Mexico.* New York: Scribner's, 1914.

MARTIN, THEODORE. *The Life of His Royal Highness, The Prince Consort.* New York: Appleton, 1875-80.

MAXWELL, ELSA *R.S.V.P.: I Married the World.* Heinemann, 1955.

MILLARD, OSCAR E. AND VIERSET, AUGUSTE. *Burgomaster Max.* Hutchinson, 1936.

MITIS, BARON VON. *The Life of the Crown Prince Rudolph.* Translated by M. H. Jerome and Eileen O'Connor B.A. Skeffington, 1930.

MOTZ, ROGER. *Belgium Unvanquished.* Forest Hills, N.Y.: Transatlantic, 1942.

OVERSTRAETEN, GENERAL VAN. *Albert I—Leopold III: Vingt ans de politique militaire Beige 1920–1940.* Bruxelles: Desctee de Brower, 1946.

OWEN, SIDNEY CUNLIFFE. *Elisabeth, Queen of the Belgians.* Herbert Jenkins, 1954.

PAGE, JAMES. *Leopold III; The Belgian Royal Question.* The Monarchist Press Association, 1959.

PAGET, LADY WALBURGA. *Embassies of Other Days.* Hutchinson, 1923.

PALEOLOGUE, GEORGES MAURICE. *Les Entretiens de l'Impératrice Eugénie.* Paris: Plon, 1928.

PAOLI, XAVIER. *My Royal Clients.* Translated by Alexander Teixira de Mattos. London: Hodder & Stoughton.

PARRY, E. JONES. *The Spanish Marriages 1841–1846.* New York: The Macmillan Co., 1936.

PAZ, H. R. H. THE INFANTA. *Cuatro Revoluciones e Intermedios. Commentarios del Principe Adalbert.* Madrid: Espasa-Calpe S. A., 1935.

PIRENNE, HENRI. *Histoire de Belgique.* 6 vols. Bruxelles: H. Lamertin, 1909-1926.

PONSONBY, D. A. *A Prisoner in Regent's Park.* Chapman and Hall, 1961.

RAPPOPORT, ANGELO S. *Leopold the Second, King of the Belgians.* New York: Sturgis & Walton, 1910.

REINACH FOUSSEMAGNE, COMTESSE H. DE. *Charlotte de Belgique, Impératrice du Mexique.* Paris: Plon-Nourrit et Cie, 1925.

RICHARDSON, JOANNA. *My Dearest Uncle.* Cape, 1961.

SAROLEA, CHARLES. *How Belgium Saved Europe.* Heinemann, 1915.

SCHMIDT, PAUL. *Hitler's Interpreter*. Heinemann, 1951.

SCHREIBER, MARC. *Belgium*. Translated by Hilda Becker. Macdonald, 1945.

SFORZA, CARLO, COUNT. *Makers of Modern Europe*. New York: Bobbs-Merrill Co., Inc., 1930.

SHERARD, ROBERT. *Twenty Years in Paris*. Philadelphia: Jacobs, 1906.

SHUMWAY, HARRY IRVING. *Albert the Soldier-King*. New York: Page, 1934.

SLADE, RUTH. *King Leopold's Congo*. Oxford University Press, 1962.

SMAHT, CHARLES ALLEN. *Viva Juarez!* Eyre & Spottiswoode, 1964.

STANLEY, THE HON. ELEANOR. *Twenty Years at Court*. Edited by Mrs. Steuart-Erskine. Nisbet, 1916.

STANLEY, H. M. *Through the Dark Continent*. New York: Harper, 1878.

———. *The Congo and the Founding of Its Free State*. New York: Harper, 1885.

———. *In Darkest Africa*. New York: Charles Scribner's Sons, 1890.

STEPHANIE, H. R. H. PRINCESS. *I was to be Empress*. Nicholson and Watson, 1937.

STOCKMAR, BARON E. VON. *Memoirs of Baron Stockmar*. Edited by F. Max Muller. Longmans, Green, 1872.

TALLEYRAND, PRINCE DE. Memoirs. 5 Vols. Edited by the Duke de Broglie. New York: Putnam's, 1891-92.

T'SERCLAES, BARONESS ELSIE DE. *Flanders and Other Fields*. Harrap, 1964.

TUCHMAN, BARBARA W. *August, 1914*. Constable, 1962.

TWAIN, MARK. *King Leopold's Soliloquy*. Boston: Warren, 1905.

———. *Autobiography*. Edited by Charles Heider. New York: Harper, 1959.

VAUGHAN, BARONNE DE. *A Commoner Married a King*. (As told to Paul Faure) New York: Ives Washburn, 1937.

VARE, DANIELE. *Twilight of the Kings*. John Murray, 1948.

VICTORIA, QUEEN. *The Letters of Queen Victoria* (Second Series) 3 vols. Longmans, Green, 1926-28.

———. *Dearest Child. Letters Between Queen Victoria and the Princess Royal 1858–1861*. Edited by Roger Fulford. Evans, 1964.

WHITLOCK, BRAND. *Belgium Under the German Occupation*. Heinemann, 1919.

WHYTE, FREDERIC. *The Life of W. T. Stead*. Cape, 1925.

WOLFF, SIR HENRY DRUMMOND. *Rambling Recollections*. New York: The Macmillan Co., 1908.

YDEWALLE, CHARLES D'. *Albert, King of the Belgians*. Methuen, 1935.

———. *A Belgian Manor in Two Wars*. Macmillan, 1949.

NEWSPAPERS AND PERIODICALS

Brussels: *Le Derniere Heure, La Libre Belgique, Le Peuple, Le Soir.*

London: *Times, Observer, Daily Telegraph, Daily Express, Pall Mall Gazette, Punch, Annual General Register.*

Printed in Great Britain
by Amazon